1

CLASSMATES

All that is Beautiful and Good

WRITTEN AND EDITED BY

Mary Brings Farquhar & Karl Terry Kleeman

~

WITH STORIES FROM

Priscilla Litwin Dolan
Ray Domingo
Warren Gerig II
Steve Gunders
Kaye Fisher Hautem
Nancy Buerer Jones
Edurne Menchaca Kowalski
Robert Karl Liese
Ellen Bancroft Page
Leata Thomas Selby
Aurora Abrera Somerstein-Campbell
Sylvia Ayers Steltzelberg
Gloria Chua Wilt
Art Zurhorst

THE AMERICAN SCHOOL

MANILA - THE PHILIPPINES - 1950S

CLASSMATES

All that is Beautiful and Good

Classmates at the American School
Manila 1943-1961

Stories of a Multicultural Group
of Classmates Born During World War II
Linked by Shared Experiences at the American School
in The Philippines

Written and Edited
by
Mary Brings Farquhar & Karl Terry Kleeman

First Edition
September 2021
Printed at Amazon

Library of Congress Control Number
2021915399

ISBN 978-0-578-25286-5

DEDICATION

We dedicate this book
To our Classmates who are no longer with us,
To our Teachers at the American School
&
The People of the Philippines

A Brief History of the Philippines

The Philippines is an archipelago of over 7,100 islands, strategically located between the South China Sea and the Pacific Ocean. The three main island groups are Luzon, the Visayan Islands and Mindanao. There are many different provinces and 175 languages. The official language is Pilipino, based on Tagalog, the language spoken in the capital city, Manila.

By around 3000 BC, seafaring Austronesians, known for their ocean-going sailing technologies, reached northern Philippines. Other early inhabitants, the Visayan people, were an ethnolinguistic group native to the Visayan Islands, the central islands in the Philippines. From 618-906, there was regular Philippine contact with China during the Tang dynasty. In 1450, Sayid Abu Bakr established the Sulu Sultanate. He was a Muslim and ruled the islands in the Sulu Archipelago including parts of what is now Mindanao.

Ferdinand Magellan, a Portuguese navigator in charge of a Spanish expedition to circumnavigate the globe, attempted to conquer the islands in 1521, but was defeated and killed by Lapu-Lapu, a regional leader of the islands. In 1543, Ruy López de Villalobos arrived at the islands of Leyte and Samar and named them Las Islas Filipinas in honor of Philip II of Spain. During most of the colonial period, the Philippine economy depended on the Galleon Trade. Trade between Spain and the Philippines was via the Pacific Ocean to Mexico, and then across the Caribbean Sea and Atlantic Ocean to Spain. After the Spanish-American War in 1898 the occupation by the U.S. changed the culture of the islands, leading to the introduction of English as the primary language of government, education, business and industry. However, much Spanish influence remained: the Catholic religion, many family names, some common vocabulary words and certain social customs.

From 1941 to 1944 the Philippines was occupied by Japan, then liberated in 1945 by the United States, who granted the islands full independence in 1946. This was followed by a mostly peaceful succession of presidents until President Ferdinand Marcos imposed martial law in 1972. The nonviolent three day revolution in February, 1986, known as People Power, led to the exile of Marcos and the restoration of democracy in the Philippines.

See Notes for Suggested Reading

TABLE OF CONTENTS

Cast of Classmates

Seven classmates contributed their stories and we will follow those stories throughout the book. Three were born in Manila during World War II. Four moved there in the 50s. We all begin with the story of our early days before we started at the American School. This provides a cultural background for the story of our shared experiences. How did such a diverse group interact and what was the impact of living in Manila and attending the American School? And how did this influence our later lives?

Mary Brings
The girl whose parents were from Austria
"My paternal grandparents, Dr. Julius Brings and Helene Brennholz Brings, were born in Austria.My maternal grandparents, Dr. Rudolf Katz and Marie Birnbaum Katz, were born in Bohemia, at that time part of the Austro-Hungarian Empire, now part of the Czech Republic." Mary was born in the Philippines after her parents escaped the Holocaust and she joined the class of 1961 in Kindergarten.

Aurora Abrera
Spanish Heritage
"My mother's grandfather was a Spanish Duke, his wife was a Lady-in-Waiting to the Queen and also related to the Queen. My father's side of the family did not have as colorful a history as my mother's. My grandfather Basilio was a simple, hard-working Filipino man from Palawan, an island west of Luzon. Grandfather Basilio was a trader, fisherman and founder of Concepcion, a town in Palawan. My grandmother was a teacher who raised six children, the youngest of whom was my father." Aurora joined the class in second grade.

Gloria Chua
Chinese Classmate
"Both of my parents emigrated from Fujian Province in southern China. My great-grandfather, Jose Yutivo, went from China to the Philippines as a young man to seek his fortune. He started out as a houseboy for a Spanish family. Eventually, he had money and land in the Philippines, but he never lived in the country permanently. It was his son, my grandfather, who really emigrated and settled his family in Manila. My grandfather continued developing the businesses my great grandfather had started. My mother's

family was prosperous, but their prosperity could not guarantee any stability or safety in the thoroughly chaotic China at that time. Reluctantly, they had to leave their comfortable life on the island of Gulangyu off the coast of China and emigrated to the Philippines." Gloria joined the class in second grade.

Terry Kleeman
The boy from Iowa
"My great grandfather on my father's side was Joseph Clement, who emigrated from Luxembourg to Dubuque, Iowa in 1865. Sometime between Joseph's arrival in Dubuque, by then a thriving town on the Mississippi River, and his first local census, his name changed from Clement to Kleemann. How this happened is still a mystery to the Kleeman family. Later Kleemann was changed to Kleeman. My mother's family was originally from Germany." Terry joined the class in the seventh grade.

Bob Liese
The boy from Ohio
"My father's parents and grandparents were clearly German, but my mother's side was probably a mix, but English for sure. My grandparents on my father's side were from St. Louis. My grandfather had a career with the Bond Company, which was a large clothier in the area. My grandparents on my mother's side hail from Akron, Ohio. My maternal grandfather was employed with one of the large rubber companies." Bob joined the class in the eighth grade.

Nancy Buerer
Baptist missionary family
"My father was from Escalon, CA, where he was one of eight children born to a farming family. Both farming and gardening were in his blood for his entire life. His parents were from German and English backgrounds. My mother was from Elmhurst, Illinois, one of five children from German and Scottish heritage." Nancy joined the class in the eighth grade.

Warren Gerig
The Viking boy from New Jersey
"My last name, Gerig, originally had an "H" in it, like Lou Gehrig. In fact, my great grandfather, born in Germany, had a birth certificate with both spellings on it, which turned out to be a clerk's mistake. When he came to the U.S. he was told it would be better to leave the "H" out, as it looked more American. So it was changed by USA immigration.

After having had my DNA tested, I discovered that my heritage is 34% Swedish, going back a thousand years, meaning that I had Viking Heritage." Warren joined the class in high school, freshman year.

~

Other classmates who provided memories for this book include Ray Domingo, Priscilla Litwin. Ellen Bancroft, Steve Gunders, Sylvia Ayers, Kaye Fisher, Leata Thomas, Art Zurhorst and Tonya Winters

PREFACE

We call ourselves the Class of 1961. One of us attended the American School from kindergarten through high school. Others came and went over the years. These were formative years that we all shared and we accepted one another, regardless of cultural or socio-economic circumstances. Our time together, although it was limited, was unforgettable. We were a small class and a close-knit group. We tell our story through the eyes of boys and girls whose observations reflect our varied backgrounds. What we saw as our "melting pot" at the time was an exceptional school, providing us with challenges which brought us together in rather remarkable ways.

Our parents, many with no prior international experience, found themselves in a new country, a new culture. They sent us to the American School to provide us a path to an American university. This was true for those born in the Philippines as well as those of us whose fathers were transferred to the Philippines for just a few years. We would like to point out that these were the Fifties. As seen through today's prism, most of our lives were privileged, perhaps at times insensitive to the local culture. We were teenagers more concerned with the latest styles, the latest rock and roll music, our basketball games and our friends.

We editors have made no attempt to sanitize the stories and we hope that you can appreciate them in the context in which they were lived.

After reading the fascinating multi-cultural background of my classmates, I understand why a plain young man from the suburbs of Memphis, Tennessee became so widely accepted at the American School in the Philippines. The background of the class taught everyone to take people for what they are as human beings. Fortunately for me, living in Memphis, my parents were "out of step" in the 1950s because their friends came in many colors, backgrounds, and religions, much to the narrow minded dismay of our community. When I arrived at the American School for the first time I was among people who shared better values when it came to attitudes about people. Though delighted, I was always puzzled by how readily I was accepted for who I was by the entire school. I now understand that it was because I accepted people for the kind of person they were, and that was what most of my new school mates had been exposed to their entire lives. Classmate, Art Zurhorst

PROLOGUE
TIME MAGAZINE

M U S I C

All That is Good

A starlit Philippine sky covered the roofless ruins of old Santa Cruz church. Viennese-born Conductor Herbert Zipper stepped onto the plank podium—and the Manila Symphony Society's first concert since December 1941 had begun.

The audience of 1,200 soldiers and natives who gathered last week inside the crumbling walls settled back to listen to Beethoven's *Third (Eroica) Symphony*. Occasionally during the softer passages, a siren wailed or a bulldozer could be heard working away at Manila's rubble. Beads of perspiration tipped Dr. Zipper's sharp nose. In the first row sat Mrs. Douglas MacArthur, in a pink cotton frock. Also present was the Symphony's president, Mrs. Benito Legarda, a handsome Philippine woman who hid the Society's instruments from the Japanese in 1941.

The orchestra was as colorful as the audience. Four American soldiers in khaki, an Australian lieutenant, a native boy and five young girls filled the chairs of some of the Society's 28 missing musicians who had been killed by the Japanese or were still fighting as guerrillas in the mountains.

Super-critical listeners noted imperfections in the reading of the *New World Symphony*, Antonin Dvorak's tribute to America. Some of the hastily rehearsed musicians were playing unfamiliar instruments furnished by the U.S. Army Special Services Division.

But the Manila Symphony gave the people a promise that night—as well as a concert. As a Dutch officer, a former Amsterdam flutist, put it: "All that is beautiful and good will come back in our lives."

Santa Cruz Church, Manila 1945
Concert Conducted by Herbert Zipper
Unpublished LIFE MAGAZINE Photo

CHAPTER 1

❧

Escape to Manila
by
Mary Brings Farquhar

Some of my American School classmates had roots in the Philippines. I did not. I have lived in San Francisco for over fifty years, but have no roots in the U.S., either.

If I were to greet you in perfect American English on a beautiful San Francisco afternoon, I could also say Guten Tag, Buenas tardes, Magandang hapon (Tagalog), or Shalom. Those languages all represent parts of the mosaic that makes me who I am. People that I meet never guess that I am an immigrant. I don't fit the stereotype, I blend in, and those who think they know me and then hear my story inevitably say, "Wow! I never knew that."

Immigration is one of the hottest, most talked about and most controversial topics at this moment. America is bitterly divided on immigration, hate crimes are up and, increasingly, immigrants are seen as "the other," forgetting that we are all immigrants.

A poem written by Igor S. Korntayer, a Polish Yiddish actor in the 1930s, describes the heart wrenching dilemma faced by European Jews who were forced to leave their homelands or face certain death after Hitler came to power.

Vu Ahin Zol Ikh Geyn?
Tell me where shall I go,
Who can answer my plea?
Tell me where shall I go,
Every door is locked to me.
Though the world's large enough,
There's no room for me I know,
What I see is not for me,
Each road is closed, I am not free—
Tell me where shall I go.

That was the dilemma in which my parents found themselves in 1938. Dr. Theodor Brings and Paula Katz Brings lived the upper middle class life in Vienna, Austria. His father was a doctor, her father was a lawyer. My father's family originally came from Poland, while my mother's came from Bohemia (later Czechoslovakia). Both families came to Vienna, where my parents were born in 1905. Both of my parents had the obligatory piano lessons and my mother had a French governess. They both loved nature and enjoyed climbing and skiing, which is how they met. My father was a Physics professor at the University of Vienna, where he had received his Ph.D. My mother taught Physical Education and Skiing in a private high school for girls.

They were both Jewish, but not particularly observant; they were cultural, secular Jews. When they married in 1934 they were already acutely aware of Hitler, who in 1933 had come to power in Germany, but they loved Austria, the Alps, the music, the theater, the memories of Emperor Franz Josef riding through the streets of Vienna in his carriage with the golden wheels. (He died when they were 11.) What was going on in next-door Germany couldn't possibly affect them, could it? It was the tail end of the fabled turn-of-the-century Vienna, the time of Freud, Klimt, Schoenberg, Schnitzler and Kokoschka. My mother as a teenager bought standing room places at the Opera, where she later sang in the chorus under famous conductor Bruno Walter. My father loved mountaineering and physics, and belonged to a physics discussion group, whose informal meetings he attended regularly in one of the famed Viennese coffeehouses. They were both politically active social democrats. An idyllic life until suddenly it wasn't.

Everything changed on my mother's 33d birthday, March 13, 1938. In an interview my mother gave to a Filipina journalist at age 90, she said, "I remember that day very clearly, March 13, 1938, my 33d birthday. The planes were thundering overhead. Hitler's troops marched into Vienna. Martial music was playing in the streets and red flags with black swastikas were suddenly displayed everywhere. We heard our chancellor over the radio, surrendering our country to the invaders. At the end of his message he said, 'The Nazis are here. We are lost. God help Austria.' Everybody was crying. How could I forget that day? It was my birthday!"

This invasion, known historically as the "Anschluss," changed Jewish life in Austria forever. Shortly thereafter my parents lost their jobs, as did all Jews. I happen to still have my mother's dismissal letter, which praises her to the heavens, not only as a teacher, but as an exceptional human being; an inspiration to her students and her colleagues. The last sentence, however, gives me chills. It states how sorry they were that "due to the unfortunate new circumstances they can no longer make use of her valuable services." I do not have my father's dismissal letter, but I know that he did important original research concerning uranium about which he corresponded with Albert Einstein, after Einstein had escaped and was teaching at Princeton. Living under the German boot, they not only

2

lost their jobs but also, one by one, many of their rights. When the Nazis came to the door asking their housekeeper if any Jews lived there, she risked her life by saying no. That time the Gestapo left; the next time maybe not. And there was sure to be a next time.

So, what did they do then? In the end it came down to a lot of luck and an awful lot of serendipity. It just so happened that at this very time in the far away Philippines, a country they knew nothing about, the President Quezon/Frieder Brothers rescue plan was being formulated.

Alex Frieder and his three brothers owned a cigar factory in Cincinnati, but took turns going to the Philippines, where the best tobacco was, and opened the Helena Cigar Factory there. It produced 250 million cigars a year, which were sold in the U.S. for the price of two for a nickel. The rescue idea started in 1937, when a group of Jews who had fled the Nazis to Shanghai was evacuated to Manila after fighting had escalated in Shanghai between the Chinese and the Japanese. As there already was an established Jewish community in Manila, they formed what was called the Jewish Refugee Committee to help the newcomers from Shanghai get settled. The Chair of that committee happened to be Philip Frieder. According to Frank Ephraim, author of *Escape to Manila*, "[The arrival of the Jewish refugees from Shanghai] gave them the idea: Why can't we bring in more Jews? Things were getting progressively worse in Germany, and they were aware of that. That got them motivated, and they wanted to help." As it happened, the Frieder brothers were poker players, and so were dapper and debonair President Manuel Quezon, the US High Commissioner of the Philippines Paul McNutt, and a friend by the name of Colonel Dwight D. Eisenhower. Together, over the poker table, they cooked up a plan. Unfortunately, it had to be approved by the State Department which was very anti-Semitic at that time, but eventually they came up with a deal. Jews would be allowed to immigrate to the Philippines IF the Jewish community in Manila would guarantee their financial support. Frieder and the rescue committee raised tens of thousands of dollars with help from the American Jewish Joint Distribution Committee. Since they obviously couldn't take everybody, they then drew up a list of occupations which were needed, including doctors, nurses, engineers, various technical specialists, a butcher, a rabbi, on and on and, fortunately for me, a physics professor. Ads were placed in newspapers throughout Germany and Austria and before long the desperate requests started coming in. By late October, 1938, the first group, more than a hundred, had been approved to receive visas to enter the Philippines. McNutt, the Frieder brothers, and Quezon became the active movers of the plan; Eisenhower played no ongoing role in the rescue but served as the group's liaison to the U.S. Army, which oversaw the Philippines.

My parents started thinking desperately about where they could go. Two years earlier, in 1936, while traveling by train to the coronation of King George VI, my father's parents met and began corresponding with a lovely Australian lady. My parents wrote her of their plight and she actually sent them an affidavit, which was a requirement for a visa. Prior to that they had received word indirectly through the rescue plan that there was an opening for a physics professor at the University of the Philippines. My father applied, but couldn't wait for a response. Mail took weeks to go back and forth. People were being killed, and frontiers were closing. After months of petitioning the Nazi authorities, standing in lines, filling out forms and paying endless so-called fees, they managed to go to Australia. It was only after their arrival in Australia, where they were unsuccessful in finding work, that his Philippine application was approved. They arrived in Manila in June 1939, very late in the game. They just made it! They were lucky, as most of my family were killed in concentration camps. Asked how she felt upon leaving Austria, my mother's words were "relieved but sad."

Between 1200 and 1300 Jews, including my parents, were able to take advantage of this well-orchestrated plan through Dec. 8, 1941, which was, because of the time zones, Dec. 7 in the U.S., when Pearl Harbor changed the course of history and war came to the Philippines.

At a reunion of refugees and Frieder family members in Cincinnati in 2005, shortly after the release of *Schindler's List*, Barbara Sasser, Alex Frieder's granddaughter, said, "You know, everyone knows what Schindler did, because of the film, but my grandfather, Alex Frieder, along with President Quezon and US High Commissioner McNutt, rescued just as many Jews and nobody knows a thing about that." So the cry went out, "We should make a film, too!" Easier said than done; but they raised the funds, found and interviewed many of the refugees or their children, such as myself, and they found 3 Roads Communications to produce an award-winning documentary, *Rescue in the Philippines, Refuge from the Holocaust*. And they convinced Liev Schreiber to do the narration.

I should mention that the Philippines' contact with Jews actually goes back to the 16th century. The Jews who settled in those islands at that time came from Spain. They were known as Marranos—Jews who professed Catholicism in public, because of the Inquisition, but who observed their faith in secret. They are known to have traveled to and lived in Manila among the Spanish settlers. The Philippines had been discovered for Spain by Magellan in 1521 and had a large Spanish community. More significant Jewish migration to the Philippines started in the 1870s when the French Levy brothers left Alsace-Lorraine during the Franco-Prussian War. They were followed by Turkish, Syrian, Lebanese and Egyptian Jews, then by American Jews in the early 1900's after the Spanish American War. By the 1920s the Jewish community had been firmly established and numbered about 500. A synagogue was built and a Jewish burial plot at the North Cemetery was acquired. One of the major contributors to the building of the synagogue, named Temple Emil, was a Russian immigrant born in 1874 who ended up (via the U.S.) in Manila in 1901, where he established several very successful businesses. His name was

Emil Bachrach, entrepreneur and philanthropist. Temple Emil was named after his first name and the adjoining social hall was named Bachrach Hall, his last name. During the Japanese occupation the synagogue was destroyed, but was rebuilt with the help of Jewish American G.I.s, of whom there were quite a few.

Neither these American Jews nor any of the groups mentioned earlier (the Turks, the Syrians, the Lebanese, etc.) encountered any anti-Semitism in the Philippines. That is an important point. All those years later, when President Quezon was approached by the Jewish Frieder brothers about allowing persecuted Jews to find refuge in the Philippines, he said, "By permitting the Jews to come we are showing the world the kind of people we really are: hospitable, just and humane."

My parents described the pre-war Philippine Islands as paradise on earth. It was lush and green, with beautiful tropical flowers and delicious fruits, such as mangos, papayas, guavas and, oh, so many others. It was also fortunate that the Philippines was a U.S. Commonwealth at the time, so everyone spoke English, which they had studied in school, along with French, Latin and, in my father's case, even Greek. Luckily, it was not necessary to learn Tagalog (the national language of the Philippines). Although they took lessons, they found the language very difficult to learn.

Manila at that time was known as "the Pearl of the Orient." That all changed after the horrendous Battle of Manila in 1945, one of the most gruesome and deadly battles of World War II.

The Japanese took control of the Philippines and began what was to be a three-year occupation and rule of the country under a puppet native government. War was on and Jewish immigration to the Philippines stopped, even though the Japanese made no distinction between Jews and other foreigners. But foreigners from "enemy" countries like the US, the UK and Australia were taken to the University of Santo Tomas and interned in makeshift prison barracks for the duration of the war.

My parents were not among them because they were from Austria, which was now allied with Germany, which was an ally of Japan. Ah, the irony and, may I add, the stupidity of war! The war years, of course, were terrible. Being technically allies of the Japanese, my parents were not interned, but nevertheless suffered the hardships and deprivations of the Filipinos. Schools were closed, so, again, they had no jobs. My father had a friend with a coconut plantation and used the coconut oil and his knowledge of chemistry to make soap. Even in the final stages of pregnancy, my mother peddled the soap in the market. I managed to be born during a raging typhoon in the middle of the Japanese occupation in 1943. It was a most difficult time, as is clearly shown in the documentary, *Rescue in the Philippines*. To quote one of the refugees, "It was no picnic, but we survived."

In fact, it is a miracle that I am alive. Because my mother was malnourished, she had no milk and, as a tiny baby, I was starving. They bought a goat, but the poor goat ran out of milk, too. One day, totally at a loss for what to do, they suddenly heard a knock at the door. It was a boy with a case of canned Carnation milk. From Gertrude Stewart, an American friend of my mother's, who had snuck milk into the internment camp, knowing that there was none on the outside and having heard that her friend Paula had a newborn baby and no milk. News travels fast in Manila! A few years ago I attended an American School reunion in San Antonio and saw Mrs. Stewart's daughter, Trudy. I told her the story about how her mother saved my life. She had a shocked look on her face and then she told me this story. The previous summer she had gone through some of her dad's wartime letters and one of them mentioned Gertrude, her mom, sneaking milk out of the camp to help a baby on the outside. She was *wondering* who that baby might have been. Mystery solved!

After the Japanese realized that all was lost, they burned the entire city of Manila and killed indiscriminately, shooting old ladies and bayonetting babies for sport. They threw hand grenades into windows and set fire to everything in their path. More than 100,000 civilians were killed, including members of the Jewish community, not because they were Jews, but because they were in the wrong place at the wrong time. From Feb. 3 to March 3, 1945 the Battle for Manila raged, resulting in almost complete destruction of the former Pearl of the Orient. It was General Douglas MacArthur who actually called Manila "the most devastated city in the world, next to Warsaw."

Post Office viewed through shell hole
Postcard from Litwin Family Archives

People were hiding in foxholes and at one and a half years of age I was in a foxhole with my parents and other people. My crying almost got us all killed. A favorite line in the film is where everyone in the foxhole beseeches my parents to "shut the baby up, shut the baby up." As they stuffed my mouth with handkerchiefs, the footsteps at the edge of the foxhole suddenly stopped. Everyone assumed it was the enemy and that, despite being innocent civilians with a baby, we would all be killed. The next thing they heard was a voice calling down into the foxhole, "Anyone want a Chesterfield?" Finally! It was the beginning of Liberation. The thousands of American and British citizens who had been interned in Santo Tomás were freed and American G.I.s handed out such precious gifts as cans of sardines, Hershey bars, toilet paper, chewing gum and the aforementioned cigarettes.

Liberation at Santo Tomas, as Internees Unfurl U.S. Flag
U.S. Army Photo From Lou Gopal's Manila Nostalgia

After the war my parents went back to teaching and, while the city was haphazardly being rebuilt, never again the "pearl" that it once had been, life became "normal" and people did not speak about the war. It was just too painful. And I? I was a small child and, despite memories of flames engulfing my city, I was a happy child who played "house" with my friend Margrit in the remains of bombed out homes on Dewey Boulevard. It was only three years after the end of the war, 1948, that I entered the Kindergarten of the American School. A special place at a special time in history where enduring friendships were made. In the School History chapter you will learn how and why that school came to be.

Most of the refugees eventually left for the U.S. or what was then called Palestine, as Israel did not yet exist. My parents, however, decided to remain. They became Filipino citizens in 1950, in order to be able to buy property and build a home. A very wise move by my father. They lived out their lives there and are buried in the Jewish Cemetery. My mother, who died in 2001, was the last of the refugees who came as a result of the rescue operation, the Schindler's List that nobody knew about.

In the 1970s the synagogue, which had been designed by Austrian refugee Ernst Korneld and rebuilt in 1945 with the help of American soldiers, found itself in a deteriorating neighborhood and was demolished. By this time most members of the Jewish community lived in an elegant area called Makati, so money was raised to build the new synagogue there. Now, in 2021, there are about 200 families in the community.

President Quezon died in 1944, but before his death he said, "It is my hope, and indeed my expectation, that the people of the Philippines will have in the future every reason to be glad that when the time of need came, their country was willing to extend a hand of welcome."

In 2009, the Israeli city of Rishon LeTsion, eight miles South of Tel Aviv, erected a monument with open doors honoring Manuel Quezon and the Philippine people for their noble actions in rescuing German and Austrian Jews from persecution and death.

So why is this story so little known? Why did it take 70 years, when Barbara Sasser, Alex Frieder's granddaughter, decided to find some of the refugees or their children and have them interviewed before time ran out? I think it was because these people experienced horror twice, at the hands of the Nazis in Europe and at the hands of the Japanese soldiers in Asia. It was time to move on and speak no more of the nightmare and of their tragic losses. They needed to heal and one of the ways to begin this long process was through music. One of the refugees and a very close friend of my parents was Viennese conductor Herbert Zipper. Before the war he took over the Manila Symphony Orchestra. During the war there were no concerts, of course, just as there were no schools. But after Liberation he knew that bringing back music was of utmost importance; it was food for the soul. That concert was an experience that my Viennese, music-loving parents never stopped talking about. After doing a lot of sleuthing I found on eBay the Time magazine from May 21, 1945 that had a short article describing that concert.

As everything had been bombed and there was no concert hall, it was held in the bombed out, roofless old Santa Cruz church under a starlit Philippine sky. Twelve hundred people attended the concert, a mixture of soldiers and residents, my parents among them. The conductor, of course, was our dear Viennese friend, Herbert Zipper. It is mentioned that Mrs. Douglas MacArthur, dressed in pink, sat in the first row, as did the Symphony president, Mrs. Benito Legarda, who had bravely hidden the Society's instruments and scores in 1941. Many of the regular musicians were missing, as they had either been killed or were still fighting guerillas in the mountains. Replacements were found among soldiers and Manila residents. It didn't matter. It was the music that mattered and Herbert Zipper had chosen wisely. They played Beethoven's Third Symphony, known as the *Eroica*, which, of course, means "heroic." And then they played Antonin Dvorak's *New World Symphony*, in honor of the United States to whom they owed so much. Even after Dr. Zipper had left for the U.S., he returned every year and gave concerts at many Manila schools, including the American School. For many students it was their introduction to classical music and Dr. Zipper's way of giving back to the country that saved him in 1939.

A few years ago I found one of the Viennese refugees, Imanuel Willheim, who was a violinist in the orchestra. When I visited him in New York we spoke of the concert and he said that he would never forget that evening, and that there wasn't a dry eye in the house. The Time Magazine article ends with a quotation by one of the musicians::

"All that is beautiful and good will come back into our lives."

That is my hope as well.

CHAPTER 2

Introduction to the American School
[Historical background from *Manila Nostalgia* by Lou Gopal]

The American School in Manila was a small, unique, well funded school. It was set up to provide an academic college preparation education, as most of the students would go to college in the United States. The history of the school's struggles and slow evolvement after the Spanish American war and its survival through World War II is both fascinating and enlightening.

The American presence in the Philippines began with the Spanish American War. Admiral Thomas Dewey slipped into Manila Bay on May 1, 1898 and destroyed the obsolete Spanish fleet anchored there. General Arthur MacArthur, father of Douglas MacArthur of World War II fame, led a brigade in the capture of Manila. However, without telling MacArthur, General Merritt had already secretly negotiated with the Spanish that Spain would offer only token resistance if the Americans kept the angry Filipino insurgents at bay. The Filipinos joined in anyway, the Spanish were quickly subdued, and in Paris on December 10, 1898, the United States paid Spain $20 million to annex the entire Philippine archipelago.

The whole story of the Americans in the Philippines after the Spanish-American War is a complicated double-edged sword. On the one hand they were paternalistic toward "our little brown brothers", a term used by Gov. William Howard Taft, which, of course, nowadays is considered racist and condescending to the extreme. But, on the other hand, Taft wanted to prepare the Filipinos for eventual independence with a governmental system similar to that of the United States.

The Philippines would not be where it is today had it not been for the vital contributions of the Americans, particularly in the areas of education and health. The colonial government concentrated its efforts on education primarily because it allowed the U.S. to spread its cultural values, especially the English language, to the Filipino people. Instruction was in English and all children from age seven were required to register in school, where they were given free school materials. The other highly significant achievement was the construction of both a modern water system and a modern sewer system. They saw to it that the streets were swept daily and that garbage was collected. By educating the people about sanitation and by making safe water available, plague and cholera were eradicated and amoebic dysentery was greatly reduced. It was the Americans who contracted the large General Hospital that is still in use today.

After the conclusion of the Spanish American War, the first wave of soldiers and their wives settled in Manila and American businessmen, teachers and missionaries arrived with their families. In the early days of the American occupation, an American public school was created specifically for the children of American and also British residents. The enormity of financing the entire public school system led the Colonial Administration to close this school.

At that point all of these newly migrated Americans obviously needed to educate their children, but the choices for an American education were quite slim. Home schooling worked for some and some enterprising mothers even set up private "American Schools." The smaller, private schools were expensive to operate and maintain and, perhaps out of desperation, a Board of Trustees was created and a private "American School" was officially incorporated in 1920. The biggest problem was finding a location for the growing number of students increasing each year.

On June 21, 1920, the American School, Inc. opened its doors in a small two-story building. There were only eight primary grades, no high school, no kindergarten. On the face of it, the philosophy of the school appeared to be culturally and racially biased although that was not the intent. Parents knew that their children would be completing their education in the U.S. and wanted to ensure that they were well prepared, to the point of providing them with American textbooks and instructors.

An editorial found in the American Chamber of Commerce, February 1922 was openly discriminatory. It stated, "The American community believes it is entitled to a school for its children and is not disposed to compromise in the matter. American children must have instruction different from that adapted to Filipino children." They did concede it might be permissible to admit European children!

"Fortunately that mindset started to change after the war. Albeit slowly, the school's policy evolved to admit mestizos, Filipinos, [Chinese] and even an Indian/Filipino/Spanish kid like me." *Lou Gopal*

The American School continued to grow and moved to larger buildings twice. Overcrowded conditions forced the Board of Trustees to finally consider a new location. Plans were drawn up to buy a Donada Street property in Manila as a permanent home for the school and, with the help of patrons and donations from the community, this goal was achieved.

Construction of a two level concrete building that was earthquake, storm and fire proof started in the early months of 1936. It soon became a significant burden to cram the primary, elementary and high school students into this one building, so J.P. Heilbronn, a wealthy American businessman, made a generous donation for the construction of another building. This building, christened Heilbronn Hall, was finally completed in the latter part of 1939. It included a gymnasium with a balcony, a stage, classrooms, and shower rooms for girls and boys.

It was also in 1939 that the American School joined MAASS (Manila Athletic Association for Secondary Schools), competing with other Manila schools in such sports as volleyball, basketball, softball, badminton, tennis and swimming. The American School did not have a swimming pool or track, so these sports activities were held at the Rizal Memorial Stadium which was close by. The trim, well-kept grounds surrounding the school made it an odd little oasis with a strikingly American atmosphere.

As the school year for 1941-1942 opened, all the signs of a typical American school were visible on Donada Street. Army buses and cars dropped students off at the school, creating a good-size traffic jam. Some of the older boys volunteered for the School Traffic Patrol. On Monday December 8, news of the attack at Pearl Harbor and Japanese air raids forced the school to close and it wouldn't reopen for almost five years. The Japanese invaded and occupied Manila. Almost immediately the American and British residents of Manila were required to register as "enemy aliens" and were sent to the internment camp at University of Santo Tomás, which Mary mentioned in Chapter One. "My family was not interned, because we were Austrian citizens, therefore allies."

The school was turned into a Japanese Army Depot, but, fortunately, due to a few kind Japanese officers, Americans in Santo Tomás were able to acquire a few carloads of books from the campus. Many of the American School teachers were interned, thus ensuring a rather seamless transition. Work on organizing the children's education started almost immediately after internment and by January 12 about 112 children had registered for school. The quality of education continued at a remarkably high level although the books, paper and pencils were noticeably meager.

The recently hired principal, Louise Croft, was in charge. Mary remembers, "She was my principal when I entered Kindergarten and I remember her as being very kind and welcoming." In the camp she tried to normalize school as much as possible and even created ceremonies for the graduating seniors. One graduating senior, Margaret Hoffman Tileson, Class of 1943, said, "I don't know how they did it, but we even had cake and ice cream!" That was a rare exception, as the internees were living on a starvation diet, which often made the kids weak and listless. The first priority was keeping the children fed as the war continued for over three years of internment.

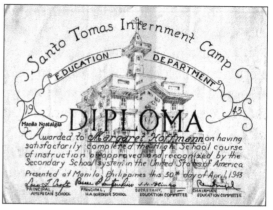

Mother Feeding Son
Santo Tomas Internment Camp
From Lou Gopal's Manila Nostalgia

American School Diploma
Santo Tomas Internment Camp
Margaret Hoffman Tileson, Class of 1943

Throughout the fire, shelling, and counter-shelling during the liberation of the Philippines, the American School buildings stood and, when the dust of battle had cleared away, they remained unscathed in the midst of a battered and torn Manila. Of course there were significant problems to overcome, including refurbishing and re-equipping the school. However, on September 9,1946, the American School once again threw open its doors and stood ready to offer its first post-war student body the best in education.

Each elementary teacher taught all subjects in their class except Physical Education, Music, Art and Spanish. Scouting was important as it provided activities and "field trips." There were also a number of competition sports teams. As was traditionally the case, school spirit and strong, long-lasting loyalties were formed, especially in the high school. There was a tremendous opportunity to be involved in the school, just because of its small size. And since classes ended at 12:30 pm, students had the afternoon to participate in extra-curricular activities. There was a Student Senate, Drama Club and Glee Club among the many available options. The journalism class was alive with activity working on the school newspaper, named the *Bamboo*, first put out in 1939. This was later changed to the *Bamboo Telegraph*. The yearbook was named the *Kawayan*, the native Tagalog word for bamboo. Sports dominated all other activities. All of these American School activities and traditions were in place when the first student of the class of 1961, Mary Brings, started kindergarten in 1948.

The school became more international in the 1940s. The Jewish children of the German and Austrian refugees that remained in Manila all attended the American School. Although most of our classmates were American, we had a variety of ancestry, ethnicity, cultures and religions in our class.

Many Filipino families could have afforded the tuition, but preferred to send their children to one of the excellent Catholic schools for a variety of reasons. This included our classmate Aurora, who left the American School after 7th grade, because her parents strongly wanted her to finish in a very fine Catholic school.

Looking back, the formation and role of the American School was complex. Our parents, administrators and teachers worked hard to give us the best possible educational experience. Many classmates came and left as their fathers were reassigned to another country or back to the U.S. We tell the story as it was but we recognize that for those times people lacked the social, racial and cultural awareness and sensitivity of today.
The American School was later renamed the International School of Manila and today reflects a completely diversified student population from sixty different countries.

Our *American School Main Building on Donada Street in the 1950s*
American School Archives

CHAPTER 3

Surviving World War II in the Philippines
Four Manila-Born Classmates

Our story continues with an introduction to three more classmates who were also born in Manila during the war. Aurora is of Spanish-Filipino descent and Gloria is of Chinese descent; they were born in 1943. Ray, of Filipino descent, was born in 1942, but he did not join the class until Junior High. We all speak of our early years during and after the war.

Mary Brings
The girl whose parents were from Austria

Mary at age five

According to what my parents wrote in my Baby Book, there were heavy air raids over Manila on my first birthday, October 29, 1944. The invited guests were thus unable to attend. I am told that I pointed to the sky and happily said "rrr-rrr," mimicking the sound of the aircraft overhead. That first year I had no toys, but played with anything I could grasp. Despite my parents' efforts to shield me from the horrors of the final Battle for Manila, my earliest memory is that of fire—the flames of war in the last brutal months of World War II when the American Army fought the Japanese soldiers in their battle to reclaim Manila.

My second birthday was much more cheerful. The war had ended, children came and my gifts included slippers, a doll, a teddy bear, and a stuffed elephant. Where did the moms find these precious items in a city whose destruction was complete? I wonder.

By age three and a half I was ready for the Teach-a-Tot Nursery School, which I loved! Because I was an only child and quite shy, my parents wanted to give me an opportunity to socialize with other children and begin "school" as soon as possible. Who knew that "school" would be my life from then on for the next sixty years?

I have some very special memories from Teach-A-Tot. I made friends readily and was delighted that one of my best friends, Stevie Gunders, also a child of refugees, was in attendance as well. The teachers introduced us to all sorts of games and songs. One song in particular created some commotion in my house. I started singing "A tisket, a tasket, a green and yellow basket. I wrote a letter to my love and on my way I lost it". But then I got very upset, because I didn't know what a tisket and a tasket were. I didn't believe my parents when they said they were just nonsense words, even though they were not to be found in their huge dictionary. I still remember how frustrated I was not to know the meaning of the words! When my mother took me to school the next day, we asked one of my three teachers, Mrs. Hall. She threw her head back and laughed, saying, "Oh, those are nonsense words, just to make it rhyme." My mother gave me that "I told you so" look.

The final exam, if you will, was another traumatic word experience. Mrs. Hall took me outside and we sat on the grass, where she pulled out a large drawing of an imaginary town. When she pointed at something, I was supposed to identify it, i.e. park, hospital, store. No problem. Almost done. Then she pointed to a wide street that led out of the town. I said "street." Wrong! "Road?" "Avenue?" "Boulevard?" Wrong! Wrong! Wrong! She tried to help by showing that it exited the town, but I was stumped. And devastated! Thinking I was a complete failure, I started crying and said, "I don't know." She said, "It's a highway." Huh? Highway? Then it dawned on her that in 1947 Manila there was no such thing as a highway and so of course I was unfamiliar with the word! Thank goodness I did not flunk out of nursery school after all!

Shortly after passing my nursery school final exam, we had a graduation ceremony, complete with white caps and gowns. The next day the *Manila Bulletin* had photos of this grand occasion in its Society pages. One of them showed me on a podium with a microphone in front of me. From Mary's mother, "I still remember her nursery school graduation. She had a white cap and gown like a real graduation, and she had to sing a song. It was very cute." My mother couldn't remember the song when I asked her years later, but I like to think that it MUST have been *A Tisket, a Tasket*! Now I was ready to enter Kindergarten at the American School in June, 1948.

Mary at the microphone,
Teach-a-Tot Graduation
Brings Family Archives

∾

Aurora Abrera
Spanish Heritage

Aurora age seven

From the Sityar side of the family, which is my mother's side, I know that my mother's grandfather was a Spanish Duke, his wife was a Lady-in-Waiting to the Queen and also related to the Queen, and my aunt had cousins in Spain, including one who was a Count. One of the Duke's sons was Manuel Sityar, a Spanish military officer who uncovered the plans of the Katipunan, the Philippine Revolutionary group that led the revolution against Spain. Since he married a native Filipina and became aware of the abuses of Spaniards against Filipinos at that time, Manuel later joined the Philippine forces under Emilio Aguinaldo. Manuel's brother was my grandfather, Guillermo, a math professor and an immigration officer. If we were to look at the family tree today, my family can be traced to the Borbon line in Europe and to the present King of Spain.

My father's side of the family did not have as colorful a history as my mother's. My grandfather Basilio was a simple and hard-working Filipino man from Palawan, an island west of Luzon. It has pristine white beaches and many coconut trees inhabited by frisky monkeys. Grandfather Basilio was a trader, fisherman and founder of Concepcion, a town in Palawan. My grandmother was a teacher and raised six children, the youngest of whom was my father.

My parents met at a train station in Manila where my mother worked. She was introduced to my father by a co-worker and, apparently, she and my father hit it off quickly. They had been courting for some time when the Japanese attacked Pearl Harbor on December 7, 1941. The possibility of war in the Philippines hastened my father's decision to get married, and they did so quickly on December 10, three days later. Gifted with a strong work ethic and great intelligence, my father's life was blessed with wonderful opportunities that helped him lead a life of service for his country. He was an outstanding student, graduating valedictorian of his high school class and awarded scholarships to universities. He attended the University of the Philippines and the Massachusetts Institute of Technology and earned degrees in Mechanical Engineering, Marine Engineering and Naval Architecture. Armed with experience and knowledge during World War II, he built the Q-boat inthe Philippines that helped General Douglas MacArthur escape to Australia and allowed President Manuel Quezon to leave Iloilo to another point in the Philippines in order to hide and escape from the Japanese. Immediately after the war and the declaration of the Independenceof the Philippines, Philippine President Manuel Roxas appointed my father Chairman of the Philippine

Reparations to Japan. In Japan, my father renewed his ties with General MacArthur and worked closely with him along with other representatives of the Allied nations to obtain reparations from Japan. Later, he was designated by the Philippine government to begin the industrialization of the Philippines by establishing the National Shipyards and Steel Corporation (NASSCO). This company was the first to build ships in the Philippines. After all, the Philippines was a country of over 7500 islands. It was only appropriate that it should build ships to help build its economy and to provide transport and leisure, similar to other industrialized countries. His establishment of an integrated steel mill in the Philippines also seeded the beginning of the industrial economy of the country. He was named the "Steel Man of Asia."

I was born in 1943 during the Japanese occupation of the Philippines. During this time life was very dangerous. The Japanese imposed curfews in the early evenings, and anyone caught walking the streets beyond a certain hour at night was stopped and questioned. After the war, my father recounted how he had been out later than usual some evenings. He had to bow deeply in front of a Japanese officer and explain why he had gone past the curfew. Luckily, he had been allowed to move on and head for home on those occasions. My father was very lucky. Often Japanese soldiers were unsatisfied with some of the excuses given to them by people caught beyond curfew hours and they simply killed them on the spot with their bayonets without hesitation.

During the occupation we were generously invited to stay with friends in Pateros, now a suburb of Manila, but at that time it was out in the country. It was supposed to be safer, but that was not always the case. If a Japanese soldier had been mysteriously killed in the environs, there would be a call for revenge against the perpetrators. The underground guerrillas would send out word through the grapevine that the Japanese soldiers were out to catch the culprits. This meant that the townsmen would be arrested in the village where the Japanese soldier was killed. They would be marched to the town square, lined up against the wall, and massacred by gunfire. My father recounted how he and his fellow villagers would hurriedly run down to the river and hide underwater by breathing reeds until the danger of being caught and arrested passed. It was truly a frightening time and there was no real escape from danger. Our friend Pio Luna's invitation to live with his family in the country, however, greatly minimized the possibility of being killed, either by the menace of the Japanese soldiers on the streets of Manila or by the relentless and frequent dogfights or bombings that took place in the skies above the city.

After the war my parents and I lived in a second-floor apartment in the middle of downtown Manila. Our apartment had a porch that wrapped around it on one side, and as a little girl it provided me all kinds of entertainment as I peeked through the beautifully designed porch holes that revealed the street below. The end of the long street led to a cemetery, so as a child I witnessed daily funeral processions on the street below. The first thing I heard was the recorded voice of a woman singing "Ave Maria." Her song came from a loudspeaker propped on top of a black hearse. As soon as I heard the song, I dropped everything I was doing and eagerly ran to theporch and peeked to the right of me to observe what was approaching. Slowly, the black hearse crawled towards where we were, followed by several lines of people dressed in black and walking slowly with their heads turned down. They were mostly women, crying loudly and dabbing at their faces with white hankies. They were followed by cars that snaked through the streets towards us, disappearing as the procession moved past, winding its way to the cemetery a couple of blocks away. There was a large Chinese community near us, so many of the participants in the procession were Chinese, displaying some of their funeral traditions. There was no television at that time, so my primary entertainment venue was what I saw on the street. The funerals were the highlight of each day.

While we waited for our home to be built in Quezon City, my parents rented a home on Dapitan Street. There was a sari-sari (variety) store on the corner sitting diagonally from the house. I would sit on the floor for several minutes and watch men, women and children march up to the store with doors wide open, to buy a cup of vinegar, a bottle of soda (tin cans were not popular then) or a sweet and sour tamarind snack. There were many vendors plying the streets, and from where Isat, I could call out to them to stop so I could buy treats from them like "puto-cuchinta," (rice cakes) or "taho." Balut vendors also came by, but I was not interested in eating boiled duck embryos that others found so delicious!

My brother, Bernardo, Jr., was born in January, 1946, shortly after the end of the war, and my mother revealed that she had difficulty producing enough breast milk for the baby. My aunt had also given birth to her first child that same year, so my mother asked her to nurse my brother as well. Junior refused to nurse from my aunt. Unfortunately, this was also the time that my brother got meningitis and within the space of a few months passed away despite frequent injections of penicillin, the new "wonder drug." My mother was a stay-at-home mom who, like my father, believed in the advantages of having an advanced education. Needing to work after high school and not able to attend university earlier, she enrolled at the University of Santo Tomas when she was already married and earned a B.A. degree in Philosophy and Letters. She was generous with us and everyone who knew her remarked that she was a great cook and a wonderful sounding board. She encouraged us to study and work hard, become independent and help others.

These values were encouraged when I entered the Second Grade at the American School in 1950.

Gloria Chua
Chinese Classmate

Gloria at age five

My great-grandfather, Jose Yutivo, went from China to the Philippines as a young man to seek his fortune. He started out as a houseboy for a Spanish family, hence the name "Jose." "Yu" is the family name, and "tivo" means mother pig—there's a story about that, something about humility, which I don't quite remember.

Eventually, he had plenty of money and land in the Philippines, but he never lived in the country permanently. It was his son, my grandfather, who really emigrated and settled his family in Manila. My grandfather continued developing the businesses my great grandfather had started.

Both of my parents emigrated from Fujian Province in southern China. My mother's family was prosperous, but their prosperity could not guarantee any stability or safety in a thoroughly chaotic country. China was engulfed in feudal and civil wars and heading toward a revolution that would split it into two entities. Reluctantly, they left their comfortable life in the family compound on the island of Gulangyu. Just off the southeast coast of China, the island was idyllic and famous for its beauty and Mediterranean climate.

Our extended family on my mother's side fortunately already had a foothold in the Philippines, as several previous generations of its menfolk had traveled to the islands to work or do business with Spanish traders. They all could speak Spanish. In contrast, my father's family was quite humble, but that was the norm in his home town of Xiamen, a town on China's southeast coast. The most notable fact about his family—as it relates to my life and upbringing—is that they were Christian. The American missionaries must have converted a large portion of Fujianese and my grandmother was probably the most fervent of all the converts.

Chinese migration is often a large-group activity: generations of families, even entire villages, aim for a common destination and, once there, settle back together in an enclave patterned after their old communities. The Fujianese mostly emigrated to the Philippines, Indonesia, Malaysia, and Singapore. In contrast, the Cantonese—Canton Province is next door to Fujian—tended to go to America, mostly to California, to work in the gold mines and railroads.

I was a war baby, born in Manila in the middle of World War II, during the Japanese occupation of the Philippines. As an infant, I should have been unaware of and therefore protected from the horrors of war. But maybe this war and occupation had been so traumatic that one bit of it managed to lodge in my infant mind. I have a memory of my grandparents carrying my younger brother and me in their arms, running for a very long time through a smoky orange scene, amidst ruins. I was in my grandmother's arms and could hear her praying and praying as she hurried along. I never realized what that memory was about until my family began telling war stories.

American troops move in
Postcard from Litwin Family Archives

We were caught in the middle of the 1945 Battle of Manila, the last major battle of the war between Japanese and American forces. Japan was about to lose the war. In desperation, they let loose one vicious last firefight, aimed at the total destruction of Manila. My parents, having previously fled from the wars (and famine and government corruption) in China, must have felt that their lives were akin to the proverbial "jumping from the frying pan into the flames." We had a dog and a cat that could not be rescued. I don't remember those pets, but my mother would recall how no one could touch that Persian cat without getting scratched, yet it tolerated my teasing and tail-pulling.

When I was young, I understood that my mother's family was the predominant Chinese family in Manila. It remained so until Ferdinand Marcos came into power, at which point his cronies got so very rich they made the Yu family look puny. But the family also did itself in—fighting within itself for control of various corporations (including the automotive plants that assembled all the General Motors cars in the Philippines). The warring factions were based on which mother my aunts and uncles were descended from. That's because my grandfather, a Christian who built our church, had three wives!

Every year, when my grandparents had birthdays, they would each have two parties: one informal, just for family, and one formal, for family, friends, and important social and political acquaintances. I had to have a wardrobe of red dresses for these occasions. And we always had to get coached on how to address everybody, not simply first uncle, second aunt, etc. There were different titles to use which would let a listener know whether your uncle was on your mother's or father's side, and whether he was older or younger than your parent. Nerve-wracking!

Our families stayed close because they grew up living in a traditional Chinese compound, a cluster of linked houses circling a central courtyard. When they married, a lot of them simply brought in their husbands and wives to live at the compound. Next to it was what we called the "clubhouse," a place with a basketball court, a tennis court (I remember my uncles, dressed in stiff tennis whites, having lessons with "Pancho" Segura, the local tennis pro), a putting green, billiard room, changing room, etc.

I have a distinct memory from 1947 when I took the President Cleveland, the ship that many American School students took to come to the Philippines, to China with my mother and my aunt. In fact, it was just before the Communists were closing China to the rest of the world. My mother and an aunt wanted to return one last time before the closure and they took me along.

I had a great time on board, ordering ice cream for breakfast and going through an entire box of plastic balloons out on the deck. I remember seeing a closet full of money. I asked my mother whether we were rich, and she said it was all worthless because of the huge inflation going on. Another of the biggest thrills was getting on an escalator in a department store in Shanghai.

In 1950, when my younger brother and I applied for enrollment into, respectively, first and second grades at the American School, we were asked to meet with the headmaster and several members of the school board. For years, I have wondered what that meeting was all about. Today, I have concluded that it was about our language skills and ability to fit into the student body. At the time, we were very unusual applicants to the school: children with not a shred of international experience or sophistication.

I do remember being asked about my knowledge of English. Or maybe I was being tested through my usage? But really, English? True, it was only my third language, after Hokkien (a Fujianese dialect) and Tagalog. But English was in the very air of Manila. It was the medium of instruction in schools and the language of government, newspapers, radio (no TV yet). It was the language that my Chinese family and community feared would override our Chinese.

All in all, it was a kindly conversation we had with this man, Herbert E. Warfel, whom I came to revere over the years. I remember how his convocations—15-minute meetings at the beginning of the school day—would have a "word of the day" to learn, or a new song to sing (such as "Across the Blue Pacific," a school song he wrote). I remember how, during rainy season when the streets flooded, he would roll up his nice white pants, take off his shoes, and wade up to our cars to carry us kids into the school building.

Headmaster Warfel

Why did my father decide to enroll his children at the American School? (My brother and I were later joined by another brother and a sister; all four of us graduated high school from the A.S.) He wanted a good education for us, and strong English skills as well, just in case we were ever to make our way to America. He himself had been offered employment in the U.S., but could not accept because, as first-born son, he was responsible for the well-being of his parents and siblings in Manila. We could have gone to local Catholic schools, which were excellent academic institutions, and their tuition would have been a fraction of the American School's. However, it was not feasible. Some of the schools required conversion to Catholicism if one was not already Catholic. Mostly, my grandmother (the fervent Christian convert) disapproved. Her conservative, fundamentalist faith rejected Catholicism. To her, Catholics were the work of the Devil, and she tried to force us out of kindergarten (yes, we did try to enroll into these schools), completely outraged by all the rosaries we had learned and all the signs of the Cross we had made. Thus began my education at the American school.

Our fourth Philippine-born classmate, a boy this time, joined our class in the seventh grade. He, too, is a Philippine war baby. Meet Ray Domingo:

Ray Domingo

I was born under a tree...

Ray at age thirteen

Now, I've never used that line to start a party conversation, but perhaps I should try it sometime.

In early 1942, as the Japanese were dropping their bombs on the Philippines, my family left their home in Manila for the relative safety of my grandfather's farm in the province of Nueva Ecija, some eighty-five miles north of the city. It is not clear to me how long they stayed at the farm, but I remember listening, enthralled as my older brothers, Fred, then ten years old, and Eric, eight, would later tell stories of whiling away the hours roaming the farm, sometimes going with my father to hunt doves and wild game that would end up on the family dinner table, or riding bareback on my grandfather's carabaos.

Duhat (pronounced doo' hot) is a dark purple Asian berry that is sweet-tart and, when sprinkled with sea salt, it becomes a delicious fruit snack in the Philippines. The duhat tree involved in my personal history was a short distance removed from the house and blended in with the surrounding trees and brush. Around the tree, my father and grandfather had stacked a circumference of gunnysacks filled with dirt. This was the shelter the family would run to when needed.

As told to me, on the afternoon of February 12, explosions and gunshots had erupted nearby. When my father and grandfather rushed to get their guns, my mother scooped up Eric, and with Fred running beside her and me in her belly, made a dash for the shelter at the duhat tree. That's when her water broke.

With my mother in labor, my father went on horseback to fetch the town doctor, who refused to come, because it was too dangerous. And so I came into this world naturally, without medical assistance and surrounded only by my family. My father cut the umbilical cord.

We have all heard of childbirth in taxicabs, buses, and elevators. Now you have heard of one under a duhat tree.

All in all, I lived a carefree and idyllic childhood in Acacia, a little barrio in the town of Malabon, in the province of Rizal. The very first home I remember was a wonderful house on stilts with a thatched roof and I remember the southwest corner of that thatched roof lifting up and down like a fish's mouth during Typhoon Ida in 1950.

It was too big to be called a hut. The house had two bedrooms, a good sized living room and a floor made of bamboo slats that one could peek through the spaces and see the ground underneath. The kitchen was on the west side of our house where all the cooking was done over a wood fire. I remember, vividly, the fragrance of rice cooking in a clay pot lined with banana leaves. Wooden stairs led down from the kitchen to the back yard. Near the stairs was a pump with a long handle and that pump provided us with all the water we needed. On the northeast part of the front yard was a chicken coop and a small fenced-in poultry farm. Chickens. We always had chickens. Chickens would come to play a part in what happened one day.

During the Japanese occupation, my father had assumed the dangerous responsibility of storing guns and ammunition in our house, and the men from the barrio would come at night to arm themselves for the purpose of taking pot shots at Japanese soldiers under the cover of darkness. In addition to this dangerous operation, some days the men would gather at our house and secretly operate a short wave radio to get any information that might help them in their guerrilla activities. My oldest brother Fred would tell of one such day. My father had ordered him and Eric to go out to the front yard in order to look out for Japanese soldiers while the men were on the short wave radio. The boys went out, got to playing as boys do, and soon forgot about the duty they were assigned. "Next thing I knew," Fred explained, "A bayonet was plunged into the ground between my feet." He looked up to see two Japanese soldiers towering over him. One can only imagine the thoughts and emotions going through my brother's mind at that moment. He knew this was big trouble and could picture in his mind, he would later say, my father and the barrio men being rounded up and taken away by the Japanese.

And then this happened: The Japanese soldiers pointed and indicated that they would like a couple of chickens. "Eric and I couldn't chase down those chickens and stuff them into a gunny sack fast enough," Fred told us. He handed them the sack of chickens and the Japanese soldiers walked away happily.

We had a maid, a houseboy and a chauffeur. We always had maids, houseboys and chauffeurs. Somehow it never seemed to be a problem fitting everyone into our life. At night, floor mats and mosquito nets were set up wherever floor space was available.

Next to the house was a wooden structure that served as a garage for the family jeep. The jeep took the place of the old family car that, alas, had been a bombing casualty. I remember one day my father and some neighbors were stripping the old paint off the jeep for repainting. Hidden underneath the top layer of paint, the name "Marion Joy" resurfaced. I remember wondering why there was all this excitement and cheering around the old jeep. "This is an omen!", they exclaimed. My mother soon gave birth to a baby girl. My baby sister. Her name: Marion Joy.

Soon we were building a new house. The smell of new lumber always reminds me of those days. The excitement. The anticipation. The proud look on my father's face as the family sat around on the piles of wood beams and concrete blocks and laughed and relived old memories and retold old family stories.

It was beautiful! Two story, three bedrooms, two bathrooms, formal dining room, large kitchen with modern stove and refrigerator, maid's quarters, tile floors on the first floor, hardwood floors on the second.

To my baby sister and me, it was the biggest house we had ever seen! It had a concrete and metal fence and a swinging gate that opened to a concrete driveway that led to the garage that sheltered our brand new, green, 1952 Chevrolet.

There was a small detached building that was home for our two houseboys and a chauffeur. On an adjacent lot we had a chicken coop and small poultry farm. Chickens. We always had chickens. Next to that lot was another lot with fruit trees and an area for growing corn, tomatoes, eggplant, mangoes, sugar apples, guavas, etc.

One might describe my growing up days as wild and free. The Japanese soldiers were gone and America had given the Philippines our independence. One day a few young people from the barrio decided to go to the river to swim. The river which ran east and west, through the town of Tinajeros in Malabon, was perhaps five miles north from our house.

I was one of the three younger boys, maybe eight years old, who tagged along. I can't recall why my older brothers were not there that day, but had they been, I would not have been allowed to go.

Going to the river meant walking half a mile east, uphill, down an incline to the railroad tracks. From there it was a four and a half mile walk north on the railroad tracks to the bridge that went across the river.

At that age I loved the water, though I hadn't learned to swim. I loved going to the river but I always dreaded crossing that bridge. Everyone in the group casually walked across to the other side where a path led down to the water. But not me. There I was on my hands and knees, trying not to look at the space between the railroad ties, imagining myself falling through and down into the deep water in the middle of the river. I knew I could get through this. I had done it a few times before. But this time it was different. Behind me, I could hear a train rumbling in the distance, blowing its whistle, and getting closer. I was halfway across the bridge.

Nestor, the oldest boy in the group, looked back when he heard the train, and upon seeing the danger I was in, ran as fast as he could on top of those railroad ties and got to me just in time to scoop me up with one arm and pull me to the side of the bridge while hanging on with his other arm. I will never forget the moment that that train thundered onto that bridge and flew by with its swaying sides inches from my face.

Once the train had passed, Nestor calmly set me back down on the tracks to crawl my way back to the group and we all had a grand time.

After the war my mother and father resumed their life as business people. They commuted back and forth between Acacia and Manila. My mother, who had been a school teacher, now bought and sold jewelry. My father ran a real estate firm, an insurance agency and the Keepsake Optical Company, at 37 Escolta, two doors from the Capitol Theater. My sister and I spent a lot of our childhood hours there waiting either to be taken to, or brought back from school, depending on whether we were in the morning or afternoon session. This varied from year to year. We took turns killing time sitting in the eye examining chair, which was the only air conditioned room at Keepsake. "I memorized everything on the eye charts," Marion would brag, and when challenged, she would recite it all. I also spent many hours trying to beat the pinball machine at a place across the street from the bowling alley located beside the Pasig River. I would occasionally go to see a movie at one of the movie theaters. Or I would be drawing. Always I was drawing, drawing, drawing. Still I had ample time to simply roam the streets of Manila.

I was now enrolled, and my sister later, at the Cecilio Apostol Elementary School, a public school in the city. I would be there up until the end of the fifth grade.

Swimming. Take swimming out of the equation and I probably would never have found myself enrolled in the American School.

As I have said, in those days I spent a lot of time at my father's place of business at 37 Escolta, either before or after school. I do not know where my father's obsession came from, but having observed my love for the water, the river, the ocean, swimming pool, any collection of water deep enough to frolic in, he decided that I should learn to swim "the scientific way." The Australian Crawl was what they called it then, simply known today as Freestyle.

Ah, yes, he was obsessed. He would take an hour and a half off from his work every day to take me to the Manila YMCA to swim and teach me the rudiments of the "scientific way." Remember, I was just learning to swim. "Swim to the other end," he would say. "You can make it." When I finally made it to the other end of the pool, he said, "Now swim back." "Dad, I can't," I would plead. One day my father was not able to leave work because of business commitments, so I took a fifteen centavo jeepney ride to the Y to swim alone. It was wonderful to be free just to do the fun little things that I would do with my friends in the river, see how long I could hold my breath underwater with my eyes open, do back flips, do handstands, etc. Then the thought came to me, "I'm going to swim to the other end." Yes. "Just relax and do it." When I got to the other end, I thought, "That wasn't hard," and I swam back. Then I swam back again, and back and forth and back and forth and back and forth, keeping count of the laps. At some point I got my second wind, and I remember thinking to myself, "I could do this all day long!"

When I returned to my father's office, I could hardly wait for him to ask me. I knew he would. "Did you do laps?" "Yes." "How many?" "Fifty." Long pause "How Many?" "FIFTY!"

And from that day on, it became, for my father, an ever bigger priority that he went with me to the Y every day. It was the end of the school year in 1954. I remember sadly saying goodbye to my classmates at Cecilio Apostol Elementary. I was not coming back.

September found me in Mrs. Grant's class, South Hall, the American School. Sitting there nervously, I listened intently as she read the daily announcement of after school activities. "Girls and Boys Class A and Class B swimming tryouts, one o'clock Army Navy Club." Tryouts normally would have been held at the Rizal Stadium pool, but on this day the Rizal pool was undergoing maintenance.

I remember the shock of diving into an over-chlorinated pool that day. Coach Amabuyok asked me how many laps I thought I could do. I said, "Fifty." He said, "Okay" and told me to do four as he watched. The next day he gave me my green swimming trunks, and my green sweatshirt with the big green and gold A on the front. I was on the American School swimming team!

That year I won all my events in the 200 meter freestyle, 100 meter freestyle, and 50 meter freestyle, and won gold medals in the same events in the Regional Championships. I was continuing to develop as a swimmer, and making my father proud. Dare I say, my life was going along swimmingly.

Each of our war baby families faced the challenges of the occupation in different ways but all came though with an eye to the future.

METRO MANILA PLACE NAMES
Mentioned

1. Santo Tomás
2. A.S. Donada St.
3. Dewey / Roxas Blvd.
4. Rizal Stadium
5. Makati
6. Forbes Park
7. San Lorenzo Village
8. Army Navy Club
9. Polo Club
10. The Luneta,
    aka Rizal Park
11. Sta. Mesa
12. Quezon City
13. Mandaluyong
14. Sangley Point
15. Pasig River
16. Malacañang Palace
17. Manila Hotel

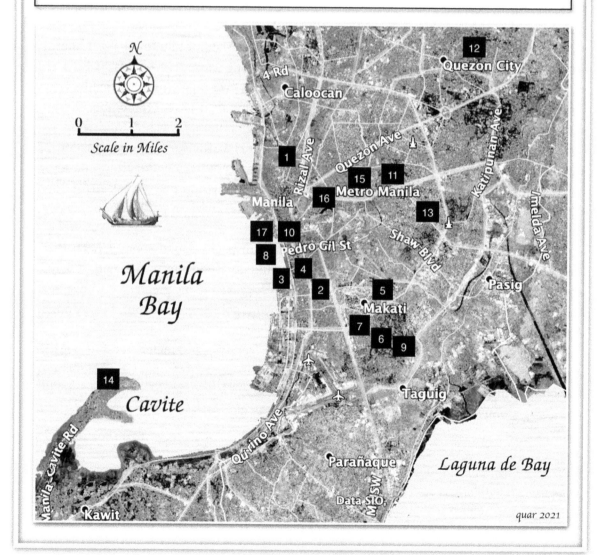

CHAPTER 4

Growing Up in the Philippines

The term "Metro Manila" commonly refers to the the greater metropolitan area of the capital city and includes the much larger Quezon City and the Makati Financial Center, in addition to many districts with individual names. The city is located on the eastern shores of Manila Bay. The Pasig River flows through the middle of the city, dividing it into the north and south sections.

Home and Food

Mary Brings
The girl whose parents were from Austria

During the war, as the city was being ravaged, we had no secure place to live and very little food. We ran from place to place, even spending some time in people's garages. My grandmother cooked by balancing a pan on three stones. According to my mother, she even somehow managed a somewhat acceptable version of *Apfelstrudel* by using a native squash, *sayote,* whose texture resembled that of an apple!

After Liberation schools reopened and life slowly returned to "normal." The Jewish refugees did not speak of the horrors they had survived, but of the future. To stay or to leave? My parents had good teaching jobs, loved the Philippines and the Filipino people, so they decided to stay. They rented the lower flat in a large, two-flat house just off Dewey Boulevard. It was a substantial old Spanish-style house. I loved it, because it was so close to Manila Bay. My parents and I took long walks on the Boulevard along the bay in the late afternoons and sat on the sea wall to admire the world famous Manila Bay sunsets. The two things I loved most about the house were the huge garden in the back with a majestic mango tree and the wide veranda with the cut-out tiles in the front and along the side of the house. It was on that veranda where I played with my friends and where neighbors joined us when they would "drop in." "Dropping in" unannounced was a local custom. There was always a snack to offer guests and their visits were never seen as an imposition.

When I was about ten a schoolmate, Gordy Lester (Class of '63), and his parents moved into the upper flat. They were Holocaust refugees from Germany and part of the close-knit Jewish community in Manila. Mr. Lester gave Gordy and me a ride to school every morning in their navy blue Hudson.

After becoming Philippine citizens in 1950 my parents could own property, so they bought a nice piece of land in the district of Santa Mesa, located in the eastern section of Metro Manila near the San Juan River. After the lot was paid off we hired an architect and built the home that l lived in from eighth grade until I finished high school. The house had a large terrace and a beautiful garden, my mother's pride and joy. No mango tree, but it did have avocados, papayas and guavas. I planted a coconut seedling in 1956 and in no time it was a tall coconut tree.

Brings Family Home in Santa Mesa
Brings Family Archives

While the house was a modest bungalow, we splurged on narra floors and entrance doors. Narra, the national wood of the Philippines, is a hard wood (now endangered) noted for its ability to take a high polish. Although it was a new house in a nice subdivision, I missed my walks on the boulevard and the seawall, where I could watch the sun sink into the bay. It also was a longer commute to the American School, but I did adjust eventually, when I realized that some of my school friends lived in the general area.

In her Oral History my mother said: "Nothing tasted like it did at home in Austria. The butter was not the same. The flour tasted different. If we followed a Viennese recipe, it always tasted different because the ingredients were simply not the same. We did not cook many Filipino dishes, mostly pancit and adobo." *Pancit* is a dish of Chinese origin that appears at every Filipino party. It's a noodle dish cooked with vegetables such as carrots, onions, celery, and chopped cabbage in addition to shrimp and/or slices of cooked chicken. There are many different varieties, depending on the type of noodle used. Adobo, made with chicken or pork and cooked with garlic, soy sauce and vinegar, is considered the Philippine national dish. Adobo is a traditional pre-Hispanic dish, which was prepared in clay pots. When the Spanish came, they decided to call it "adobo," the Spanish term for a marinated dish.

Recently I went to a Filipino restaurant in San Francisco that catered primarily to Filipinos. When I looked at the menu, I was very surprised not to find adobo. I asked the owner about the omission and he laughed. He said that they used to offer it, but every Filipino said that their *lola's* (grandmother's) adobo was better. Since he couldn't win, he removed it from the menu and stuck with more complex dishes.

My mother continued, "We generally cooked Austrian food. The main meal was at noon and the lighter meal was in the evening. We frequently invited people for Sunday afternoon coffee or tea with small sandwiches and pastries This was known in the Philippines as *merienda*, in Austria as *Jause*."

As we mostly had Austrian food as our main meal, I sometimes asked to be excused to eat with the house girls in the kitchen. I much preferred their fish or chicken with rice and fresh green vegetables. To this day I prefer to eat this way. I think the house girls were flattered to know that I preferred their simple cuisine to the heavy Austrian meat, potatoes and gravy. And it's so much healthier!

Other Philippine dishes include *lechón* and *balut*. *Lechón*, a roasted suckling pig, comes from the Spanish tradition and is a popular Fiesta dish in the Philippines. The skin is crispy and the meat is succulent, but animal lovers such as I tend to stay away. *Balut*, considered a delicacy in the Philippines, is a fertilized duck egg that is incubated for a period of 14 to 21 days, then boiled or steamed and eaten whole after the eggshell is removed. The embryo is already formed and close to being hatched when it is cooked. When we were growing up, vendors would walk up and down the streets with a bamboo pole on their shoulder that had round metal containers hanging off the ends, filled with warm balut. They would cry out "Baluuuuut Baluuuuut" in a sing-song voice that rose at the end of the word. I had no interest. However, on the night before I left the Philippines for college I rode up and down Dewey Boulevard with my friends from school. They came across a balut vendor and they made me eat it. After all, it was my last night and they certainly weren't going to offer it at my college cafeteria in California!

For snacks and dessert we had a number of choices. *Halo-halo*, which means mix-mix, is the traditional casual dessert. It consists of shaved ice with a variety of mix-ins, which range from sweetened red beans, sweetened white beans, sweetened coconut strings, gelatins, and fruits such as jackfruit, plantains, and lychee. It sometimes includes ice cream as well. The more formal, classic dessert is *leche flan*, basically the same as the Spanish flan, or the French *crème caramel*. For an every-day dessert there is always ice cream. The Philippine Magnolia brand goes back to 1925 and offers all the usual flavors plus mango, coconut, ube (purple yam), banana and even avocado.

Magnolia Cart with Jeepney
In the public domain

When we kids heard the familiar bell of the Magnolia cart down the street, we would run out with our centavos and grab either a popsicle or vanilla ice cream on a stick, encased in hard chocolate. Sometimes the chocolate was embedded with toasted glutinous rice, known as pinipig, and that was my favorite—pinipig crunch.

I also watched for the puto & cuchinta man with a similar bamboo pole and round metal containers. When I heard "Putoooooo, Cuchintaaaaaa" I ran out with a few coins to purchase the two types of steamed rice cakes, one white and cake-like, the other golden, round, silky-smooth and sticky, both covered with shredded coconut.

Across the street from the American School, right on the corner, was a *sari-sari* store. This means *random-random* and that is exactly what it was. Any little thing you might need. For us kids that meant chocolate bars, chewing gum and the all-time favorite, *champuy*! We old timers liked to gross out the new kids with this very shriveled up, very dry, extremely salty plum. To a fresh-off-the-boat American, it does not look appetizing, to say the least.

Coconut water vs. coconut milk: People often confuse coconut water and coconut milk. Any time I wanted coconut water (the liquid inside the young coconut) or coconut milk (the drink one gets from squeezing or pressing the white meat of the young coconut), I would ask the gardener to shimmy up the tree and bring me down a coconut. He did it masterfully and I still don't know how, as there are no branches to hang onto. After refrigerating it, the house girl poked a hole in it, inserted a straw and offered me what I still consider the world's most refreshing drink. You can buy it in the supermarket here, canned or bottled, but it's not the same. Afterwards she took a bolo knife to it, cracked it open, and I could spoon out the smooth silky white flesh of the fresh young coconut. Masarap! (Delicious).

Calamansi juice is the popular alternative to soda pop. The calamansi is a small citrus fruit, about half the size of a lime, but perfectly round. It eventually turns orange, but people picked and used it while green. Mixed with simple syrup, it is a delicious, refreshing drink. Most homes keep a pitcher of calamansi juice in the refrigerator for the family and unexpected guests.

Because the weather is so hot there it should be mentioned that people drink several bottles of Coca-Cola and similar carbonated soft drinks per day. The Philippines also produces an excellent pale Pilsen beer that is exported throughout the world. The San Miguel brewery goes back to 1890, when a group of Spaniards decided that Manila needed a brewery. Most of its brewmasters have been imported from Germany, primarily Munich.

Gloria Chua
Chinese Classmate

We were burned out of our house during the Battle of Manila. The Japanese finally lost the war and the Philippines was liberated, but where were we to live? We ended up at the "Clubhouse," a recreational facility my maternal grandfather had built adjacent to his family compound. We made a temporary home out of a facility that had a basketball court, gym lockers and showers, and sitting lounge. That facility opened up to a practice golf green on one side, and to a clay tennis court and a lawn with gazebo and kiddie swings on the other side. More than enough space to recreate in, but not a real home. Luckily, we didn't have to stay there long, because the family compound and one other family house around the corner from the Clubhouse were rehabilitated—from having been seized for Japanese military use—and returned to family living. We moved to that house around the corner, which was by the Pasig River and up the street from Malacañang (the Presidential Palace) and San Miguel Brewery, and lived there until we moved to Forbes Park.

It was the early days of Forbes Park when we moved there in 1953. Our house was one of the earliest ones to be built in the new development. We may have had just one or two neighbors; it was eerily quiet—and totally dark—at night. We always joked that my father had built our house to last through another world war, because it was not of wood, nor of cinder block. It was of solid, 3-ft-thick concrete, and that kept the house cool inside. Every day we were happy to return home from school (around 1pm) and transition from hot schoolroom to cool house.

The landscaping was done shortly after we moved into the house, and it was fascinating to watch. In a matter of 2 days, we had a full green lawn, 12 grown coconut trees spread throughout the yard, numerous other trees, bushes, flower borders, garden walks and paths. To my mother's dismay, my father slowly converted all the flowers to fruit trees. Flouting Forbes Park's elitist residential rules and conventions, my father installed beehives in a corner of our backyard. First there were just two hives, growing eventually to six. My siblings and I did not like having to skirt around the hives to avoid bee stings, but we were being finicky. We had a big yard and the hives were hidden in a corner. The bees were peaceful if we left them alone. And eventually, they provided us with an unusual amusement and learning experience: harvesting honey.

When the frames vertically hung inside the beehive boxes became honeycombs laden with honey, my father loaded them into a large circular tank that we cranked to spin out the honey by centrifugal action. That honey flowed out of the tank's spigots into glass jars, ready to be sent off to friends and family for consumption.

Harvesting the honey was our only involvement with the bees. Our father, however, put on his beekeeping apparel (hat with mesh face cover, long-sleeved shirt) and carried a smoker. This was to keep the bees relaxed while he checked the hives for health and adequate nutrition.

Back in the 50s it was an easy commute to school from Forbes Park; it took just fifteen minutes by car to reach the American School on Donada Street.

We had Chinese meals at our home, prepared by Chinese or Filipino cooks. Occasionally, we were served lasagna, roast beef, green salad, if our cook had experience with Western food. We did not have Filipino food; a lot of Filipino cookery is influenced by Chinese recipes, so we just had the "real" thing!

For instance, *lumpia* is really Chinese. *Lumpia* is a Fookienese (my Chinese dialect) word that I translate as "soft roll"—which is quite different from fried Filipino *lumpia*. The challenge of eating *lumpia* is that you have to roll your own fresh (not fried) lumpia. In a *lumpia* dinner, there's always a competition to see who can roll the biggest, fattest lumpia, as big as a burrito, that holds its shape and doesn't leak when one bites into it. Traditionally, Philippine lumpia are filled with pork and some vegetables and fried. These are served with a dipping sauce, either a sweet and sour sauce or a sweet chili sauce.

Although Chinese meals don't include a lot of desserts, our dinners typically ended with ice cream, which we preferred plain—no toppings or sauces. On occasion, we had it served in a special way: scooped into half of a young coconut. Wonderful.

Local fruits and vegetables were, of course, different from those in the U.S. The local spinach I loved was really a water spinach (called *kangkong* in Tagalog). Local avocados and papayas were larger, and served differently. I used to eat avocado mushed with milk and sugar! Our strawberries came from Baguio, the cool (temperature-wise) hill city we retreated to during the hot months.

I grew up accustomed to three cooked meals a day, plus afternoon *merienda*, an afternoon tea time of sorts. I snacked on fruit, wedges of jicama, strips of sugar cane (very challenging for jaws). Fortunately, packaged cookies and chips had not yet arrived in the country!

Aurora Abrera
Spanish Heritage

The first place I would call "home" in the Philippines was the second floor of an apartment building on Oroquieta Street in downtown Manila. Home was a large apartment that occupied almost the length of a block. A visitor would not realize how spacious it was until he reached the top of the stairs on the second floor. He would have to climb a long narrow staircase to get there. Once there, he would suddenly be greeted by light streaming from the large doors lining one side of the living and dining areas. Out of those doors was a long porch running adjacent to them. I enjoyed staying on that porch, because I could peer through its pretty openings to watch people and cars go by on the street below.

It was wartime and the Japanese occupied Manila, so, to be safe, my mother and I stayed mostly at home. My father was the only one who left the house in order to go to work. Then, for safety reasons, my father accepted an invitation for us to live with a close friend and his family in Pateros, Rizal, a small town outside Manila, but now a suburb. Their home was a typical native Filipino home, made of bamboo with a thatched roof. The slatted bamboo floors kept the home cool all day long. The large windows were kept open to allow the tropical breezes to flow through the house, thus circulating the air even more. We stayed in Pateros for a large portion of the Japanese occupation.

The war ended in 1945. A year and a half afterwards our family moved for a few years to Tokyo, Japan when my father represented the Philippines as Head of the Reparations Mission to Japan. Our home in Tokyo, the magnificent Philippine Embassy, was a dramatic change from our Manila apartment, which was very modest. I loved every inch of the large and grand home. I enjoyed running through the foyer's marble floors, jumping down the steps of the winding staircase and even using my tricycle in the ballroom. I also enjoyed going to the top of the house where there was a rooftop swimming pool and a tower circled by windows that overlooked the Tokyo skyline. The landscaped gardens had two levels with water fountains, statues and cascading waterfalls lined with red roses on the side of a hill. It was truly a little paradise for a little girl with a vivid imagination.

When our family returned to the Philippines in the early 1950s, my parents rented a beautiful large home on Dapitan Street, owned by one of their close friends. I can never forget the streets surrounding the house that always flooded during the rainy season between June and September. The house had a canal in front of it that looked like a creek. When the rains came, the canal overflowed and the streets turned into rivers where cars could not drive through. People would come out of their homes and start rowing *bancas (outrigger canoes, the traditional Philippine boat)* into the streets. Our house had a wide wooden bridge over the canal which our car drove over to get into our garage on the first floor. Because of the water pressure, the ropes that tied the bridge to the poles would disengage and the bridge would start floating away from the house into the street. To see the wooden bridge floating away and our maids swimming after it, waist deep in water, made me and my siblings laugh hysterically. Of course, the house help always managed to push and pull the bridge back and to tie it to the poles once again, always a fun scene to watch until the bridge was back in place.

The last house I lived in was designed and built in Quezon City by my parents, who had thought and dreamed about a beautiful and spacious home for a long time. They were inspired by the homes they saw during their residency abroad. The house reflected my parents, their experiences and their future plans. For example, my father, who was an engineer in the midst of establishing the steel industry in the Philippines, designed the new house with foundations and the strength of a large commercial building. My mother was superstitious, and thus, when the pillars were being constructed, she directed the workers to mix into the concrete different gold coins and the blood of roosters for "good luck." The house was relatively large, with rooms to house a family of at least six and to entertain a large group of people in a sprawling red-tiled terrace adjacent to the house. The house also featured beautifully carved panels and furniture from the native trees of the Philippines, glass and gold chandeliers from Spain, and modern kitchen appliances from the U.S. All the staircases of the home had steps that ended in "oro," i.e. "gold", again for the good luck that we enjoyed in that home for many years..

Our family would order a roast pig and serve it whenever we had a party at home. It was usually made the centerpiece of the buffet table. Although I would eat the lechón at the party, it was never my favorite. I always thought it was too greasy, and I did not like seeing the roasted pig with a bamboo pole shoved down his throat and body.

My mother told me stories about how scarce food was during the war for many Filipinos, including our family. In the early 50s my parents, sister and I had just returned from living in Japan, the U.S. and Europe for four years and we needed to establish roots once again in the Philippines. By 1950, our family had developed an eclectic taste in food, having been exposed to so many different dishes during our travels abroad. My mother liked to cook and bake, so while aunt Tia Anita made the "regular' meals, my mother tried out recipes that were different and seemed special to her. Thus, in addition to the regular Filipino fare that included *adobo* and *sinigang,* a hot and sour soup of pork, vegetables, garlic and tamarind, she treated us to special meals such as *Stuffed Pork Chops* and *Arroz a la Valenciana,* similar to paella. She perfected European desserts such as *Vienna Cake* or *Sans Rival.* And yes, rice was always served at every meal. If we were home, we had siesta (nap time) after lunch from 1:00 – 2:00 P.M. This was followed by *merienda* (Afternoon Snack or Tea time) at 4:00 P.M. that consisted of coffee, tea or soda with fruit or pastry, which we would have on the veranda, the terrace beside our garden. This snack would tide us over until dinnertime, which was usually at around 7 or 7:30 P.M. We always sat together at mealtime.

Taho is a delicious tofu that is sweetened with syrup. The vendor carries a wooden pole over his shoulders, balancing two circular metal tubs containing the white tofu in one and the sweet dark brown syrup in the other. He announces his wares as he plies the streets, shouting "tahooooooo, tahooooo!" I always enjoyed this as a warm afternoon snack.

We loved home-cooked Filipino meals, so we always had Filipino dishes at each meal (including eggs at breakfast) consisting of rice, a vegetable, and a meat dish of either pork, beef or chicken, as well as sea food. We ate a lot of different kinds of fish. I loved fried fish and ate them with rice. In addition to this was always something special, usually our mother's experimental dish from different new recipes, oftentimes from another culture like India, China or Spain.

What I enjoyed most in the Philippines were the fruits, and I still love to buy them there whenever I visit. Next to Thailand, the Philippines has the best papaya in the world. It's a sweet and healthy breakfast or dessert food and is probably one of the most popular fruits in the country. It is relatively easy to grow and very helpful for digestion.
Mary would argue, "I, too, loved all the fruits but my favorite was (and still is) the mango. There is nothing like a ripe, sweet, juicy kidney-shaped Manila mango that you have to eat over the sink with juice running down your arms. But then there were the green (unripe) mangoes. We drove our mothers crazy by eating these green (very sour) mangoes with rock salt. My mother insisted we would get a stomach ache, but nobody ever did."

Aurora remembers the first house she lived in growing up in Manila. It had a large yard with different fruit trees. The neighborhood children loved to climb over our fence, jump into the yard, and scurry up the tall trees to pluck the fruits, often to eat the small juicy ones as they climbed skillfully down the trees. I can still see my old aunt, her long dark hair tied into a tight bun behind her head, running after the little boys with her broom to shoo them away and to keep them far away from the succulent and tempting coconut, atis, siniguelas, santol, star apple, banana, papaya and macopa fruits hanging temptingly from the trees waiting to be picked and eaten.

Religion

Mary

Catholicism is the official religion of the Philippines. In terms of our own family, we never encountered any anti-Semitism whatsoever in the Philippines. Manila had one Jewish synagogue, Temple Emil, which was described in Chapter 1. We were secular Jews and attended more of the cultural events than the religious services, except for the High Holidays, Rosh Hashanah and Yom Kippur. It was very important to my parents, however, that I attend weekly classes for a few years in order to receive an education in Judaism and in how to read Hebrew.

Gloria

Both of my parents' families were converted to Christianity back in Fujian province, China. Thanks to the work of American missionaries, most of Fujian province had adopted an evangelical, cross-denominational Protestantism whose central belief was of Jesus Christ as the key to personal salvation and entrance to Heaven.

My paternal grandmother was an energetic evangelist. She toured all over southern Luzon spreading The Message. She did this primarily in English, even though she was not fully proficient. My grandfather used to remark that while she might have known only 50% of the English language, she was able to use 100% of it!

My grandmother required her family to fully participate in our local church, the Chinese United Evangelical Church of Manila. For many years of my youth, I spent three hours every Sunday at church, attending Sunday school and then the grown-up service, in which sermons were first delivered in Mandarin and then translated to Fookienese. I must say my knowledge of the Old and New Testaments proved especially useful when I became a Literature major in college—I knew all the Biblical references.

My maternal grandfather, a wealthy man, financed the construction and establishment of this Chinese church, but he never set foot in it. My mother's family had a looser approach to religion. All faiths existed here: Protestants, Catholics, even Buddhists. The family produced two Catholic nuns. One of my aunts became a cloistered nun in Canada and one of my cousins in Taiwan.

Aurora

Quezon City, in the early 1950s, was a relatively new suburb of Manila and was mostly a residential community. Our home was one of the newest in the neighborhood. It was surrounded by many empty lots with tall grass that swayed with the country breeze. A couple of blocks away, within a ten-minute walk from our home, the new Roman Catholic Church, the Santo Domingo Church, was built in 1954. It housed the famous statue of the Virgin Mary, carved in the sixteenth century. Apparently, when the Dutch fought the Filipinos and the Spaniards in the sixteenth century, they were defeated through the prayers and supplications of the Filipino and Spanish community to the Virgin Mary. Thus, growing up in Quezon City, I attended a fiesta celebrating the victory of the Spaniards and Filipinos against the Dutch Naval invasion through the intercession of the Virgin Mary, for whom they created the statue carved out of ivory.

Home Life

Mary

We classmates may have lived a different lifestyle from one another but, as far as we were concerned, that made no difference. We lived in Metro Manila in nice houses, some more luxurious than others. It was the norm for foreigners and Filipinos alike, not only the wealthy, to have servants. This custom provided employment for many locals.

Our house girls spoke excellent English and I enjoyed talking to them while they worked. It was great fun to watch Andrea, the house girl, polish the floor with half a coconut husk, an activity she greatly enjoyed and which I enjoyed watching. The coconut fiber in the outer edge of the half husk, is a marvelous stiff, natural brush. With one foot she would step on top of the husk, on the rounded part, while under the other foot she had a piece of flannel, saturated with polish. She would deftly dance around the living room, brushing and buffing, until the entire floor was polished to a high gloss. One day, when I was living in a college dorm room with linoleum floors, a package arrived for me from Andrea. It was a coconut husk, completely useless on the ugly linoleum, but what a conversation piece it turned out to be!

When one thinks of the tropics one thinks of heat. Damp heat. Along with the heat come the bugs. In our first house near Manila Bay, the house with the large veranda along the front and the side, we enjoyed watching the little lizards play on the wall every evening. They slithered and danced around quickly, sometimes hanging from the ceiling, but never falling. They were small and cute, nothing scary about them. Just fun. From that same veranda we also enjoyed watching the fireflies in the garden after dark. As a child I didn't realize that their flashing lights were a mating ritual; they were just so enjoyable to watch.

But then there were others, such as cockroaches. I was terrified of them and would scream for the house girl when I saw one. She simply took off her bakia (wooden slipper) and with one deft blow disposed of it quickly. I will never forget the time I was getting ready for school and went into my dark closet to slip on my moccasins without looking. I didn't wear socks; it was way too hot. As soon as the sole of my left foot stepped down hard into my left shoe I heard a loud crunch. Yes, you guessed it. Still gives me the creeps to this day.

In the evenings I sat in a comfortable living room chair next to a standing lamp and read books. I should explain that my parents hated screens. They were European and insisted on fresh air. No air conditioning, either. The light from the lamp was sometimes an invitation for a salagubang to come in and fly around my head. When I looked up the English translation, it simply said "beetle," but it was a big, fat, dark, ugly beetle that flew around me with a buzzing sound and I just knew it would land on me. Again, house girl to the rescue. She simply took a cloth from the kitchen to shoo it off.

But then there were the flying ants, which, like most insects, are attracted to light. They only came in once but I will never forget it. We were having dinner and they entered in a swarm, heading straight for the dining room chandelier. Some of them got too close to the light and fell on the table. The house girl, as usual, knew just what to do. She brought in a huge bowl of water, set it under the light and that's where they landed when they fell. They were small with translucent wings. Not scary, just icky. After enough of them had drowned, the remaining ones decided to take off for greener pastures and disappeared. The house girl cleaned off the white table cloth, removed the bowl with the carcasses and we were able to enjoy the rest of our dinner. That's life in the tropics, along with mosquito nets at night, of course!

> From Mary's mother, "We had many friends, partly from the Jewish community, partly from the neighborhood, and of course our teaching colleagues. I taught at two girls' schools and Teddy taught at the University of the Philippines, Far Eastern University, Trinity College and Ateneo College at various times in his long career as a physics professor. Many of Teddy's friends were the Jesuit Brothers of LaSalle College, mainly Americans. They often came to our house, drank some San Miguel beer, and philosophized until deep into the night, solving all the world's problems. Teddy's graduate students also enjoyed socializing with their physics professor at our home."

Dr. Brings in Discussion with Grad Students on Terrace
Brings Family Archives

Mrs. Brings continues: "When Mary was growing up we had both dogs and cats. Teddy and I both loved animals very much and, of course, Mary learned to love them, too. Every time a pet had to be put to sleep, once because of mange and once because of distemper, we all cried and cried.

We never owned an automobile. Remember, we were living on Philippine teachers' salaries! We might have been able to afford a car, but not a good driver. We never learned how to drive and we were both nearsighted! I think we could never have driven in that crazy traffic where drivers made up their own rules much of the time. We got around Manila by bus and by jeepneys. I liked the jeepneys. They started out as American jeeps, left over from the war, but are now made in jeepney factories. They had regular routes, but you had to know what they were. There were no designated stops. You just called out 'Para' when you wanted to stop or 'Para sa canto' if you wanted to get off on the corner. Plus they were very airy, and the traffic was nothing like the congestion of today. Of course we took taxis also, especially when we were dressed up to go out."

Mary

Manila social life was legendary. People loved to dress up and go out. In the United States much socializing is done in restaurants, simply because it's easier, but in the Philippines parties were held in people's lovely homes. Most homes had gardens or terraces, where tables could be set up and where uniformed servants circulated with trays of drinks and mouth watering hors d'oeuvres. Guests then helped themselves to the bountiful buffet table that had every imaginable local delicacy with the obligatory lechón as centerpiece. Women wearing lovely cocktail dresses could float around in the balmy evening air, never having to worry about getting cold or needing a jacket.

In 2015, when many of us returned for a reunion, schoolmate Guilly Luchangco (Class of '57) invited us to dinner at his lovely home. I kept thinking to myself, "Yes! This is exactly how it was!" The tables in the garden, the lanterns, the balmy air, the gracious atmosphere.

Guilly's Party
Seated from l to r: Mary, Aurora and Jaye Van Wolkenton (Class of '57)
Standing from l to r: Ming Ramos (A.S. counselor & former First Lady),
host Guilly, former President Ramos, and Guilly's wife Maloy
Photo by Peter Farquhar

People always tell me that my life growing up was "so interesting," "so exotic," But for me it was just normal. My father used to say that every day I woke up in Austria (hearing my parents speak German), then traveled through the Philippines, surrounded by Tagalog on the way to school, then arrived in America, where I spent most of my day at the American School. Then did it all in reverse. It was just natural. I am reminded of the many times new families from the U.S. or Europe would be asked how they liked the Philippines. Very often the answer was that they liked everything except the humidity. That always puzzled me, because, having only lived with humidity, I didn't know what it was. For me, humidity was as normal as spending time in three cultures every day and feeling at home in all of them.

There is something I would like to add about growing up in the Philippines. Somehow the concept of "time" is just different from the U.S. Every time I return I am made aware of this. In the U.S. each day goes by so quickly. There is always a rush to get things done and there is never enough time. Over there the days seem to have more hours —somehow there is time to breathe—to take it easy and relax. That is probably what I miss the most.

Gloria

Such is the economic divide in the Philippines that we, the privileged, had a houseful of servants, all desperate to make a living, catering to our every need: housemaids, *lavandera* (laundry person), cook, gardener, driver. I did not fully "get" my privilege. I wanted to iron my clothes, and the *lavandera* would not let me get close to the iron and ironing board. I wanted to cook or bake, and the cook would not let me into the kitchen. I only snuck in there on her days off (much to the dismay of the other household staff) and baked up cookies that only my loyal dog would eat.

I lived a pretty straight-laced life: school was important and schoolwork consumed a large part of my time outside of school itself. Then there were piano lessons, which I started taking at the age of three, inspired by all the music and singing we did after dinners at my grandparents' house. A number of my uncles played the violin, and all my aunts could play the piano to one degree or another. My Aunt Harriet started teaching me how to play, and I proved proficient enough that my parents looked for a serious piano teacher for me when Aunt Harriet left for the U.S. to go to the Princeton Choir College, where she studied choral conducting.

During our high school years, we wore multitudes of petticoats under our skirts. This trend was really silly, so thought my parents, but they put up with it. They also had to put up with all the bells we pinned to the petticoats during Christmas season. I suppose we were jingle belles.

Aurora

Born a Filipina and growing up mostly in the Philippines I lived the "Filipino lifestyle." That meant growing up with a close-knit family and having a lot of help at home. Since my father was always at work or traveling to various places in the Philippines and abroad, my mother took care of our household while also keeping a busy business and social life. At home, she was assisted by her sister-in-law, my widowed aunt, Tia Anita, my mother's right hand and the all-around assistant. My mother and she planned the weekly meals together, and then Tia Anita would shop at the market for the meats, vegetables and fruits needed for that week. Tia Anita also cooked—breakfast, lunch and dinner at home. There was a hierarchy of help at our house. My mother would be the "Head Person," followed by my aunt, Tia Anita, who was in charge of the yayas (nannies) and the cleaning people. There were usually three maids who took care of the children and also took turns cleaning the house. We had a gardener who came a couple of times a week.

My mother did not drive. She tried once and hit the electric pole outside our driveway, thus ending her driving experience! A driver came every day to take us to the various places, such as school, shopping, and social events. My father had his own chauffeur who drove him to and from work and any other place in-between.

My aunt and all the help were a blessing for my mother. Without them, she would not have been able to handle everything in our house. My mother, an entrepreneur, loved to be in business. With help at home, she was able to be creative, to manage the stores she established, as well as to raise her five children. She did not observe regular work hours, so she could come and go as she wished at a boutique at the Santa Mesa Mall and then at a dress shop in Santa Mesa Heights. Many of her customers were family and friends as well as ladies from JUSMAG (Joint U.S. Military Advisory Group), an American military compound in Quezon City.

In the early elementary years, I do not recall any extraordinary fashion trends going on. I started becoming more fashion-conscious when I reached the sixth and seventh grades. I enjoyed how we girls tried to outdo each other with the number of tulle petticoats we could wear under our skirts—the fluffier, the better! We enjoyed showing off the starched white tulle petticoats that billowed around us when we sat down and looking at and comparing each other's different petticoats that peeked out from under our skirts!

When the Christmas season rolled around, we added another accessory to the petticoats. One of the girls pinned little brass and silver Christmas bells on the hem of her petticoat, and that trend spread like wildfire around the school. Pretty soon the corridors were filled with sounds of Christmas bells every time a couple of girls walked by. Everybody accepted it as a trend, and the tinkle and jingle of little bells added a lot of charm and uniqueness to the season.

My mother gave me free rein on what styles I wanted to wear for school, giving me a taste of independence and a sense of confidence early on. Clothes were not sold *en masse* in different sizes at the stores in Manila as they are now, and each dress had to be individually sewn. Thus, a few weeks after summer vacation in April and May and before school started in the month of June, my mother and I would drive over to the Central Market in downtown Manila and buy several yards of different solid-colored and printed fabric and lace. Then a dressmaker came to our home to sew me some new dresses for the school year. Surrounded by cotton, nylon, and silk fabric, different colored thread and lace, my mother, the dressmaker and I would huddle together for an hour or two with different fashion magazines. We would flip through hundreds of pages and, after lengthy discussions, decide which different styles the dressmaker should sew for me. Once the decision was made, the dressmaker came every day for about a week or two to finish her job. I really enjoyed this entire ritual every year!

I left the American School after seventh grade and transferred to Maryknoll College, a prep school run by Roman Catholic nuns of the Dominican order. This school required uniforms, quite a change from the American School "fashion show"!

I accepted this lifestyle as part of life and I did not appreciate it when I was growing up. I thought this was "normal." I was in for a rude awakening when I got married and became a wife and mother in the United States. I had to learn how to cook, bake and clean house very quickly. Maids? They did not exist when I was starting the rest of my life in the United States!

Mary

Aurora and Gloria described the dress scene perfectly! When I arrived in the States and walked into a dress shop, the saleslady asked me what size I was. Size? I had no idea. All my clothes had been made to measure. I was so embarrassed. She must have wondered what planet I was from!

We girls loved to shop for shoes. There was one street in downtown Manila, Carriedo St., that had nothing but shoe stores. I shudder to think of the high, high heels we bought and wore. Those days are long gone!

∾

Leisure Time and Filipino Friendships

Mary

As children we grew up without TV and computers, but we were never bored. We played outdoors and used our imaginations. After the war many homes were bombed, so that only their skeletons remained. No roof, but connecting walls; perfect for playing house. We girls played active games, such as hop-scotch, jump rope and a native game called "sipa." (Sipa is a coin, washer or some sort of disk, wrapped in many rubber bands to make a ball. The ball is kicked backwards and forwards and kept going continuously. When it falls, it's the other player's or other team's turn to kick).

Some of us had large airplane inner tubes in our yards. They were great for jumping on or dreaming up all sorts of activities with our own rules. Or, when it rained, we played indoor games, such as jacks, Chutes and Ladders, checkers and card games. A favorite for girls was playing with paper dolls, giving them names and inventing stories about them.

Filipinos are known throughout the world for their kindness, sincere friendliness and hospitality. This is why when you enter many U.S. hospitals or assisted living communities, chances are that quite a few of the nurses and caregivers are from the Philippines. When somebody greets you in their home, no matter what time of day, they will not only say "Kumusta ka?" (How are you?), but immediately follow it with "Kumain ka na ba?" (Have you eaten?) And then immediately offer you food, regardless of your answer.

When we moved into the house that we built in Santa Mesa in 1956, we discovered that one of our neighbors was the Dy family. Mrs. Remedios Dy had been a student of my mother's many years earlier. So, they reconnected and our two families became friends. We got to know each of their twelve kids and watched them grow up, just as they watched me grow up. After my father passed away in 1973 and I was long gone, my mother lived in the house alone with the maids. From the day my father died to the day my mother died in 2001 (with maybe just a few exceptions) Mrs. Dy came over every afternoon at 4:00 on the dot for *merienda* (afternoon coffee) and stayed for about an hour. Every day! There was no truer friend. When I went back after my mother died and the house was being emptied and prepared for sale, I stayed at Mrs. Dy's. She wouldn't hear of me staying at a hotel. I called her "my second mom", I see her every time I go back and several times a year we get together with one of her sons and his wife, who live in San Francisco.

Mrs. Dy is only one example of our many, many Filipino friends. Also, the family of our house girl, Andrea, became like family to us. I put her niece, Ginger, through college, helped her buy a home and visit with her and the entire family every time I visit the Philippines. Her children call me "Oma," the German word for "grandma," which is what Ginger called my mother.

Mrs. Brings and Mrs. Dy Sharing Merienda
Photo by Peter Farquhar

Gloria

We socialized mostly within the Filipino-Chinese community. But my father, a brilliant businessman who was also a would-be farmer, sought acquaintance with a number of Filipino agriculture and animal husbandry experts, and in the Filipino way, those acquaintances became significant friends of our entire family. I remember most fondly

Mr. Isidro—I don't think I ever knew his first name, as there was no reason I would address him other than Mr. Isidro. He was a horticulturist and a researcher affiliated with the University of the Philippines. My father would often consult with Mr. Isidro to find appropriate trees and plants for his various "farm" properties outside Manila. I would tag along on visits to Mr. Isidro's house to look at plants, get advice, and generally putter around a garden lush with a wide variety of greenery. I was always happy to see him—a kindly, grandfatherly man—and I felt he was just as happy to see me. He was only in his early sixties when he suffered a fatal heart attack. My father was devastated by this loss, as was I.

Aurora

When I was nine I learned how to play two games when I stayed at my cousins' home in Oas (southeastern Luzon) during Easter. One was *patintero*, a Filipino child's version of football, where each team stood on invisible parallel lines and tried to block the other team from reaching their "home" on the other side of the field. They spread-eagled their hands and ran back and forth on the invisible parallel lines. I loved the game, but could not recreate it when I got back home because of lack of space in our yard. The other game I learned was *Mahjong*, a game of skill, strategy, and calculation that involves a degree of chance. It is played with a set of 144 ivory (nowadays often plastic) tiles with a distinct clicking sound, based on Chinese characters and symbols. My aunt and cousins knew how to play it well and taught me what to do. I was so fascinated by the game, I wanted to play it every day I was there!

Later, in grade school at the American School, classes ended at noon and I had plenty of time to indulge in my favorite activities when I got home. Being young and not involved in school activities, I had time in the afternoon for myself because I had many "loves" and hobbies, souvenirs of which I kept stashed away in drawers and cabinets.

My parents loved talking about the musicals they watched on Broadway in New York and they had a collection of the 33 1/3 sized hi-fi records they had bought as souvenirs from those shows. I loved the songs from Broadway's *My Fair Lady* and *Oklahoma*. I also enjoyed the musicals on the large movie screens downtown, like *Carousel, Seven Brides for Seven Brothers* and *Singin' in the Rain,* etc. I would come home and listen to songs from these musicals, so much so, that I learned all the words to the songs by heart during those afternoons. I still remember them to this day!

A fan of movies and movie stars, I collected pictures of my favorite actors from movie magazines and newspapers and glued them into albums. I also wrote fan letters and much to my delight, received responses from Hollywood stars. Of course I did not realize at that age that these were mass produced and mailed to thousands around the world.

I enjoyed corresponding with many friends abroad. Through the Brownies and Girl Scouts, I made some pen pals in the US, Europe and Asia and took the time to write them at least twice a month. This was a way I added to my collection of stamps, which was another hobby of mine.

I was not the only one who enjoyed doing all these activities. Many of my elementary school friends indulged in one or more of these hobbies. Thus, on certain days during the week we would bring our albums to school and exchange pictures and stamps, treating each item like precious jewelry and handling them very carefully so they would not tear or get lost.

My father was a golfer, and he had a family membership to the Wack-Wack Golf and Country Club in Mandaluyong. When he was not traveling, he would spend an entire Saturday at the club playing with his buddies. My family would either go with him or follow a little later, driven by our chauffeur. We enjoyed this weekend ritual because we had the opportunity to swim in the club house and enjoy all the delicious snacks, like hamburgers, fries, fruits and chips.

Our friends in the Philippines were like family to us. Our bonds were very strong, and we all treated each other like brothers and sisters.

During World War II, my father's friend, Pio Luna, whose wife was also my mother's friend before the war, invited us to live with him and his family in Pateros, Rizal, a small village outside Manila. My father accepted the invitation, believing that living outside the city in a small rural town was safer than living in Manila, where Japanese soldiers kept watch on the streets.

Throughout our growing up years, my parents' closest friends were many and generous. Our families would visit each other often. There was never any need for an invitation. If the mood struck us, we would take the car and visit. The same worked for them. There was always a meal and snacks available regardless of the day or time.

Even to this day, these friendships endure, continuing to the next generation. I am profoundly grateful for the generosity and compassion they have shown our family throughout the years.

Lawlessness and Diseases

Although it is clear that our lives at home and at school were generally happy and care-free, our growing up story would not be complete without recounting some negative experiences that we were aware of.

Mary

By local standards, Manila in those days was a pretty safe place to live. All the homes were surrounded by tall walls, generally concrete block topped with broken glass to prevent climbing over. And a lot of places had a security guard. Most of us got around the city with no problem. I never felt threatened walking around the city or taking public transportation by myself.

The windows of my bedroom had bars, but no screens. It would have been too hot. My parents hated air conditioning. The bars were there to discourage burglars, but the burglars outsmarted us. They simply took a fishing pole with a hook while I was asleep. Twice they managed to reel in my watch and the few pieces of jewelry that I had laid out on my dresser for the next day.

Something else that we had to watch out for in the tropics were intestinal parasites, such as pin or tape worms. Once when I was about nine I was walking behind a friend and it looked as though she had a loose thread on the bottom of her skirt. I told her to stop, so that I could pull it off, but as I yanked on it, it kept coming. Yikes! It was a tapeworm. So embarrassing for both of us!

In the 6th grade when we were eleven we were sent outside in small groups of four to be inoculated against polio. The Salk vaccine, brand new at the time, was in the form of a sugar cube. Polio was prevalent during the years we were at the American School and three people contracted the disease. One of them was my close friend and classmate, champion swimmer/diver Linda Pratico, who was stricken with it when we were in high school. I visited her often at the San Juan de Dios Sanitarium that was in walking distance from school. She was in an iron lung and, amazingly, she was able to make a complete recovery. One of my most poignant memories is that of her father, sitting in the hospital corridor, with his face in his hands, weeping. The look of anguish on his face will always haunt me

Aurora

My elementary school years in the Philippines were idyllic because I was not aware of the lawlessness or any criminal activity that existed in the early 50s. There was, however, one incident in 1952 that made the reality of crime dawn on me and I became more aware of what life around me was like.

It was the day a crime was committed in our house. My mother had collected some jewelry from her family and from her shopping sprees abroad. She kept these rings, bracelets, earrings and pearl rosaries in a lacquered and ornate jewel box in her closet. Being very trusting, she kept her closet door closed, but not locked. One morning, as she was dressing and getting ready to go out, she discovered that her jewelry box was not in its usual place. She looked high and low for it, and finally concluded that it had been stolen. She told my father and together they called the police to investigate. Shortly afterwards, police detectives came and questioned everybody in our home including the household help. The police concluded that it was an "inside job" and that one of the maids was responsible for the theft. They said they suspected that this particular maid had stolen the jewelry box during the night and had handed it over the fence to an accomplice waiting outside on the street. They said it was a typical *modus operandi* executed by servants in homes they served. The detectives continued to tell my parents that, with their consent, they could extract a confession from the maid, but when they described the torture they would have to perform, my parents were horrified and decided immediately not to pursue the investigation. Since there was no proof of guilt, they could not bear to think such torture would be done to a possibly innocent person. They preferred to end the investigation and lose the jewelry rather than to subject anybody to cruel tactics in order to extract a "guaranteed" but inconclusive confession. It was a wake-up/reality call for our family, especially for a young person like me, to understand what "justice" might mean in the Philippines during the 1950s.

The disease I heard about most in the Philippines was tuberculosis. I heard about it from reading the newspapers, listening to the radio and hearing people comment about TB whenever we drove by the Quezon Sanitarium where the victims of this disease lived and were treated. In the Philippines so many people were afflicted by it. What was most surprising was that people around me accepted that bit of information stoically when someone told them they had it. Maybe it was too common or maybe I was too young to notice any fear in their eyes.

Fiestas (Festivals) and Holidays

Mary

The Filipino fiestas are linked to the Catholic religion, as each barrio had its own patron saint. When it was that saint's day, the town celebrated. It was an effective way to spread Christianity throughout the land. Who doesn't want to attend a fiesta, with processions, music, dancing, pretty girls vying to be "queen", food and drink?

Due to the thousands of town, city, provincial, national, and village fiestas in the country, the Philippines has traditionally been known as the "Capital of the World's Festivities." On Catholic holidays or feast days, there are always processions in town.

Since my father taught at the university, he had students from many different *barrios* (villages). Therefore, the whole family was frequently invited to their town fiestas. They were always on a week-end and, if the town was not too far away, we were happy to attend. We watched the procession and the crowning of the barrio queen. Every home had a table laden with food and we were expected to go from house to house and eat. We learned to keep the portions small so we could eat a bit at each home and not offend anyone! What I remember best was one fiesta when I was about ten. The town was in watermelon country and they had a variety of golden watermelons that I had never seen before. The sweetest, most delicious watermelons ever!

One custom that was very prevalent at Christmas all over the country in the 1950s was that of the "cumbanchero." That was the term used for "caroling" during Christmas time. Until the mid-sixties, the tradition was for a group of young boys to go around the neighborhood singing Christmas carols in front of the gates of each house. Their voices rose above their makeshift instruments that they attempted to play. It didn't matter whether they could really play them or whether they were in tune. As long as they sang loud enough, nobody cared. Most families had a little dish filled with coins near the front door. After a few carols the house girls would pay them and they would move on. Even now, all these years later, when I hear certain Christmas carols, especially *Jingle Bells*, I think about how those little boys sang those songs. They had no idea what a "one-horse open sleigh" was and, for that matter, neither did I.

People always ask me if I celebrated Hannukah growing up. I did not. Jews do not consider Hannukah a major holiday and I do not recall anybody celebrating Hannukah in Manila. It happens to be a festival of lights that occurs at about the same time as Christmas (the date varies) to symbolize the coming of the light. It commemorates the rededication of the Temple in Jerusalem, where a small quantity of oil to light the Temple's menorah miraculously lasted eight days. My parents grew up in Austria, a Catholic country where Christmas was magical. It was where *Silent Night* was written and was the source of the real *Tannenbaum* (Christmas tree) and so many other traditions. Our tree was a Baguio pine tree and, in accordance with Austrian tradition, we used real candles, held in place with wire. Such a beautiful glow, but we had to be sure to blow them out carefully when unattended.

The Christmas program at the American School on the last day before vacation was legendary. Mrs. Geoffey's advanced art classes made glorious stained-glass windows out of tissue paper on a frame. They were large and very delicate and had to be transported carefully to the gym, where they became the decoration for the Christmas program. The glee club sang carols in English, Spanish, French and German. A student would read the Christmas story from the side of the stage with the curtains closed. Then the curtains opened and revealed a tableau—motionless figures representing the Nativity scene. I remember being cast as the Virgin Mary twice with a blue shawl over my head and holding a doll in my arms.

On July 4, 1946, after the war, the Philippines became independent and the Filipinos were proud to celebrate their Independence Day along with the U.S., who had, after all, liberated them from the Japanese. Therefore, it was actually a joint celebration of the friendship between the two nations with parades and fireworks. However, in 1964, for political reasons, some Filipinos felt that the Philippines was too much in the shadow of the U.S. and that the Independence Day should revert back to the short-lived Independence from Spain on June 12, 1898. The Philippine Congress approved the motion, which still stands today. Of course, we, the Class of '61, still celebrated Double Independence Day!

I attended the festivities on the U.S. Embassy grounds during the day. I very much enjoyed listening to the band and joining everyone in a rousing rendition of the national anthem. After it got dark, my parents and I would climb to the top of one of the double-decker buses that went up and down Dewey Boulevard. We admired the amazing fireworks, especially when they closed with both the U.S. and the Philippine flags in brilliant color, representing the deep friendship between our two countries.

Gloria

All our Filipino friends were city folk, so we never experienced fiestas in the barrios. But right after the war, when we were living in a downtown area (near the Presidential palace), we often witnessed religious processions, which you might consider fiestas without food. Maybe there was food at the conclusion of the procession, but seeing it from our windows as it passed by the house, we had no idea what was at the end. This procession of people would hover around or follow after an open wagon carrying a statue of a saint, an altar, or even a staging of a religious scene. If it was Holy Week, we were sure to see a depiction of Christ on his way to crucifixion. We would see a man wearing a crown of thorns standing before a cross, or flagellating himself. The crowds around him carried candles and/or rosaries. The procession moved slowly, so we saw all the other accoutrements that accompanied the religious scene.

I remember wanting to experience a real "white Christmas," since all the traditional images of the holidays seemed so ridiculous in the tropics. My Christmases at home in the Philippines seemed to be a dichotomy of a celebration of the birth of Christ, and a celebration of Santa Claus. I always preferred the birthday to the Santa. Why? I just thought it was a better story: the birth in a manger and the arrival of the three kings. The accompanying pageantry, symbolism, and music all made it solemn and magical at the same time. I loved seeing all the plays about Joseph and Mary (always played by the most beautiful girl in the room) wending their way to Bethlehem I loved the traditional Christmas carols and decorations: Christmas trees, manger crèches, and especially the star of Bethlehem.

Fourth of July always reminds me of the best fireworks I saw at the Polo Club one year. They were not mere flashes of colored light shooting up high into the sky, but patterns of lights—of the U.S. flag, for example—burning in unison and then flickering out all at the same time. I had never seen anything like it.

Aurora

A unique celebration in the Philippines that I enjoyed very much growing up was *All Saints' Day* on November 1. On this day everyone, and I mean everyone, in the country went to the cemetery to visit the graves of their loved ones. Filipinos walked, drove, and/or rode to visit a grave to pay their respects to their dearly departed. The adults brought folding chairs, tables and food to the cemetery, because they expected to see relatives who would join them for snacks and drinks, and who would catch up with each of them on the goings-on in the family and with friends. Some curious people would consider this as a "special outing" to view other grave sites owned by people they didn't know, but who allowed them to view the bodies of their deceased relatives encased in a glass container. When a family allowed a "viewing," throngs lined up to look. Word would get around pretty fast about this "curiosity." Our cemetery plot was a small and modest one, but a great number of people would start lining up at the mausoleum next door to us. The deceased person's glass casket had been prepared for the curious to see. Moreover, the embalmed body would be made-up for the occasion, complete with new make-up and a fresh hairstyle. For years I wondered what that deceased person looked like. Finally, after having celebrated All Saints' Day for a couple of years, I gave in to my curiosity and summoned up the courage to look next door when the line of people didn't seem too long. It was not as scary as I thought it would be. The embalmed body looked more like a doll than a human being.

One thing that stands out in my mind was the ritual we did at midnight before Easter Sunday. We had to stay up all night until the church bells rang at midnight. Then my aunt and other relatives told us to jump on our beds as high as we could. When I asked why, I was told that I would grow taller if I did. Thus, when the church bells rang long and loudly that night, my cousins and I jumped as high as we could on our beds. Luckily, the springs didn't snap, despite the vigorous jumping. I am not sure I was very successful that evening. Eventually I grew to be 5 foot 3 inches, but not more, as I had hoped that night!

The Philippines is the only Christian nation in Asia, so we celebrated Christmas with many trappings imported from the Christian west. Every home had a Christmas tree laden with colorful balls, ornaments and lights. Presents lay under the tree waiting to be opened on Christmas morning. Santa Claus visited homes that had children in it, and as soon as the children woke up, they opened their presents. Then our family attended Christmas Mass at Santo Domingo Church, followed by a Christmas buffet at home that lasted the entire day as family and friends came and went to exchange Christmas cheer, gifts and conversation.

What made Christmas different at our home were the days that led to December 25. We had daily visits from Christmas carolers, mainly street urchins coming in groups. They approached every home in our neighborhood ringing doorbells, jingling their bells and singing one or two Christmas carols before stretching out their hands for a gift of some coins or a few pesos. We would also have carolers representing some charity groups, who wrote my parents letters requesting a donation in exchange for a few minutes' worth of caroling inside our home. My parents always welcomed them with open arms because they added joy to our home. I especially loved the *paroles,* derived from the Spanish word *farol,* meaning "lantern." They are hand-made Christmas stars made of multi-colored tissue paper and bamboo, lit from within by a lightbulb. People hung them from the windows of Filipino homes and buildings. They made the entire country glow and enhanced the landscape everywhere we went.

Christmas in the Philippines, a Typical Parol
In the public domain

Week-End Recreation

Mary

The Army and Navy Club was founded in 1898 and reorganized in 1952. The Club offered the same kind of family club environment as the pre-war club, but with a greatly expanded civilianized and Filipinized membership. The Club, on Manila Bay, had a swimming pool, tennis courts, a library and a large club building with restaurants. Many American School families were members and socialized there on the week-ends.

My parents felt that it was important to have a place where we could go on week-ends to relax, swim, meet friends, entertain guests, use their library, etc. The Polo Club was quite a distance away, very expensive and hard to get to without a car. I always enjoyed going there, however, with my friends who were members. The Army Navy Club's fees were a little more reasonable, it was very accessible by public transportation, and it was situated on the bay. It was pleasant to be near the water, close to the home in which I had grown up until we moved to Sta. Mesa. We went there most week-ends and enjoyed the pool. My parents, who had grown up swimming in the ice-cold Danube, found the water much too warm, but for me it was perfect. I loved meeting my girlfriends there and everybody agreed that their hamburgers were the best in town. I'm still wondering what made them so good. Maybe I don't want to know.

I survived three challenges at the club. One was to jump off the high diving board. Not dive, mind you, like my friend, Linda Pratico, the diving champ. Just jump, holding my nose. I chickened out time after time, but once I made myself do it, despite being terrified, I was done. No need to do it again.

Army Navy Club Pool Area Overlooking Manila Bay
Brings Family Archives

Another time I lost a contact lens at one of the tables on the bay side. The floor consisted of boards with space in between them. Plenty of space for a lens to slip through. This was decades before disposable lenses. There WAS no replacement. One of the waiters volunteered to go down and look for it. The proverbial needle in the haystack, especially since the lens was clear plastic. By some miracle he found it. My parents tipped him generously.

Another challenge was to climb over the fence on the bay side and swim to Navy Landing, from where the Sangley boats came and went. I was secretly hoping to attract the attention of one of the cute sailors, but, boy, did that backfire! The swim itself was easy. I was a good swimmer and it was not that far. The landing was held in place by wooden pilings that had been driven into the ocean bottom. My plan was to hang on to the landing and lift myself up. However, I had never heard of barnacles. As my legs grazed the pilings that had been there for many years, the razor-sharp edges of the barnacles cut up my legs. In pain and bleeding profusely, I can't recall the details, but was somehow rescued and returned to the Army Navy Club, which fortunately had a small clinic. No permanent damage, but much pain and humiliation.

A 1947 agreement provided sites for 23 US military bases in the Philippines, which was to last for 99 years. During the 1940s and 50s, the Philippines remained the home of a number of American military bases.

When we looked across the bay from Dewey Boulevard we could see Sangley Point Naval Base next to the city of Cavite. There was a Navy boat that one could take across the bay to Sangley and actually be "in America" in about 40 minutes. For me going to America was a lifelong dream, so going to Sangley was the closest thing to it at that point. It was so near and yet so far, because one had to flash a U.S. government ID to the nice sailor at Navy Landing in order to board the boat. Well, I got together with a girlfriend (the previously mentioned diving champ, Linda Pratico) who didn't have a government issued ID, either, and we cooked up a plan. We would get to know the sailor on duty Sunday morning and become friends with him. As it turned out, he was a lonely young man named Bill, happy to talk to some nice American girls. He liked us and we enjoyed chatting with him on occasional Sundays. (Navy Landing was right next door to the Army Navy Club, where Linda and I swam.) Of course, one day, when it wasn't too busy, we asked him to let us on the ferry and he did. Looking back, I know he could have gotten into big trouble, had there been a problem, but, fortunately, there wasn't. We just wandered around the base for about an hour, went into the snack bar and felt thrilled to actually be on American soil. Eventually we took the boat back, simply smiling and waving at the sailor on the other end, who figured we were legit, and scampered onto the boat back to Manila, laughing and giddy that we had pulled it off without a hitch! We had spent an hour "in America" with no ID.

Day Trips and Vacations

Mary

Originally, the Baguio region in the Philippines was a vast mountain zone with lush highland forests, teeming with wildlife and numerous species of flora. When the Spanish arrived in the Philippines, this area was never fully subjugated by Spain. When the United States occupied the Philippines after the Spanish–American War, Baguio was selected to become the summer capital of the then Philippine Islands. Governor-General William Taft, on his first visit in 1901, noted the "air as bracing as the Adirondacks."

The last leg of the drive from Manila to Baguio, after leaving the flatlands and the shimmering green rice fields, was along the twisty, winding road called Kennon Rd. It was named for its builder, Lyman Kennon, of the U.S. Army Corps of Engineers, completed in 1905. The last, steepest part is known as "Zigzag Road" because it is so steep that it requires numerous switchbacks. Looking out the window at the vegetation, I was always excited when we were leaving the tropical forest behind and entering the vastly different pine forest. That's when we knew that we were almost in Baguio! I loved the cool weather, the pine trees and the beautiful flowers that thrived in the cool, damp air.

Aurora

In the Philippines in March, April and May, schools closed and the humidity and heat made it unbearable to live in Manila. My father rented a house in Baguio and although he would spend only a few days with us, the rest of the family stayed a few weeks, accompanied by the maids. It was cool, we enjoyed fresh fruits and vegetables every day, and went boating, car driving or biking at Burnham Park in the center of the city.

My father hardly had time to vacation much because he was busy getting the Philippines back on the road to recovery from World War II. His main task was to help move the country from an agricultural economy to an industrial one. Thus, after working with Reparations in Japan, he was assigned to build the shipping and steel industries in the Philippines, a task that kept him from enjoying much family time. He tried his best, however, to give us many opportunities to have fun and relax despite his busy schedule. For example, in 1958, when he traveled to the United States to work with banks and industrialists to obtain loans and equipment for Philippine industrial plants, he brought me with him to Washington, D.C. and New York City in order to familiarize myself with these cities. By this time I was a teenager, and I understood the importance of his work and appreciated this learning opportunity for me. It was an unforgettable experience because I attended special events with my father and met many government officials connected with his work. I had the opportunity not only to meet Philippine President Garcia and his wife, and Philippine Ambassador Carlos Romulo, but also to hob nob with President Dwight Eisenhower and Vice President Richard Nixon at close quarters. I still have pictures of those memorable times!

Since I was already in the United States and closer to Europe, my father decided to give me the opportunity to travel there as well. He invited the wife of his good friend and classmate from MIT to accompany me to visit Belgium, France and Switzerland. Traveling with Mrs. Frankie Brown was exciting. It was made even more special when I met friends of my father in those countries. They brought me to different tourist sites I had only read about. They also spoke in different languages. This was impressive to me, for I only spoke three and I thought this was adequate. Even the elevator operator I met at the hotel spoke five languages. Wow! That trip opened my eyes to the magic of different cultures, languages and food beyond the diversity I had already experienced in the Philippines.

Since my father had different work locations in the Philippines when he was building the steel mills and the dry dock for ships, he brought us along sometimes and put us up in the guest houses while he worked and inspected the plants for a couple of days. Traveling from Manila, we spent time in Panganiban, Camarines Norte, in a beautiful bungalow resting on top of an old gold mine overlooking the China Sea, as well as in Mindanao where the steel mills were located near the Maria Cristina Falls. Sometimes, on weekends, we would take a three-hour tug boat ride to the shipyards and steel mills in Mariveles, Bataan. There we stayed at another guest house and played on the sandy beaches while my father continued his job, constantly working, even on weekends.

Our parents were believers in traveling as an educational experience and presented opportunities for us to explore parts of Asia as well. Thus, in the 60s when my father was assigned to Thailand by the United Nations, he and my mother made us stay in Bangkok with them when we were off from school or work. Bangkok became the jumping board for exploring other cities and countries nearby.

Gloria

The very first time I went to Baguio was by plane, which was a military leftover, I guess, because the seats ran along the sides (like a jeepney) instead of in rows. As a child, I looked forward to the two or so weeks we spent up in Baguio every summer. I enjoyed playing roller skate tag all around Burnham Park. We were real devils as we skated on every surface necessary to get to where we wanted to go—up steps, up hills, etc. Then there was bowling—with duckpins—in the local bowling alley. I have never gotten the hang of bowling with regulation sized balls and pins!

We enjoyed the trips to the St. Louis school, where the nuns taught the orphans how to work with silver. We used to come home with all kinds of silver jewelry, spoons, and various decorative objects. The nuns were also instrumental in developing strawberry farms—a real treat to get fresh berries and good jam (this was before Mrs. Stewart's jams and jellies).

As locals, we could get into John Hay only under special arrangement. However, each time was wonderful. I loved all that American food. (Come to think of it, the very first time I ever had pistachio ice cream was at Clark Air Base—astounding that the U.S. military used to fly in all kinds of fresh food to its bases around the world!)

Mary

When my parents first arrived in the Philippines in 1939, my father knew that he would be teaching Physics at the University of the Philippines, but what a wonderful surprise it was for the Austrian, mountain-loving Brings couple to learn that he had been assigned to the Baguio campus with cool, clean air and mountain vistas. They were there for a year, so they learned to love it and to familiarize themselves with the best hiking trails. That is where I was introduced to hiking, which I still greatly enjoy, on our first vacation there when I was about six years old. We went back often, sometimes by plane, sometimes by train, sometimes by car with friends. And inevitably, both going up and going down, I would be violently carsick. We stayed, not at the elegant Pines Hotel, but at a lodge my parents knew that had the most beautiful garden. I loved it there.

Camp John Hay was established in Baguio on October 25, 1903 after President Theodore Roosevelt signed an executive order setting aside land for a military reservation for the United States Army. It was a major R&R (Rest and Recreation) station for American military personnel and their dependents. Because of its cool mountain climate, it was an ideal location for servicemen looking for a break from the unrelenting tropical heat and humidity

In the Summer of 1960 my friend Judy Tye was about to go back to the States for good. We had been friends since the 8th grade and it was sad that she would not be there for our Senior Year. Her parents were missionaries for a church that had vacation cabins in Baguio. Judy and I stayed at one of them for a week to enjoy the trails, the cool foggy air (you actually needed a sweater!) and everything that Camp John Hay had to offer. We played a lot of miniature golf (more our style than the real thing) and also enjoyed the hamburgers and milkshakes at the 19th Tee Restaurant. It was a lovely hilly walk from the cabin to the entrance of Camp John Hay. What I enjoyed most was walking through the cool damp fog in the early morning. It made me think of walking through a cloud.

In the 50s the traffic was not what it is today, so one could go on day trips on the week-ends—a mini-vacation. It only took an hour to get to Tagaytay and enjoy a view of the Taal volcano. We would stop at the Taal Vista Lodge for lunch and admire the beautiful view of this most unusual volcano: a volcano in a lake on an island!

The other great spot for a day trip were the Pagsanjan Falls, where one could hire a boat and a couple of boatmen and go serenely up the river, looking at and listening to birds and monkeys in the tall gorges on both sides. At the end was a small lake and thundering falls where one could cool off and swim. Then the fun began. On the way back the boatmen would "shoot the rapids" at top speed while darting in and out of the rocks. They had been trained since early childhood and knew the rocks well. It was quite a thrill.

Besides Baguio, the Hundred Islands National Park in the province of Pangasinan on the Lingayen Gulf was a favorite destination. We stayed in native huts with bamboo floors. I had one to myself and my parents shared a larger one. I think I was twelve, because I remember bringing my ballet shoes with me and practicing, while looking out of the large window at the beautiful blue ocean. Each day we hired guides, who would take us in a banca (outrigger canoe) to different islands with interesting features. I distinctly remember the one with the cave. My first experience with stalagmites and stalactites and bats! We jumped out of the banca and swam into the cave. No beach. Just rocks and a dark cave. Scary, but fun. The next day it was an island with miles of white sand beach. Great for swimming. The boatmen caught some fish and grilled them for us on the beach. On another day we rented goggles and snorkels, and they took us out to an island where we could see beautiful corals and tropical fish. From then on I was hooked on snorkeling!

CHAPTER 5

The Grade School Experience

Mary

It was 1948, I had just "graduated" from Nursery School, and it was time to enter the American School Kindergarten at age four and a half. Little did I realize how significant the school would be in my life and that in the year 2020 I would be the only person from my class to go back to Manila to celebrate the unforgettable 100th birthday of the school, founded in 1920.

I have two very clear recollections from the first day of Kindergarten. For some reason it was my father, not my mother, who accompanied me that morning. We were ushered out to the playground where they had some large chicken-wire cages with bunnies. I guess to distract the children and keep them from crying. Well, it worked. As I was a huge animal lover, I was mesmerized by the bunnies. Then I suddenly realized that my father, also an animal lover, would want to see them, but by then he was gone. The teachers' ploy worked and, no, I did not cry. That's because of my second memory, which was the sudden realization that my best friend, Stevie Gunders, was in the class, too. No coincidence, I'm sure! All of the other children were American, so that was my introduction to American English and culture.

Every day, time was set aside for naps. The teachers, Mrs. Bartlett and Miss Jordan, would lay woven mats on the floor that had our names on them in large red block letters. I was named after my two grandmothers, Americanized versions of Marie and Helene, thus Mary Helen. My parents combined the two names to form the first name by which I was called, Marylen. That was the name on the mat.

The Kindergarten room, later to become Mrs. Ruth Geoffey's art room, was divided into a large space and a smaller side room, which was an enclosed veranda. There was a portable blackboard out there. The teacher would throw out a letter and we would have to come up with words that started with that letter. One day the letter was "c" and I meekly said "Cinderella." The teacher said we couldn't use names, but that the word "cinder" was fine and wrote it on the board. I had never heard the word "cinder" (we didn't exactly have fireplaces in Manila) and was mortified because I thought she was just humoring me.

First and Second Grades

Mary

After a successful Kindergarten year, I was very excited to go into First Grade! My teacher made me think of Snow White, because she had creamy white skin and long, beautiful dark hair. Not only that, but she had a beautiful name—Rose Lloyd. I decided that when I grew up, I would be a first-grade teacher, just like Rose Lloyd. I already knew how to read a bit. One evening, when I was about four, my parents and I were taking our usual walk on Dewey Boulevard, when we saw a Coca-Cola stand. It had the iconic red sign with *Coca-Cola* in curly white script and, underneath, in block letters, "Have a Coke." Without ever having had a reading lesson in my life, but knowing the alphabet, I announced "Have a cookie." Close enough! My parents stared at each other, dumbfounded, realizing that I was instinctively reading phonetically, and we rushed home, where they gave me other words to try. The best part of First Grade was that we were given a book, *Dick and Jane,* of course. I couldn't wait to get through it because it was followed by more and more books. I was on my way to becoming a voracious reader!

The second-grade teacher was Mrs. Fletcher, an elderly lady with bluish-gray hair, who had been teaching Second Grade forever. She did special little things, like mailing each child a Christmas card. I treasured mine for years! Three important things happened in Second Grade.

One was that my friend, Stevie Gunders, announced that he had something for Show and Tell. He came to the front of the room and said four words, "We got our visa." It was something I heard a great deal from our refugee friends. Our classmates, who were all American, were clueless, but I knew that whenever someone got a visa they left for good. I didn't expect to ever see him again and was sad, but through the magic of the Internet, our two families reconnected over forty years later.

The other thing had to do with my name, Marylen, a combination of Mary and Helen. One day we had to choose an activity from among those posted on the wall, and we were asked to write our names under our chosen activity. I picked something and wrote "Marylen" underneath. I wish I could erase what happened next because I would still to this day be Marylen, a name I actually prefer and which some of my oldest friends still use. The bratty girl behind me shrieked, "That's not how you spell Marilyn! Haven't you heard of Marilyn Monroe?" Because I wanted more than anything to not be considered "different" and because I knew that "Marylen" would forever set me apart, I went to the teacher and said, "Marylen is just a nickname. My first name is really Mary and that's what I want to be called from now on."

But Second Grade had its happy moments as well. The third "important thing" was a happy one. One day two pretty high school girls came into the class, whispered quietly to

64

the teacher for a moment, looked around, then whispered to one another. They explained that one of the high school clubs was putting on a fashion show and that they were looking for models from all the grades. They had decided to pick two second grade girls. The dresses would be furnished by a local dress shop, hoping to make some sales. Of course, all the girls were smiling up at them, saying to themselves, "Oh, me, me. Please let it be me." Imagine my complete shock and disbelief when they announced that they had chosen one of my best friends, Shelagh Cromwell, and me.

Mary Walking the Catwalk in her Designer Dress
Brings Family Archives

Gloria

Despite Headmaster Warfel's confidence, I had a difficult entrance into second grade at the American School. Aside from the fact that I felt strange in a place of mostly white faces, I was behind academically. I did not know how to read, having spent first grade at a local school where all we did was play. I was almost demoted. Thankfully, I received private tutoring that got me caught up in no time.

In my Fujian community in Manila, I lived a life both guarded and insular. We guarded our language and culture; we stuck together in groups, as Chinese, as Fujianese, as families. And yes, we were all of the Christian faith. My life experience was certainly different—you could say, opposite—from that of a typical American School student.

I lived a double life, an American life at school in the morning, and a Chinese home life. It was a conflicted life. My family and community opined that while I was privileged to attend the American School, I was also in danger of losing my Chinese-ness. I was going to be a "foreign devil." I didn't know which way I was supposed to be going.

Their remedy was re-education—to be achieved by sending me to Chinese school in the afternoons! So, during my third-grade year, my school day began at the American School from 7:30 to 12:30 in the morning and transitioned (via car, eating lunch and changing into a school uniform along the way) to Chinese school from 1:30 to 4:00 in the afternoon, which concluded with classroom cleaning and leaving with lots of homework.

It was exhausting and I cried every night as I tried to do all my homework. Finally my parents decided to end this cruel schedule and just let me be "Americanized." I never completely learned to read and write Mandarin, and forgot most of what I did learn. I was liberated to become "Americanized" and could proceed through high school graduation at the American School without community interference.

I spent many years learning to play the piano. After getting an introduction to piano from my aunt, I got a new piano teacher who could not appropriately teach young children. She was more appropriate for would-be professional classical performance pianists. I was assigned to learn Clementi, Scarlatti, Diabelli, Mozart, Beethoven, etc., learning each of a composer's pieces from beginning to end, perfecting and memorizing them, and then starting all over again from page 1 to attain even more perfection. It was a sure-fire way to kill my interest in piano. All I wanted to do was play *John Brown's Little Indians* with all the other kid pianists, not play some boring classical piece, over and over and over again. I rebelled, refused to practice, and wanted to quit my lessons. My parents' response was to get me new teachers who might renew my "interest." At some point, they hired Mrs. de Wit (the feared elementary school music teacher at A.S. who got the little kids to sing like angels) to teach me piano, saying that I would get my knuckles rapped if I didn't perform well for her. It didn't work. She didn't rap my knuckles (and she really was quite kind to me), and I still hated piano lessons. I must have had half a dozen teachers over my forced fifteen years of piano lessons.

Third Grade

Mary

At the end of second grade and into third grade, I was making more friends. Shelagh, with whom I shared the fashion show honors, was from a Scottish family. Her father worked for Shell Oil. I was also making friends with Eva Sternberg, another refugee kid, and then Aurora and Gloria. Our third grade teacher, Mrs. Zwonecheck , was strict and demanding, a good teacher.

Mary with Omi on the Veranda
Brings Family Archives

However, the most significant events of that year were not school-related. My grandmother Brings, my Omi, was my world. Since both my parents worked, she raised me. She read me stories and she let me play with her antique magnifying glass, still one of my prized possessions. She let me "help" her bake exquisite Austrian cakes by licking the bowls and the beaters. She taught me how to make *Vanillekipferl* (vanilla crescents) Her English was perfect and she spent evenings teaching English to German/Austrian refugees. In the 1920s she played a powerful role for women's rights in Vienna and published articles and short stories. She could recite pages of poetry by Goethe and Schiller from memory, even on her deathbed. After suffering a series of strokes, she became paralyzed on her left side and died in July, 1952. Our school year began in June, so Third Grade had just started. This was my first great loss, and I was devastated. It happened on a Saturday and I still remember my mother entering my bedroom early in the morning. She lifted my mosquito net and I saw her tear-stained cheeks. She kissed me gently and said, "Omi is gone." I was supposed to begin ballet lessons at Anita Kane's Ballet Studio that day. Of course, my mother called and postponed. How could I dance? Omi was gone.

A few months later Shell Oil told the Cromwells, Shelagh's parents, that the company-owned house in Baguio would be available for their use for an entire week. The good news was that daughter Shelagh was allowed to bring a friend along. The bad news was that the assigned week was a school week. I couldn't imagine missing a whole week of school (horrors!), but my parents were very forward-thinking and felt that it would do me good and give me an experience that would be more educational in many ways than going to school. Both sets of parents arranged a conference with Mrs. Zwonechek, who gave them the assignments for the week, which, of course, Shelagh and I did every day under the watchful eye of Mrs. Cromwell. It was my first time away from my parents and I had to try to fit into a very traditional Scottish family for a week. Yes, there were some awkward moments and misunderstandings, but we went hiking, we went horseback riding and we visited Camp John Hay, Burnham Park, the St. Louis silver school, and the famous Baguio market. Every day was an adventure, a memory that I treasure to this day!

Fourth Grade

Mary

Fourth grade was a pivotal year. Because of limited space at the Donada campus, one grade was occasionally moved to the Seafront Compound which belonged to the U.S. Embassy. Seafront was conveniently located on Dewey (now Roxas) Boulevard. 1952-53 happened to be our 4th grade year. The classroom was a quonset hut with a corrugated iron roof. In retrospect it must have been terribly hot, but we kids didn't mind.

Every school has a few teachers that are extra special, extra memorable, and that have a reputation that precedes them. We had heard the stories. "Oh, Mrs. Wood. Very hard, very strict, very thorough, very fair, and, consequently, very beloved. And, she's British!"

Mrs. Wood taught us how to read for comprehension. We read about Joan of Arc, Johann Gutenberg, James Watt, Eli Whitney, Robert Fulton, Louis & Marie Pasteur. Mrs. Wood also told us the whole story behind Guy Fawkes Day. So that we would never forget how to spell one of the most frequently mis-spelled words in English, we simply had to remember that there is "a rat" in the middle of "separate". Multiplication tables had to be memorized and recited ad infinitum so that they would remain with us for life—and they have. She made long division and fractions great fun. She had a gift!

Mrs. Wood put maps all around the room, and she made geography come alive. My most vivid recollection is her description of Tierra del Fuego at the tip of South America. The fact that it means "Land of Fire" was fascinating, and I decided then and there that I would someday see Tierra del Fuego. Forty-five years later, as a Spanish teacher, I had an opportunity to take a Sabbatical. My project was to create short classroom videos of Argentina, the highlight of which was Tierra del Fuego.

Aurora

I remember a day every month when the entire compound had to be sprayed with DDT, most probably against mosquitoes and other tropical bugs. Of course, what was significant about all that spraying is the lack of protocols for us to go anywhere except to stay where we were. Hence, when the truck came and sprayed the compound, a huge chemical fog enveloped us wherever we were, and a distinct odor permeated the whole area. It was difficult to breathe, but it didn't last very long so we were able to tolerate the discomfort for a few minutes. Then, as if nothing had happened, the class continued. Thank goodness we survived that experience without getting poisoned! Imagine what kind of fuss would arise if that ever happened to anybody these days. What an uproar that practice would create! But Mrs. Wood said nothing and simply carried on!

Mary

Mrs. Wood was also renowned for her teaching of poetry. She loved poetry and firmly believed in the European tradition of asking students to memorize and recite poems. One that has remained with me is John Masefield's *Cargoes*. We had to recite it, mirroring the type of ship we were describing. The first verse had to be recited in a rocking cadence, reminiscent of rowing, as we learned that a quinquireme was a galley with four sets of oars. The second was smooth and slow, like the stately galleon it described. The favorite was the third, fast and choppy, similar to what would now be considered rap.

Cargoes

Quinquireme of Nineveh from distant Ophir,
Rowing home to haven in sunny Palestine,
With a cargo of ivory,
And apes and peacocks,
Sandalwood, cedarwood, and sweet white wine.

Stately Spanish galleon coming from the Isthmus,
Dipping through the Tropics by the palm-green shores,
With a cargo of diamonds,
Emeralds, amethysts,
Topazes, and cinnamon, and gold moidores.

Dirty British coaster with a salt-caked smoke stack,
Butting through the Channel in the mad March days,
With a cargo of Tyne coal,
Road-rails, pig-lead,
Firewood, iron-ware, and cheap tin trays.
John Masefield

About a month before the end of the school year, Mrs. Wood became very ill, and she was hospitalized. I remember visiting her in the hospital with classmate Eva Sternberg. Our mothers, who were friends, arranged the visit. We brought her flowers and wished her well. We hoped that she would recover, but we never saw her again.

Gloria

After Mrs. Wood left, Mrs. Barnett, a very pretty young blonde, took over our class. One day she forgot something (her lunch?) at home and her husband came into the room to give it to her. He was as handsome as she was beautiful. They were both straight out of central casting. Everybody just loved her, because she was not only beautiful, but so kind.

When Mrs. Barnett was our teacher, I got on the honor roll for the very first time. It might have been because her lessons were so much easier than Mrs. Wood's. Nevertheless, I was determined to never fall off the honor list again! Our class was grateful for her teaching and for her availability to step in at a moment's notice to take over for the iconic Mrs. Wood.

Mary

Mrs. Barnett arranged a class field trip to Malacañan Palace at the end of the school year, sometime in March, 1953. The palace grounds had a little zoo and, of course, that was my favorite part. I was so enthralled with the animals that I wrote the president a letter, asking where the animals had come from. Much to my surprise, I received a reply the following month from President Quirino's Protocol Officer:

Office of the President of the Philippines
Manila

April 16, 1953

Dear friend Mary:

I want to thank you for your note and I am happy to know that you enjoyed your visit to Malacañan Palace and the sights you saw. The animals in the zoo were gifts given to President Quirino by admirers from abroad. With my kindest regards, I am

Your friend
Manuel Zamora
(Protocol Officer)

Miss Mary Brings
Manila

Letter from Malacañan Palace
Brings Family Archive

Aurora

Our after school routine was to wait outside for our rides by some bushes and a chicken-wire fence on which grew thick vines of purple trumpet-like Morning Glories.

I remember sucking nectar out of the sweet purple flowers while we were waiting to be picked up from Seafront. Gloria and I followed Mary's lead. Until then, I had no idea that we could try drinking from pretty flowers growing from a bush on the side of the road. I don't believe I have ever tried doing that again since then! That Fourth Grade at Seafront stood out for so many reasons!

Fifth Grade

Mary

In Fifth Grade we were back on the Donada campus in the newly built South Hall. By this time my circle of friends was growing larger and included Carolyn Willard. Her mother, Mrs. Willard, was our Fifth Grade teacher. Since I was frequently invited to spend the night at Carolyn's, it was an interesting and highly unusual opportunity to observe a teacher in "real life". Even though my parents were teachers, I didn't make the connection that teachers had a life outside school and I enjoyed becoming part of the Willard family. One time when my dog Brownie had puppies, the Willards adopted one of them, so I loved being able to go visit the pup. Because Mr. Willard worked for the Embassy, they had PX privileges, which for me was something magical. Sometimes they took me along and it felt like actually setting foot in America. You had to use a special "scrip" to buy anything, so my Philippine pesos were worthless there. However, they always bought comic books and gum for Carolyn and me. The popular gum at the time was Double Bubble, a thick pink rectangle, about an inch long and a quarter inch thick that came with a comic inside on waxy paper. Mrs. Willard bought Double Bubble in huge quantities to use as an incentive to get an A on a test or quiz. And, if you received 100%, she gave you two. We had spelling tests frequently, so those of us who were good spellers ended up with kitchen cabinets filled with Double Bubble gum. Now I am very careful with what I eat and I work with a Nutritionist to keep my cholesterol down. It occurred to me that it might be interesting (and probably horrifying) to discover what that stuff was made of. I was not disappointed! According to Google, the ingredients are:

Sugar, Dextrose, Corn Syrup, Gum Base, Tapioca Dextrin, Titanium Dioxide, Confectioner's Glaze, Carnauba Wax, Corn Starch, Artificial Flavors, Artificial Colors, (FD&C Red 40, Blue 1, Yellow 5, Yellow 6, Red 3), and BHT (to maintain freshness). Yuck!

Gloria

Fifth grade was the year when we first learned something about U.S. geography and history. For some of us who had never been to the U.S. this was all new. Also we learned to place the states (only 48 of them) on the U.S. map and name state capitals. We were given maps with the outlines of the states and had to fill in the names. When we mastered that, we added the capitals. We were so proud of ourselves when we got them all correct! Knowing place names and capitals is not geography, of course, but it's a start.

Mary

The Fifth Grade history lesson that made the greatest impression on me was a personal story that Mrs. Willard told about how her family, the Hendersons, weathered the

Depression. I had never heard of the Depression, so listening to the poignant stories of that dark period, knowing that this was my teacher's family, moved me profoundly.

Most of us were involved in Scouts during grade school, as it was something to do after school. It was not like in the U.S. where Scouts go camping and learn how to survive in the wilderness. That was not done there. Too hot, buggy and dangerous. I don't know what the boys did, but the girls saw it more as a social time to get together with friends after school. We met in a classroom and had a scout leader, somebody's mother, who gave us things to do, such as games, songs and a lot of cutting and pasting. I think we made cards for every conceivable holiday. We did earn badges, which we sewed onto our sashes, but that was secondary to the socializing. To earn the baking badge, for example, I just brought a note from home, saying that I had baked something under my grandmother's watchful eye. Grandmother Brings was long gone by then, but my mother's mother, Grandmother Katz, who had escaped to London during the war, had come to live with us and was also a good cook and baker. By Seventh Grade we had outgrown Girl Scouts, as our interests began to blossom in other directions.

Sixth Grade

This was our last year of grade school, our last year of having just one teacher for all academic subjects. That teacher was Mrs. Susana Grant. Again Aurora, Gloria and Mary, who were in this group, contributed to this section.

Gloria

Mrs. Grant taught all subjects well, but her strong point was history. Two years later, in Eighth Grade, she would be our Philippine History teacher.

I loved being in Mrs. Grant's class, especially when we had the European history lessons, the first time we had this subject in depth. Interestingly, the course taught history through the biographies of European historical figures. I can remember Albert Schweitzer being one of them. His background confused me because he was from Alsace-Lorraine. I was always unsure whether it was in Germany or France or somewhere else! Oh, there was also Marie Curie, probably the first woman scientist I had ever heard of. Anyway, Mrs. Grant would teach us about these famous lives through story time! So easy to learn, and fun.

Mary

There were three specialty subjects taught by other teachers: Art, Music and Spanish.

The Art teacher, Ruth Geoffey, had been trained in the Berlin Art Institute and was another refugee of Hitler's Nazi regime. She was well prepared and she always challenged us with varied and interesting projects. For example, she taught color theory and had us mix colors accordingly. She showed us how to achieve perspective in a drawing, and how to make prints using linoleum blocks and a very sharp tool. As some students had a greater innate ability in art than others, she took into consideration the time and effort extended and not just the artistic quality of the final product.

Aurora

Nobody who attended the American School from the 50s into the 70s could forget the wild red-haired Ukrainian music teacher with the sharp tongue, Olga Ifland deWit. She was a force to be reckoned with, and she instilled fear in all of us, especially during exam time, when we had to approach the piano and sing to her accompaniment. The more frightened one was, the softer one sang, but the softer one sang, she softer she played, so there was no escape.

Mary

I remember an incident with our Spanish teacher, Carmen Jauregui. We only had Spanish half an hour per week, two fifteen minute sessions, so it consisted mainly of fun activities and songs. No grammar, no tests, just an introduction to the sounds of a language that was still widely spoken in the Philippines. She knew me because she sang in the Symphony Chorus with my mother and had seen me at the rehearsals. One day she taught us *Cielito Lindo*, the famous "ay, ay, ay, ay" song. She handed out the lyrics, the class sang it in unison several times and the homework assignment was to memorize it and be able to sing it individually the next time the class met. Since she knew me and knew that my mother sang in the chorus, she called on me first. I was shy and embarrassed, but having done the homework, I somehow got through the song. Then Miss Jauregui started calling on others to do the same thing and not one person in the class either could or would stand up and sing. I still remember how furious I felt at the time.

Students were coming and going, even in grade school.
But friendships were formed, many of which endure until today.

CHAPTER 6

Four New Classmates Arrive

Terry Kleeman, Bob Liese, Nancy Buerer & Warren Gerig

Our story continues with the introduction of new members to the class of 1961. Again we see the diversity of the class with their varied backgrounds and experience.

Karl Terrance Kleeman was born November 21,1942 in Dubuque, Iowa. He was baptized Catholic. He went by his nickname, Terry. His parents were Carl Joseph and Lucile Mary Kleeman who were also born in Dubuque. All four of his grandparents were from Dubuque as well. His father was an only child, but his mother had six brothers and sisters, so he would eventually have many cousins making up his extended family.

Terry Kleeman
The boy from Iowa

Terry at age fourteen

Until the war my parents never really got very far from Dubuque. During the war my Dad was in the Navy and was assigned to Alameda Naval Air Station in California. By that time my brother John, called Jack, had been born, and our family packed up an old car and moved west. My mother tells me during the trip they heated up my brother's baby bottles on the car engine. At the Naval Air Station, as aircraft carriers came into port from their Pacific duties, the planes would be flown to the base where mechanics worked on them. My father worked on the electronics and radios.

After his discharge from the Navy, my father went to work at the Dubuque dealership for International Harvester, the company that made tractors, farm equipment and trucks. My father's work included unloading parts from freight cars. One day the boss asked if any of the young workers could type. My father raised his hand. He actually didn't know how to type so he went out and bought a second hand typewriter and worked day and night. When he reported for his new job he could type. The move from the loading docks to the office started him on a new career path. He began to move up the ladder. After a few years he was promoted and transferred to Davenport, Iowa where my brother Jim was born and I started Catholic school. After about four years, my father moved up the ladder again and with another promotion, he was transferred to Des Moines. By this time he had moved into accounting and had made a name for himself by setting up improved accounting procedures. Our family lived in Des Moines for four years. I attended Catholic school, sang in the children's choir and served as an altar boy. I remember school as being stressful, in part because the nuns were very strict.

One nun, Sister Mary Stevens, would take misbehaving students by the ear lobe and press her fingernail into the lobe, sometimes drawing blood. We all lived in fear of her. Another memory shows the intimidating impact of the nuns those many years ago. One day, probably in fourth grade, my teacher nun said she had to leave and that no one was to talk while she was gone. Well, some students in the class started talking. One student asked me a question and I responded. When the nun came back, she caught some people talking and asked that anyone who was talking raise their hand. She then had them come forward and each got a swat across their hand with a ruler. I did not come forward as I was not really talking. I started worrying that if I died before I got to confession, I would go to hell. My worries got to be anxiety, and I needed to get to confession right away, so I went as soon as I could. This event made me fearful of doing anything wrong. My saving grace was our catechism with stories of Jesus filled with love. During Mass, the stories from the New Testament, gospels and epistles were based on love and caring for others. I always chose love and not the damnation side of Catholicism.

I was always a pretty shy and sensitive boy. We moved a lot and went to different schools. I made friends, but was never there that long, so I had to start over with each move. My brothers were my best playmates. My family would go back to Dubuque from time to time, especially at Christmas. I was able to spend time with my cousins. Christmas in cold, snowy Iowa remains among my fondest memories. When we visited Dubuque, we boys would stay at my cousins' house. We joined our three male cousins and slept in one room, sharing beds. They had a large Christmas tree and a wonderful Lionel train set. Then there was midnight mass and Christmas day with all my uncles and aunts and cousins. I especially treasure the memory of big Christmas dinners in a house full of joy.

In Des Moines our family got our first dog, Boots, an American Springer Spaniel. I was very close to Boots, and we went everywhere and did everything together. One day we were out and about and she got caught on a wire fence and tore the skin on her inner thigh. I could see the muscle under the torn skin. She did not seem to be having any pain, but I called my father at work. He came home and we got Boots to the veterinarian. One other time, we had driven across town to go sledding. Of course, Boots came along. At one point she ran off playing with some other dogs. We searched high and low for her but could not find her. We returned home and I was despondent. While eating dinner, we heard a scratching at the door. Somehow Boots had found her way home across town; my joy was unbounded. I bond deeply with dogs. I have always loved dogs and their care was and is an important responsibility.

My father had always been a good athlete and got his boys involved in sports at an early age. I played Little League baseball and was a Cub and Boy Scout. One day, the summer after I completed 7th grade, my Dad came home from work and asked my mother if she would like to move to the Philippine Islands. The first thing we all had to do was to get out the globe and Dad had to show us boys where the islands were. This resulted in another crisis for me! My dad decided we could not take Boots. I vividly remember my Dad taking Boots to the dog pound. My brothers got out of the car to say good bye to Boots. I could not do it and sat in the car crying. I never really got over that, and I am tearing while writing this. This was an emotional move for me.

Except for a brief time in California when my father was in the Navy during World War II, my parents had never lived anywhere except Iowa. My dad bought a new 1955 Chevrolet and the family drove across country from Iowa to Los Angeles, where we visited Disneyland, which had just opened. My Dad then loaded the car on the ship, and we took the President Cleveland to San Francisco; Honolulu, Hawaii; Yokohama, Japan and Manila, the Philippines. On the way we visited Pearl Harbor. Other than the one we were on, having never seen ships, let alone war ships, we boys were very impressed. When we got to Japan, our family was entertained by Japanese gentlemen from the local International Harvester subsidiary in Yokohama. In conversation with our hosts, my brother Jim came up with "Have you ever been to Pearl Harbor?" (Jim was 6 years old). There was a long moment of silence, and then the conversation continued as if the topic had never been brought up.

What an adventure for this Iowa family! My Dad was the new comptroller (treasurer) with the International Harvester Company in the Philippines. Our family arrived in Manila on October 5, 1955. The voyage on the President Cleveland was filled with activities for us boys and I beat my younger brother Jack in the finals of the shuffleboard championship. I often remind my brother of that since I don't think I could beat him at anything now. In the talent show, we three boys sang *Take me Out to the Ball Game*. I think that is the last time we were invited to sing for good reason.

What follows is what arriving in a new country halfway around the world was like in my mother's eyes as taken from a letter sent to her mother: "As you can see from our press notices, we were welcomed to Manila. The International Harvester Company (I.H.) gave us the red carpet treatment. Met at the pier by the officials and wives and driven to the

Manila Hotel. The view is magnificent, on one side Dewey Boulevard with its beautiful center parkway and Manila Bay; and the other side of the hotel overlooked the city. We had a suite consisting of two huge bedrooms, two baths, large living and dining room combination. We had so very much red tape to go through to enter this country. Fortunately, the International Harvester Company employs two men whose job it is to assist incoming and outgoing employees and they know all the angles. With their help we sailed through customs and the U.S. Embassy and Philippine immigration routine in about two days. We had to be checked and rechecked, finger printed, registered, etc. An interesting sidelight, our Jim, while waiting in line, became bored with it all, very nonchalantly sang out, 'God Bless America, land that we love', and you can imagine how quickly he was quieted. The I.H. office has been looking for housing for us. As elsewhere, living accommodations are limited and rents are high. But we aren't in any hurry because our furniture will not arrive for at least a month. We are still living in the hotel and the boys are waiting for school to start on the seventh of November."

One early memory in the Philippines was of a nice large painting in our hotel room of a young Filipina woman, naked from the waist up. We boys had never seen anything like that. One day when our parents were out, I took an envelope and cut a "bra" out of the part with the glue and stuck it on the glass over her breasts. How naive I was, a good Catholic boy right out of Iowa! I wonder what the hotel cleaning people thought when they saw that!

I had completed 7th grade back in Iowa. Because the school year at the American School was mid-term, my parents had to decide if I was to go directly into the second half of 8th grade or repeat the second half of 7th grade. I actually started school when I was 4 as my birthday was November 21, and so I was always one of the youngest in my class. My parents decided that I should repeat the second half of 7th grade, a decision for which I am so grateful since I was beginning in a new school mid-year in a new country This gave me a head start. My first day at the American School was November 7, 1955.

Terry's first and best friend was Bob Liese, who was born on July 25, 1943.

Bob Liese
The boy from Ohio

My father was attending the University of Missouri and my mother was down the road at Stephens College for women, both located in Columbia, MO. They were married in Akron

Bob at age fifteen

in 1942 prior to my father's being shipped to Germany, where he rose to the rank of Major in the US Army (Field Artillery). I do know he was awarded the Bronze Star and served under Gen. Patton in the Battle of the Bulge. Following WWII my father returned to school and graduated from Akron University in the field of Chemical Engineering. He went right to work for BFGoodrich and before long we were off to Tuscaloosa, AL for his first assignment.

We arrived in Tuscaloosa in 1949 and I immediately enrolled in first grade; I can remember printing 1949 on my school work.

My earliest recollection is being accosted on the playground and called a "Yankee." I had no idea what they were talking about, so I asked my mother, who told me to call them Rebels. I made many school friends, but I was surprised at some of their living conditions. Not shacks, although sub-standard. Once on a hall pass the Black janitor took a piece of gum out of his mouth and told me to throw it away which I obediently did. Today I figure it was some kind of retribution. I witnessed a neighbor actually whipping his Black maid in his yard and I was totally confused, as she was an adult. So was the South in the early 50s.

On a lighter note I have fond memories of accompanying my dad when he'd play golf and I was amazed how he'd drive the ball so high and far. I knew that's what I wanted to do when I was older. I believe I really got the bug at age thirteen watching our neighbors Terry and his brother Jack chipping golf balls in their large yard in Quezon City.

Another memory is of my Dad and I watching the Crimson Tide and their practice at the university. I proudly wore an Alabama Crimson Tide T-shirt for as long as it lasted. Our place was fairly close to a main rail line and I enjoyed watching those huge locomotives go by. Once an engineer tossed me a railroad magazine right out his window.

By then I had two little brothers who could pass for twins, although they were thirteen months apart. It was not long before Dad got into the International Division at Goodrich and we took a ferry boat with our car for an overnight trip to Havana, Cuba, where we spent an enjoyable three years during the pre Castro era. Wasn't without its revolution, though, as I remember staying home from school (yaay!) during the Batista takeover.

But talk about beautiful blue/green water! I'll never forget Veradero beach! It was there I saw my first tarantula spider, scorpions and a huge iguana. I would hunt the smaller lizards with my Whamo slingshot. I only wished I had been older then. Nonetheless I would hop buses out to the Biltmore Yacht and Country Club, which was right on the ocean and had a golf course. I attended Ruston Academy, full of American kids. I was seriously behind in 3rd grade, as their academic standards were higher than those of my previous school in the States. We were all Cub Scouts and my friend's mother was the den leader. Our troop took many field trips and one was to Morro Castle, the fort at the entrance to Havana harbor built by the Spanish. In it was a frightening statue of someone being tortured next to an opening down to the sea and I saw sharks that still bother me to this day. Less stressful were our troop's trip to a sugar mill, the Cerveza Hatuay beer factory and a U.S. Navy submarine. Our troop for some reason attended a ceremony which included the dictator Fulgencio Batista. We were all in the front row at attention when he arrived. A lady in the crowd rushed out to him, and I watched his body guards remove her not so gently. All in all Cuba was a great place, even for a boy my age.

My sister, Kathy, was born in Havana, and soon thereafter we returned to Akron in 1954. I returned ahead of my parents and siblings and stayed with my grandparents. It was then that my grandfather taught me to fly cast. He was a charter member and investor of the newly formed Rockwell Springs Trout Club in Castalia, Ohio where I spent many a day fishing. The place had a clubhouse and several cabins for overnight accommodations as well as several miles of spring fed streams. One kept what one caught and paid by the pound once the trout were cleaned. One day I caught thirteen in four hours but my grandfather just let me keep going. Fortunately, a large group came in for dinner and they all wanted trout.

In 6th grade I had the same teacher my mother had had years earlier so she was very old but still teaching. Once it started snowing I would stare out the classroom window, but she never admonished me, knowing the climate I'd come from. I was in 7th grade at a different school which was a converted high school that they called junior high. They had strange courses to me, like wood and metal shop. I went to wood shop which was pretty boring but I managed to make a tie rack for my Dad. One kid was really into it and he made a soap box derby race car for the annual Akron event.

Now by the Spring of '56 I was just getting used to stateside living when Manila was mentioned. I knew exactly where it was, having had a board game called *Wide World*, the object being to start in New York, roll dice and take boats and planes and get to Manila (of all places) first! It's an old Parker Brothers game and to this day I still have sheets of collector stamps stored within the board. Our family took an American President Lines steamship, the Wilson. Another crossing was on the Cleveland but that came later. I was pretty distraught leaving the USA and thought my stamp and coin collecting days were over. On the Wilson I made a really good friend, a Chinese kid whose father was in the UN and from Jamaica, Queens NY. I was excited when we corresponded later as I would get a UN postage stamp. There was also a friend on board who kept mentioning Elvis Presley who I had not heard of. He was probably from the South where Elvis was really hot. Then a young Black kid my brother's age kept talking about Little Richard. It took a while before Rock and Roll began playing in Manila. I guess I expected the Philippines to be somewhat like Cuba, but the place seemed backward, with much bomb damage, poverty and lack of all the U.S. amenities found in Cuba. The sounds were strange, mostly of vendors shouting in Tagalog, the noisy buses and jeepneys and the blaring juke boxes in the sari sari stores and cafés.

After arriving in Manila we spent our first days in the Filipinas Hotel. We then lived in two homes, while the Company arranged for a house while ours was being built. Apparently the renters were on home leave and we just moved right in—their maids, their furniture and all. Our household goods did not arrive for what seemed like months. Our first place was a compound just off Dewey Blvd. and very near Seafront. From this compound we moved out to Quezon City, where Terry, the first person my age that I met, lived across the street. I started at the American School in 8th Grade in the Fall of 1956.

Nancy Buerer joined the class of 1961 in the eighth grade. She was born in Elmhurst, Illinois in 1943. Her father was from Escalon, CA, where he was one of eight children born to a farming family. Her mother was from Elmhurst, one of five children. They met at Wheaton College, a Christian institution just a few miles west of Elmhurst. One thing that drew them together was that they both felt called to be missionaries in Africa, and that is what they trained and prepared for. When they were married in September 1940, their plans were put on hold as World War II was going on across the world. They moved to California, where Nancy's father did carpentry work as well as farming and preaching.

Nancy Buerer
Baptist missionary family

Nancy at age twelve

My older sister Peggy was born in June, 1941. When the U.S. entered the war, my father was exempt from the draft because he was a minister. He felt the need to take additional courses in Bible and ministry, so they moved back to Elmhurst and lived with my mother's parents while my father was taking courses at Moody Bible Institute in Chicago. I was born in April 1943. Shortly thereafter he took a church in Polson, Montana for a couple of years.

Finally, in April 1946, after the end of the war, my parents left for the Belgian Congo. My mother's aunt and uncle and cousins were already there, and I'm sure my parents were grateful for their support. My great grandfather and my mother's mother were very active in the U. S. administration of the mission, the Congo Gospel Mission, and they often sent packages and ran errands on behalf of the missionaries.

The day after we arrived was my third birthday. I have very dim memories of someone baking me a cake, and receiving gifts of a glass piggy bank and an ivory napkin ring. I kept them for several years, but, sadly, I have no idea what happened to them.

Africa was an interesting experience to say the least. I marvel at the faith and courage of my parents who surely realized very soon that they had taken on much more than they had bargained for. We lived at a mission compound where there were three housing units, a print shop, a church, and a school. For the full three years we were there we had no electricity or running water. We had a kerosene stove, and our house boy went half a mile to a spring and brought water up to the "house," where my mother boiled it so we could drink and cook with it. The first year we lived in a thatched annex to the church. The second year one of the other missionary families went back to the States on furlough, and we moved up to the second house, which was built from palm leaves. The third year we became very "uptown" and moved to the third house, made from concrete blocks. We even had an indoor bathroom, although that was still like an outhouse. We had tuna cans filled with kerosene, under each leg of our beds, to keep the driver (large, biting) ants from climbing up to us during the night. I believe we had a kerosene icebox as well, called an "icyball." Even though life was difficult, we had our loving parents there, and we didn't know we were "deprived."

The mission compound was outside a village called Kifwonzondo, and the language spoken there was Kikongo. My parents learned quite a bit of the language, but I only learned a few words. To this day I can sing a couple of songs in the language, and remember a few words—"Beka," Go away, "Pamba," bad, "Mbote," hello and good, and "Zola," love.

When Peggy turned 6, my mother taught her and a couple of the other missionary children, using the Calvert Course, a correspondence curriculum from Baltimore, MD. I had no one to play with during the day, so I hung around the school room and learned to read and write, just like the "big kids." Consequently, when I returned to the States, I started first grade, but it was soon obvious that I knew everything that was being taught, and so I advanced to second grade at 6 years old.

The Calvert Correspondence School was founded in 1897, and is still in existence. It provides instruction for over 10,000 students in all 50 states and hundreds of countries throughout the world. As I remember it, we had a book with lessons for each day in multiple subjects, math, English, history, art, etc. We had textbooks, and could learn independently, although my mother as teacher was there to guide us, grade our papers, administer tests, and answer questions.

The school on the mission station was for local boys, and at times during the day they would march together across the property while singing. So Peggy and I would march at the rear of the column and participate with the boys. Other activities were climbing trees (the trees there were short and perfect for young children), coloring, and playing in the yard, where we had to wear safari helmets to keep our heads safe from the glaring heat of the sun.

There was a group of people in the Congo called "Maganchis," that would rob and otherwise harass the local people. We kids were afraid that they would come and do something to us, but that never happened. I have pictures of two of them, but my understanding is that they were just dressed like "Maganchis" and were never a threat. We were robbed a few times—once at Christmas time, when all our presents were stolen. However, we figured that they needed these things more than we did, and I don't remember being angry about it.

By then I had two more sisters. I cannot imagine what my mother went through having them. One was born in 1947 in a small missionary hospital, where she almost died, and the other was born in 1948 in the back of a car trying to get to a city hospital. We returned to the U.S. from Africa in 1949. We traveled to Leopoldville, now the capital of the Democratic Republic of the Congo, then to Kinshasha, where we got on a riverboat to Matadi, where we boarded a ship to cross the Atlantic. Our family of six and two Belgian priests were the only passengers. I had my 6th birthday on the ship.

We landed in New Orleans, where I saw the Jax brewery sign along the Mississippi River. That sign, or one of its descendants, is there to this day. I had my first taste of ice cream in New Orleans, and my first soda pop, which I didn't like at all ("It stings my tongue!").

After about eight months in Elmhurst again, we moved to Almont, Michigan in January, 1950, where my father pastored a small church and I attended the second half of second grade through the first half of fifth grade. The elementary and high schools were in the same building, and I remember seeing an exhibit on the bulletin board in the high school about the year 2000. I was awestruck and thought, "Oh my goodness, I will be 57! I wonder if I will live that long!" For the second half of fifth grade, we were back in Elmhurst, where I made several friends in my school, and watched the coronation of Queen Elizabeth II on the TV with one of them. My grandparents had a small black and white TV (as did everyone else), but my family never did as long as my parents lived. Needless to say, the coronation impressed me tremendously.

We left for the Philippines in 1953. My parents told us they were applying to be missionaries somewhere in the Pacific, and I was sure it would be Hawaii. My ten-year-old mind was full of romantic ideas about hula dancers, flowers and moonlight strolls on the beach. So when I found out it was the Philippines (the where!!?) I was pretty disappointed.

We crossed the Pacific Ocean on a freighter called the Pacific Bear, where we and another missionary couple were the only passengers. The other woman was an artist, so Peggy and I took art lessons from her, which helped to pass the time. We were on the ship over the Christmas holiday. Our supporters from the States felt sorry for the poor little missionary children on the ship, so they sent us a lot of presents. The day after Christmas we were experiencing a storm, and the ship was rolling from side to side fairly violently. My youngest sister did not heed the instructions of my parents to stay in the room on the bed, and she opened the stateroom door, which promptly slammed shut on her little finger, and nearly cut it off. I will never forget my father's face and voice, crying "Oh no!!" when he realized what had happened. There was no doctor on the ship, but the purser, who had a little medical training, set and bandaged my sister's finger. It healed as well as could be expected. However, for several years she could not bend the joints at all, and eventually had surgery to bend the finger and prevent it from extending straight out.

We arrived in Manila in early January, 1954, and some of the missionaries came to the docks to meet us. The first people we met were the Bancrofts, whom we had heard about before we got there because they had kids Peggy's and my ages. I started out being better friends with Sylvia instead of Ellen because I was in the same grade as Sylvia.

In sixth and seventh grades I took correspondence courses (Calvert School again), and my mother taught me slowly so I would end up where I belonged. I have to give a shout out to Calvert School. The curriculum was wonderful, and I learned so much. They had an art history course in each grade, and I learned all about famous paintings, sculpture and architecture. In 2003, when my husband Bill and I went to Italy, I saw many of these art works in the Uffizi and other museums and still remembered what I had learned as a child.

In Manila, we lived on the second floor of a refurbished Quonset hut, left over from the war, and on the first floor was my father's print shop. His mission was, among other things, to be in charge of the literature for the missionaries in the Philippines. At times I would "help" him, and learned how to set type, operate the press, assemble and staple booklets, programs, letters, and whatever was needed. As time went on, we were able to purchase more updated equipment, such as a linotype and more sophisticated presses.

We didn't know many people, except the other missionaries and people at the church we attended. My mother taught English and Christian ethics at a seminary associated with our church and our mission board. I was quite shy, and it was hard for me to talk to other people. However I did enjoy musical programs, as I took voice lessons from one of the women missionaries. Those lessons were the foundation for lifelong participation in choirs and other musical events.

When I was twelve my mother gave birth to a baby boy, which was very exciting for all of us after having four girls. We all went to Malaybaly, Bukidnon, Mindanao, where there was a missionary doctor, and stayed about a month. While I was there, I met several Filipina girls my age and became very close friends with them. When we returned to Manila, I corresponded with them for several years. Unfortunately, when I went back to the States, we lost touch.

After a year of homeschooling four children, caring for a newborn, and finding that she was pregnant again, my parents decided to send Peggy and me to the American School. Peggy started 10th grade and I started 8th. This was a big turning point in my life, as I had classmates and much more of a social life. I met so many kids with such diverse and international family backgrounds, such as business, politics, military, missionary, and academics.

Warren Gerig joined the class of 1961 as a high school freshman. Warren was born on March 11, 1942 in Camden, New Jersey. The father of one of his best friends was Sheriff of their County, so he got used to the uniform, blaring police radios in the house and a squad car in the parking area.

Warren Gerig
The Viking boy from New Jersey

Warren at age twelve

When I was ten years old (1952) my family moved from a small town in Southern New Jersey to Bombay, India. I guess my saddest moment of moving was leaving my friends in New Jersey. My father worked for Mobile Oil. He was a mechanical engineer who understood the formula to making different kinds of fuel: gasoline, kerosene and aviation fuel. He was important because of his work. He was classified as critical to National Defense and was not to be put in harm's way. During World War II he signed up for the Navy Seabees. After the War he assisted in developing new designs for Mobile Corporation refineries. He was also asked if he wanted to work on a Government Secret Project.

My grandfather, who had just passed away with emphysema, had a large house on a sizable piece of property. The family decided to sell it and split the proceeds. So we were homeless and had nowhere to go. At dinner one night Dad asked us how we would like to go to India. He was fantastic at selling my sister and me into all kinds of ideas. Our first reaction was: Where is India? So at that dinner we decided to go on this wonderful experience.

My father started working for Standard Vacuum Oil Company, a joint venture between Mobile and Esso (Exxon). It would have been against the law in the USA for the two companies to work together for antitrust reasons; however, internationally it was permissible and the Government had said that it was in our country's best interest.

His job was to build an oil refinery outside of Bombay. We arrived in the middle of the night during a festival with a bright full moon and found a lot of people sleeping on the sidewalks and in some cases in the street. Indians chew beetle-nut, and it looked like the whole population was spitting up blood. When we got to the Taj Mahal Hotel and into our rooms, my sister, Mom, Dad and myself huddled on a big king bed and cried for some time, trying to figure what we had gotten ourselves into. Well, needless to say, one can get used to anything, and we did.

I was put into a very refined Indian girls school of 3000 along with four other American boys, as our mothers did not want us attending the British Boys School, since those teachers practiced corporal punishment. We had had no Algebra, no Geometry and no Foreign Language, so the school put my sister and me back a grade, and we started to learn French and Hindi. Looking back on that experience, I cannot understand why this was not an enjoyable one for me, being with so many lovely young ladies, that is.

It wasn't long before I requested a transfer to the boys' school, corporal punishment and all. It really wasn't that bad; one just had to have the motivation to learn. The only problem was that after four years in the British School System, when we returned to New York the principal said, "Well, you know Algebra and Geometry and a foreign language" (French) so they put us up two grades. We skipped all the stuff in between, so that we still know our Kings and Queens better than our Presidents.

While living in India my father took me to several security briefings that were given by a well known British Security Company for our own protection. We learned why the driver would always take us to school and shopping with mother using different routes. Also we learned what to do if we were ambushed and why I had to watch for kidnapping by a pedophile. Even so, I took a lot of risks in Bombay. I found that if I wanted to neutralize a situation I would simply say "I'm American" in my distinctly American accent. Some didn't like the British and wanted them out of India, but for some unknown reason they liked Americans. I traveled all over as an 11–14 year old on Red Double Decker buses just like in London. But then there were dangerous Hindu/Muslim riots, some of which kept us locked up in our compound for weeks!

The most memorable event was to see the Taj Mahal during the first full moon after the Monsoon Season. When it was clean, it glistened. It is the most beautiful building I have ever seen! I spent a lot of my time flying kites with rice paste and ground up glass on waxed string. My friends and I would have kite fights from the tops of buildings. We would try to cut the opponent's string with the glass part of our string. What fun that was! Kite fighting — HURRAH!!!

Because it was painful to leave all the friends I had in India, I decided not to get close to people on the next assignment. That was almost impossible to do. Our next assignment was in the Philippines in 1957. "Why were we in the Philippines to build another oil refinery on Bataan?" was my biggest question. "Why do we build these refineries and turn them over to the local Government and leave?" My father explained that this was how we get what we want. It wasn't until he had passed that I found out the real answer. Allen Dulles, Director of the CIA, was asked by President Eisenhower to give him a list of the countries where we would need aviation fuel if the Cold War expanded and also countries that were allies, where a refinery would help their economy. The Philippines was important because it was an ally and an oil refinery would generate a better economic situation, plus fuel for Subic Naval Station and Clark Airbase.

I was excited we were going to the Philippines, not only because of the history of World War II, but also to honor my grandfather who had been there at the turn of the 19th century. From him I had heard it was a great place to live. My grandfather was a Marine Sergeant who sailed into Manila Bay on Admiral Dewey's Flagship during the Spanish American War. He was stationed in Manila for some time before being shipped off to the Boxer Rebellion in China. He stated that he really liked the Philippines and wished he could have stayed longer. Also, I was interested in the fact that the refinery would be built on Bataan across from the World War II American Fortress on Corregidor Island. In fact I visited the island several times and wrote my American School Senior Term Paper on Corregidor.

We lived in the Manila Hotel for six months until we got a home in San Lorenzo Village where we spent most of our time in the Philippines. Being in school had been the most traumatic experience for me living abroad. In 1957, when we moved to the Philippines and I was placed in the Freshman Class of the American School, it was almost the end of the school year. The American School was a lot harder than schools in the USA, but Patricia and I found that the transition to the American School was easier than to the British schools in India. Above all, we felt much more welcome.

We classmates are now pre-teens and we look forward to fully enjoying the many activities that the American School has to offer its Junior High students.

CHAPTER 7

Adapting to Life in the Philippines

Chapter 3 speaks to growing up in the Philippines for those classmates who were born there during the war. Although they had very different backgrounds, they were Philippine residents and were more integrated into the local culture.

In this chapter we follow four American families who arrived in the 1950s. It was not difficult to adapt to life in the tropics, as for most of us we had pretty much all we needed to maintain our back home lifestyle. We also had special advantages such as servants, something that our families had never been able to afford in the U.S. Many of our families did not really integrate into the Philippine culture, probably because for most of us this was a temporary assignment. But each family was a bit different. For us students, it was easy to fall into the American School "bubble" where we found friends and many school-related activities. These are our stories.

Passenger ShipPresident Cleveland, American President Lines
Kleeman Family Archives

The American President Lines (APL) was well known for operating some excellent all First Class Passenger liners to many parts of the world. Most of our classmates arrived on the President Wilson or the President Cleveland.

While Bob had lived for a time in Cuba, Nancy for three years in the Congo with her missionary parents and Warren for five years in India, Terry came directly from Iowa. All of us arrived with uniquely different experiences and expectations, but all immediately began adapting to life in Manila. In this chapter we see how four young teens and their families attempt to integrate new traditions into their lifestyles.

New Homes in the Philippines

After arrival most of us were put up in temporary housing while our parents searched for permanent homes. Also, most of us had to wait some time for our furniture and other belongings to arrive by freighter. But eventually we found and moved into new homes which were quite different from what we were accustomed to. Our classmates' homes were spread throughout Metro Manila but for all of us our second home was the American School.

Terry Kleeman
The boy from Iowa

Kleeman Home in San Lorenzo Village, Makati
Kleeman Family Archives

Living in the Philippines meant a lot of changes for our Iowa family. We lived in the Manila Hotel when we first arrived. When our furniture arrived, we moved to Quezon City, one of the cities within Metro Manila, but somewhat out in the country at that time. Our home was one of several new homes that constituted about a block on a dirt road mostly surrounded by open fields. Most of the houses were owned by one landlord, the Saranguias. We got to be good friends. My mother would go to their house frequently for a visit and we boys would play tennis on their tennis court. Our house was surrounded by six foot walls made of concrete block with broken glass imbedded in cement to discourage unwelcome guests. We had a large steel gate at the entrance, a two car garage and a spacious driveway. One of the first orders of business was to put a basketball hoop on the garage. We had a commute into school each day and our Filipino driver took us. About a year later, our good friends, the Lieses, moved in down the street. Bob Liese and I were in the same class at the American School and became good friends. We had a large side yard where we played, including American football and chipping golf. Later we moved to a subdivision closer to our American School friends called San Lorenzo Village in the suburb of Makati. Our new home, unlike our previous home, just had a small front yard and small wall, but there were open spaces in the neighborhood for play. In that location we were also close to the wonderful Polo Club for many recreational activities.

Bob Liese
The boy from Ohio

We also first lived in Quezon City near Terry. Sometime in early 1957 we moved into a newly built company home and, as it turned out, Nancy Buerer was our neighbor. We lived there probably four years before moving to Urdaneta Village in Makati, a new development in the area of the old airport. It was much easier being closer in, with easy access to communities such as Forbes Park, San Lorenzo, and the other gated communities, known as "Villages."

Nancy Buerer
Baptist missionary family

Our home in the Philippines was a missionary compound with metal fences (made of materials used for airstrips during the war) topped with barbed wire for better security. Our family was never robbed, but someone did break into the other house in our compound when nobody was living there and took some things that were held in storage there.

Warren Gerig
The Viking boy from New Jersey

We lived in the Manila Hotel for five months when we arrived, as no decent housing was available for us, and our furniture was still in transit. When a fantastic home opened up in San Lorenzo Village, a gated community in Makati where many American School classmates lived, we took it immediately. The house was a big four bedroom home with servant quarters and a two car garage. It had a perfect darkroom for developing pictures, my passion. We also had lovely designed tile floors downstairs, fabulous narra wood floors upstairs and solid doors made of teak. One couldn't kick in those doors! The yard was fabulous with every variety of colorful flowers surrounding on three sides. My father did not want a wall around the house, so we had a three foot brick fence built, that allowed us to see at least a quarter of a mile, as there were no other houses on our edge of the Village at that time. We were always worried about being robbed, not having a high wall with broken glass on top. However, we never had a problem with unwanted guests in all the years at this location.

My father was building a new refinery in Bataan, on the north side of Manila Bay, and had a second home to stay in when he was there. It was part of the refinery complex. These were typical American homes and were for the foreign contractors building the refinery and eventually the people who would run the refinery. When I was getting ready to graduate and the rest of the family would be leaving the Philippines after completion of the refinery, we decided to move closer to the school, into an apartment just a block from the American School. There we were robbed twice in eight months, even though we had bars on the windows and doors. Luckily the thieves didn't get much, as most of our furniture and goods had been moved to storage while waiting to move out of the Philippines.

Nancy: Several of us girls went to a slumber party at one classmate's house, and late in the evening we kept hearing some intermittent sharp noises. But we were having a good time and didn't worry too much about it. In the morning we found that someone had cut the window bars and entered the house, stealing money and some of our other possessions. They were certainly quiet, because we really heard nothing.

Bob: Election Day was always a holiday from school, and we were encouraged not to go out into the general public, as things sometimes got pretty heated among political rivals. I remember that we were always safe on Election Day at the Polo Club. "Oye, one more Calamansi please and a Grenadine 7Up for my friend."

Terry: Recurring references to six foot walls with broken glass, bars on windows, and barbed wire may give the impression that we were not safe. Actually, Manila was quite a safe place to live. Although there were occasional robberies due to the high poverty rate, none of us ever had an experience where we were harmed or threatened.

Adapting to New Foods

Terry: So how did an American family from Iowa deal with food prepared by our Filipino cook? My parents spent their whole lives in Iowa with a "Midwestern Iowa diet." We tended to eat potatoes, Iowa meats, especially hamburger, spam, cheese, assorted garden vegetables (fresh from summer gardens but canned goods in the winter), sweet corn in season, salads with iceberg lettuce, pie and cake and most of all ice-cream. Perhaps not the most healthy diet, but it worked for generations.

All of a sudden we had a Filipina cook. Of course, Mom initially kept our family on our usual diet. This required some innovation, like home made potato chips, sliced potatoes fried in a pan (definitely not the same). As time went on, Mom and our Filipina cook integrated local dishes into our meals.

In one of my mother's letters to her mother in Iowa, she described her first impressions as seen through her eyes. "And the first thing on our family agenda was food. Manila has a number of grocery stores, mostly Chinese owned and operated. There are also several native markets. Due to the fact that meat in the grocery stores is sold from refrigerated counters, we were told that these establishments are often referred to as 'cold stores'. Fruit, vegetables, and meat are sold by the kilo (2.2 lbs). Import control has greatly reduced the availability of imported foods. At practically any given time some one thing will be unavailable. Meat is imported from the United Sates, Australia, New Zealand and Argentina. From neighbors who have some kind of connection we were able to get sixty pounds of tenderloin from Argentina. The only pork sold is local pork and we buy it from the cold stores. The fish is good. We buy shrimp in the live state and the cook takes care of them. They stink to high heaven but the end product is delicious. Baguio vegetables are the ones we were used to, midwestern style vegetables grown in the 5000-foot altitude of the Mountain Province and shipped to Manila. The following are among those available: beets, cauliflower, celery, string beans, peas, cabbage, sugar peas, tomatoes, cucumbers, lettuce and turnips. We can get fresh tomatoes all year round and they are so good. All butter and cheeses are imported. There is a large variety of local fruits. The bananas are ripened on the trees. Calamansi is a small green native lime and is especially good as a fruit drink. The native oranges when ripe, are as green as grass, but they are sweet and good. As far as drinks are concerned, we are learning to like the local coffee and there is no shortage of soft drinks. Also, the water is safe to drink. The Philippine marketplace where fruits, vegetables, fish, etc. are sold is something to behold. Wares are laid out right in the narrow streets. And one never pays the asking price—everything is bargained for."

Mary and her Mother at a Typical Market, Brings Family Archives

Bob: Having disembarked the SS President Wilson the previous day, I strolled in for my first Philippine breakfast at the Hotel Filipinas where we were staying. There were some strange things on the menu and I discovered I could not order my usual grapefruit, so I tried this thing called a papaya. It wasn't bad at all, only a little stringy. I later came to enjoy other local fruits, mainly mangoes, guavas and star apples. Speaking of mangoes, we had a full-grown mango tree in our back yard in Mandaluyong (a suburb of Manila). The tree was very close to our surrounding wall and the locals (probably kids) would throw stones trying to dislodge the fruit, usually hitting our roof and making a racket.

For our daily meals we did our best to go American. My mother planned the meals and relayed them to our cook, Sabina, who was the best. She always asked me what I wanted for dessert, saying in her native accent, "Do you want Mango or Cookie?" She had a way of preparing the mango that to this day I can't replicate. The halves would be pushed up and opened up like an umbrella with cross cut square chunks that were easily spooned out. I can't even halve the thing correctly what with the large seed. We ate a lot of pork and, of course, rice. When I returned to the States I wouldn't order or eat rice, having become so tired of it. My mother always spoke of Kobe beef, a staple. She would lament that she missed the "Golden Bantem" Ohio corn and the fact she could not get her beloved artichokes. My good friend Skip Haven's father was the person in charge of APL (American President Lines) in Manila, so mom could then get her artichokes from the ship's stores when in port and Skip would deliver them. On Sundays when Sabina was off, Dad would prepare what he called a "Hobo Dinner" consisting of beef, potatoes, carrots and onion all thrown together, and heated up and served in individual foil wrapped portions—truly American!

It goes without saying, at one time or another, we had tried all the usual Filipino dishes. I particularly liked lechón and lumpia and the Sari-Sari store snacks. I am still amazed that I could buy a "warm" San Miguel beer in those stores for twenty centavos, which back then according to the exchange rate was about a U.S. nickel.

Nancy: The food we ate at home was mostly the same as what we would eat in the States, although we had tropical fruits such as papaya, mangoes, guavas, and of course bananas. We could not get beef readily, so we ate mostly pork and chicken, rice and potatoes, vegetables and spaghetti. If we ate out at a restaurant (not often), we sometimes had Filipino or Chinese food. We especially liked lumpia, which was wrapped meat and vegetables and deep fried. We could not get fresh milk (no cows), so we drank powdered milk. The brand name was Klim, "Milk" spelled backwards! There were two American style supermarkets in Manila, called Acme, which my parents frequented.

Warren: I couldn't get enough of papaya whenever it was available. Our cook also prepared a dish called mangoes and sticky rice, which was deliciously sweet and tasty. As far as drinks, it was calamansi or coke. Any kind of noodles was fine with me, and I loved added small shrimp cooked in butter. You could never get enough shrimp! I always felt there were too many vegetables, but ate them anyway!

Religion in a new land

The American School, a private, secular school, included students, parents, staff, and faculty from all over the world. It is quite amazing, when compared with the culture of today, that we cared about and respected each other's rights to believe as we saw fit. All of our families found a church of their choosing.

Terry: We were Iowa Catholics. My mother's brother was a priest. I had about twenty first cousins. We went to mass every Sunday. So, when we arrived in the Philippines, we fit right in and immediately found a Catholic church. But since we did not speak the language, we did not participate in many church activities.

Bob: My Dad was a deeply religious person, having been brought up in the strict Missouri Synod Lutheran church. There must not have been a Lutheran church in Cuba because we attended an Episcopal church, which was probably a close substitute. That all changed in Manila, as there was a tiny, painted white, Lutheran church. Dad would round up my two brothers and me every Sunday for the service. My mother did not attend with us and her "out" was that it was not air conditioned. I could understand that, as it was rather stuffy in that little church.

Apparently, Lutheran missionaries were very active in the Philippines and my Dad knew and befriended every one of them and their families. So much so that we'd host many of them for family cook-outs and pool parties at our place in Urdaneta Village. I was surprised to see Ray Domingo, my good friend and classmate, with his family attend our little church. Years later at a school reunion he told me his folks had been visited by a missionary. My dad was even somewhat of a lay-minister and actually preached a sermon on occasion which, by knowing him otherwise, I never would have envisioned.

Nancy: From the beginning of my life, my belief in God and in Jesus, as His Son and my Savior, has been extremely important to me. My parents were missionaries, not only in the Philippines, but also for three years in the Belgian Congo, Africa and, after we returned to the States, as church "planters" and home missionaries in northern California. We attended and were active in the First Baptist Church of Manila for about three years. Then my father felt called to start a church in Quezon City, so we pioneered that for several years. I played the organ there, and taught children's Sunday School.

My father was a printer, and his print shop was on the ground floor of our home, which was a repurposed Quonset hut that was left from World War II. He printed whatever was required by our mission and its partners, which could be schools, churches, or approved individuals. These items included such things as "tracts" used to hand out to potential church members, programs, and instructional materials.

My mother was on the faculty of the Baptist Bible Seminary, which was initially located at the church, but later moved to its own campus in Mandaluyong (an area of Manila). She taught English, which every Filipino of a certain age was required to know, in addition to his or her native language. She also taught Christian ethics.

We attended church every Sunday morning and evening and every Wednesday evening. One thing I remember very well is that, on All Saint's Day, which was November 1, we would go to a cemetery and pass out "tracts." The Filipino people received these very well, and we felt that this was an evangelistic opportunity.

Warren: My mother and father always went to church. My father was a Presbyterian and mother was an American Baptist. In India we went to an Episcopal Church. In the Philippines we attended the church where my best friend's father was minister. He was a Presbyterian pastor in a non-denominational church.

Fiestas (Festivals) and Holidays

In those days the Philippines and the U.S. still shared July 4 as their combined Independence Day. Many classmates remember celebrating the festivities at the U.S. Embassy.

Ellen Bancroft: [*Another Classmate*]: It was a tradition to go to the U.S. Embassy for the annual 4th of July celebration. There always was a man walking around on stilts, dressed up as Uncle Sam. When Vice-president Nixon visited the Philippines in the mid 1950s, there was a reception for him and his wife at the U.S. Embassy and many of us got to shake their hands.

Terry: Hearing the *Star Spangled Banner* played by the Marine Band was very emotional, especially so far from home. Those were probably the most moving celebrations of the Fourth I can ever remember.

As we learned in Chapter Three, the Filipino fiestas are often linked to the Catholic religion, as each barrio had a patron saint.

Terry: Since my father was an executive with the International Harvester Company, we were invited to festivals by his Filipino employees. Often these involved a roast pig, the previously mentioned lechón. We boys had never seen a whole pig being roasted over glowing embers. We enjoyed the local music and dancing. From Terry's mother in her own words: "Yesterday was the feast of Christ the King. The procession was beautiful and Mass was said in Luneta Park, directly in front of our hotel. The people celebrate All Saints and All Souls in a tremendous way. They spend all day and night in the cemetery. The market places are jammed with flowers and huge candles. These are lighted on the graves and left burning all night. Refreshment stands are set up at the cemeteries and many picnics are held."

Warren: My father worked downtown and spent some time on Bataan where the refinery was being built. The Mayor of Bataan always made sure our family was invited to area festivals. It was a time of fun, games and eating all kinds of local foods; sometimes we actually knew what we were eating. Mother always reminded us not to eat too much, as these people didn't have much at home.

Of all the countries in the world that celebrate Christmas, the celebration in the Philippines is by far the longest. Preparations begin in September and the celebrating ends on *Three Kings* in January. Filipino families tend to be large, but very close. Therefore they enjoy traveling to distant provinces to celebrate with far-away aunts, uncles and cousins. The caroling begins early, as do the paroles (lighted star lanterns) in the windows and the many, many parties.

Terry: Our family set up a Christmas tree, an artificial tree we brought from Iowa, with all our traditional ornaments that had been shipped with our furniture. Santa found us on the other side of the world and we went to Christmas Mass at Santo Domingo Church. We got presents sent to us from our relatives in the U.S. which was quite a treat. Then we would open presents and have an Iowa Christmas breakfast. We all thought it was really something to be able to go swimming at Christmas.

In an attempt to experience a little change in the season, one year our family went to Baguio at Christmas. I remember that on Christmas Day we were in our little cottage with a fire in the fireplace (a real treat for the Philippines) and we heard Christmas carols. We looked outside and a whole group of children were singing Christmas carols outside our door. It was nice, accents and all, and much appreciated.

From Terry's mother: "1956, it's Christmas time again. Everyone is busy making preparations. Out here, homes and gardens have been decorated for weeks (colored lights and lanterns). The boys and I have been working at it. We've hung all the decorations we brought out with us plus a few more, in addition to which we sprayed most of the windows with artificial snow. From the inside it looks lovely and much like about a White Christmas but Carl, Terry's father, is amused by the fact that inches from the windows and doors, the flowers are blooming beautifully, with the palm trees in the background. But on these cooler evenings, with the dimly colored lights, the magic snow is more effective. Baked about 8 pounds of fruitcake and it turned out quite well. School closed on Friday with a lovely Christmas program, class parties and gift exchange."

Bob: I remember New Years Eve in 1956. My younger brothers and I perched ourselves on the roof of our house in Quezon City and watched and listened to fireworks that would not quit. Fireworks were big in the Philippines and I certainly bought my share of 'triangles' [triangles were small firecrackers made of folded brown paper with explosives inside and a fuse coming out one end] and 'bawongs' [a larger firecracker] over the years.

New Lifestyles in the Philippines

Terry: One big change for us Americans was that we all had servants. Some American wives claimed that they always did their own housework in the States and didn't need a maid, but soon enough the humidity made them realize that it was, indeed, far better to hire someone who was accustomed to the intense tropical heat.

In Iowa, my folks had never had any kind of help at home. All of a sudden, we had a houseboy, a lavandera (washerwoman), a cook, a gardener and a driver—wow! I remember the driver using a feather duster to keep the car clean. I remember strange smells from the servants' cooking. I remember not having to make my bed. I remember being formally served our meals.

One transportation mode that was different were the ubiquitous jeepneys. These began as jeeps that the U.S. Army left in the Philippines after World War II, but were eventually made in factories. They were repurposed to have a bench seat in the front that would hold about three people, including the driver, and two upholstered benches in the back facing one another that would hold about eight. They were brightly decorated with all sorts of pictures, poems and religious medals, especially St. Christopher to ensure a safe trip.

From Terry's mother soon after their family arrived in the Philippines: "This is a strange country, very modern in some respects and very backward in others. Some places in the city are very beautiful and others are the extreme opposite. There are hundreds of small stores and shops, but no large department stores. And one never pays the asking price — everything is bargained for. We have hired a driver for the car. During the rush hours, cars are bumper-to-bumper and fender-to-fender together with buses, jeepneys, horse drawn carts, push carts, etc. There seem to be no traffic regulations and few stop and go lights. It is much safer to have a driver. The children have to be driven to school and picked up. There are almost no sidewalks. We have a "boy," Galiardo, who seems very nice and we can understand him somewhat better than most. He has had two years of college and speaks better English than anyone with whom we have come in contact. The boys think he is wonderful and he tells them all kinds of stories about the war years, which must have been terrible years for these people. In turn, the boys tell him about the United States and he dreams of being able to get there some day. He also acts as our "amah" (sitter) and has stayed with the boys a few times."

Bob: Talk about the life of Riley! We were able to shop in western style supermarkets. One was the Acme in Forbes Park; it was Chinese owned.

Nancy: My life style reflected that of my parents and the mission they were sent to accomplish. Being missionaries, my parents could only afford one house-girl. They didn't have a driver, so my father drove us kids to most places. A classmate lived close by and our fathers took turns driving us to school and sometimes picking us up. But we usually found our own way home with the buses and jeepneys. One time Mary and I were in a jeepney, and the driver had a sign posted on the ceiling above his seat that said, "I love you before, but now no more!" We laughed about that for years.

Bob: Speaking of buses and jeepneys, the traditional mode of public transportation used to be the *calesa*, a horse-drawn carriage. They were still around in the fifties, although they were rapidly being replaced by motorized vehicles. Because there was a certain old fashioned charm to them, my dad once took a photo of a *calesa*. He entered it in a big Kodak photography competition in New York and, much to his surprise, won first place in one of the categories. A Filipino artist friend, C.V. Lopez, later turned that photo into a painting. The original photograph has gone missing, but the family still owns the painting.

Calesa
Photograph of a Painting of a Photograph
Courtesy of the Liese Family

Nancy: My life was a bit different from that of my classmates because, even though I was a typical junior/senior high kid, I had to follow several strict rules for behavior. I was not allowed to go to movies, dance, or play cards (other than Old Maid), but I did play a lot of games—Monopoly, Flinch, Boy Scouts, Authors, Clue, Parcheesi, and Chinese Checkers. We never had television, so the games, reading, playing the piano, and homework were our major diversions in the evenings.

I was a big reader. My favorite books were *Nancy Drew* and other mysteries—*Judy Bolton, Cherry Ames,* and *Vicky Barr,* also *Anne of Green Gables*. We had a list of required reading for most of our English classes, and we were introduced to many books that we probably would not have chosen without this push.

I was not allowed to listen to popular music, but I did so when I was at the homes of my classmates. This was the era of Elvis Presley and Pat Boone, and I kept up with all the current hits. At home I listened to classical and sacred music. We had a record player for 78 rpm that we cranked to start. When the music slowed down, we had to wind it up again. I took piano lessons from the time I was six until I was in high school.

I started clarinet in the band in my elementary school in Michigan, but the American School did not have a band. Singing was always my first love as far as musical participation is concerned and still is.

Warren: There are two places I lived where you could say I was considered to have "White Privilege." One was India and the other the Philippines. India was full of unbelievable poverty and starving, especially children. The Philippines had a poverty problem, but nowhere as severe as India's. As I got older, I enjoyed Philippine life.

In high school, we smoked fantastic hand rolled cigars as good as any Cuban. We drank San Miguel Beer although in most places it was warm; it didn't give you a headache the next morning because it had no preservatives. No hangovers. The rum was first class. In spite of the fact that there was no issue about underage drinking of liquor, it wasn't abused by us. It was done responsibly. Never while driving.

Generally we guys were more into exploring. Most of us made trips to Corregidor, an interesting place of war memorabilia. It was also dangerous, as the island was still not cleared of unexplored weapons. Once I found a cache of 81mm mortar shells. These shells were still in original packing cases and looked brand new. Some of us also found shells that were rusted, but no explosives or warheads. I also found a rusted Marine KaBar knife alone with other pieces of war-related junk. I took the knife to a knife shop in Old Manila. The shopkeeper removed the rust and polished it, then blackened it and ground down the leather handle and resealed the remaining leather. It was like new again. Beautiful! A knife maker in Portland, Oregon made a leather sheath, and it looked brand new. The knife was stolen from me in Viet Nam.

Terry: Other than after school activities, each of us enjoyed leisure time in our own way. Several of us were big stamp collectors. Bob and I met a Filipino boy who had found a chest in his house with a large number of Philippine stamps from during the World War II Japanese occupation. His collection contained many unusual stamps and first day covers with wonderful things stamped on them like "Passed By Censor Japanese Military Police." He was interested in U.S. stamps, so we spent a great deal of time trading.

Rare stamps in which references to the U.S. were blocked by Japanese censors
Kleeman Family Archives

Bob: The Japanese occupation first day of issue cover had the sought-after one peso over four peso overprint and is hand stamped. The stamp itself issued previously under U.S. control pictures Montalban Gorge. Unfortunately, the stamp club was rather short lived ('56-'57) because the American facility where we met at the Port closed down.

In an era with no social media and fancy electronics, we still managed to stay pretty up to date. I kept up closely with the "Fast 40"—that is, all the U.S. music. I listened to the latest hits, whether it be Sangley (KTLG) or the many tapes exchanged from the U.S. After Terry returned to the U.S. he was an excellent source from Milwaukee's WOKY; Dick Bourdon from Louisville's WKLO, Mike Harrington's KIDO from Boise and Harry Morton from SF's KYA. I have to admit, I had it covered.

The Gaiety Theater was the place for American movies. And for only a peso (25 cents). As we got older, some went next door from the Gaiety to Guernica's night club which featured an excellent Spanish combo. Another popular hangout was Casa Marcos at the end of Dewey Blvd. Araneta Coliseum was the place for concerts that featured the latest U.S. singers such as the Everly Brothers, Rick Nelson, Little Richard and Neil Sedaka, to name a few.

As teenagers, we all wanted to wear the latest styles from the United States. Boys would get clothes sent to them from the U.S. and girls had their clothes made, but with current American fashion magazines for inspiration.

Terry: I actually had a pair of blue suede shoes. I also remember my white bucks and how I tried to keep them clean. We even carried around a little bag of white powder to touch them up on the run. Then button down shirt collars came into style, the Ivy League look. Then there were the pants with the buckle in the back, also part of the Ivy League look.

Terry Wearing Barong Tagalog Formal Wear
Kleeman Family Archives

Because it was too hot for a coat and tie, formal wear for men, young and old, was often the barong tagalog. The finest were made of piña, a sheer fabric fashioned from pineapple fibers. They were beautifully embroidered and worn outside the trousers. Men wore a cotton T-shirt under them, which made them cool and comfortable.

Bob: I never did have blue suede shoes, but over time wore white, tan and gray bucks. My favorite pants were white Levi's which eventually became available in several colors. At that time the haircut for boys was the flat top and for some, myself included, the ducktail.

Nancy: We girls were very fashion-conscious. We had to wear dresses or skirts and blouses every day to school. The crinoline petticoats were a status symbol. The more you wore, the "cooler" you were. And we all wanted 22 inch waists and shoes in every color.

The Polo Club and the Army Navy Club played a major role for us American School kids in Manila. The nearby US Embassy would let us teenagers fish from a sort of concrete dock in the rear. Terry and Bob's adventure one day sparked Terry's Bamboo Telegraph article "I'll never forget the day that Bob fell into the bay."

A.S. kids at Polo Club Entrance
From Lou Gopal's Manila Nostalgia
Photo by Gunter Prittwitz

Many week-ends were spent at the Polo Club which was was in Forbes Park and close to many of our homes. It was a center for family recreation and offered many activities, including swimming, tennis, badminton, bowling and outdoor movies. And of course watching the polo matches was great fun.

Terry: I remember swimming at the Polo Club all the time. My brothers and I had a large tractor inner tube we got from our dad. We once knocked over the large bulletin notice board which stood on the floor with glass cover. It made a big bang and people came running. We were scared to death, but when they put it back, thank goodness, the glass had not broken.

Around the pool were shelters with thatched roofs. Also, there was a wading pool for young children and a playground behind the main pool, where they had Easter egg hunts. You could order food and drinks and just sign the chit. What a life! Bowling was duckpins with human pin setters. Then there was the Teen Room.

Bob: Yes! I remember Honorio who we nicknamed "#26," his waiter number. His service area covered the Teen Room. Of course there were stables in the back for the polo horses. There were also riding horses that all the members were allowed to ride. My girlfriend at the time talked me into it—never again! It was a great place to meet friends and just enjoy.

Terry: Although most of us were not from military families, we sometimes went onto bases as guests of friends who had the required ID. The large military bases like Subic Navy Base and Clark Field had their own schools.

Sangley Point Launch Departing from U.S. Embassy Dock
From Lou Gopal's Manila Nostalgia

Sangley Naval Air Station was on the end of the point on Manila Bay across the bay from Bataan. Quite a few classmates on the "Point" attended the American School. I remember those trips to Sangley! We would catch the Navy launch at the American Embassy. It was a great boat ride across Manila Bay. Sangley was like a small piece of America. I remember the air strip. Also there was a hobby shop there that we used to love to visit.

Vacations

Terry: The Baguio region in the Philippines was a vast mountain temperate zone and a popular vacation destination for us classmates.

Families could stay at different locations including the Baguio Country Club, which had a lodge and cottages. The club had tennis courts, but what impressed me the most was the golf course with sand greens. After putting, the caddie would drag the "green" with a flat piece of canvas on a long pole to smooth the sand for the next group. I had never seen sand greens before nor have I since. I can still remember the street that ran between the cottages on a hill on one side and the club house on the other side. There were lots of flowers and trees, really a lovely setting.

Nancy: Some families stayed at mission houses and others at company houses. Our mission owned a house on the top of a hill outside Baguio. It had a fireplace, a first for me, and a lovely terrace in the back. It had several garden areas which were kept up by the live-in caretakers, and I remember the snapdragons especially. I believe that these gardens influenced my love for gardening today.

Terry: The Camp John Hay golf course had traditional grass greens and formal gardens near its entrance. There was some affiliation with Camp John Hay that allowed non-military to play golf and go into the 19th Tee, an American-style restaurant at the golf course that had real American-type hamburgers, fries and milk shakes. Roads ran right through the course. There were two roads between the #1 tee and the green, one at the bottom of the hill and another on the way back up near to the green. We used to try to hit the street with our drive and get a great bounce. Hole #5 was called "Cardiac Hill." They put in an automatic rope lift (pulley) system after a few casualties! Downtown Baguio had an open air market with many folks in their native clothes including loincloths for the men.

Mountain Province Native Wearing Loincloth
Kleeman Family Archives

We boys bought knives that had a large blade covered by the handle split in two parts so you could swing it around in your hand and open it like a switch blade. Those knives were called "balisongs" and we all had to have one or two. And then there were the daggers that looked like ballpoint pens that you could carry in your pocket. Don't know why we were so fascinated with these knives, just teenage boys I guess.

Nancy: There were numerous craft shops in the market where we could buy wood carvings and purses and scarves made from a pineapple fiber called jusi (hoo-see). You could also buy silver and shell jewelry and other beautiful handmade items.

Terry: In Burnham Park, in downtown Baguio, there was a block surrounded with closed off paved streets where Bob and I rented motor scooters, Vespas and Lambrettas, and rode around the loop for hours. At some point, after we were very experienced, we were able to rent the scooters and drive on the city streets. No worry about a drivers license, although if you wanted to buy a drivers license with an older date of birth, no problem. Also, there were fellows who brought horses to ride at different locations around town. These were small local horses. Some of them were a little ill-tempered, but we all used to enjoy riding together.

Terry and Bob on motor scooters in Baguio's Burnham Park
Kleeman Family Archives

Flying time between Mania and the Island of Hong Kong, off the coast of mainland China was only about ninety minutes and some of us made occasional visits. Also in traveling to and from the Philippines Hong Kong was a regular stop. We traveled to Hong Kong several times. I made one trip with classmate Raymond Kim and his mother. Raymond was the son of the Korean ambassador to the Philippines. For us boys the big attraction was to go shopping for stamps for our collections. We also rode the Star Ferry and went to Repulse Bay on mainland China. We could see Communist China from there.

Warren: Hong Kong was a fantastic place, my favorite city in all Asia. I loved to go broke buying inexpensive items, especially cameras, electronics, telescopes, wrist watches and binoculars, you name it. High quality but great prices.

Most of us whose fathers worked for American companies in the Philippines were allowed home leave to visit family in the U.S. every few years.

Terry: In 1958, the Kleeman family was allowed a trip back to Iowa to visit family. By that time I had completed my freshman year in high school. Since we were about halfway on the other side of the globe, we elected to travel west from the Philippines and go around the world. We travelled entirely by propeller plane and we spent a lot of time on airplanes. We made numerous stops including in Hong Kong, Bangkok, Japan, India, Egypt, Italy, Greece, Monaco, Switzerland, Spain, Holland, France and England. We had never travelled outside the USA except for our trip to Manila, so everything was new to us. My father had to exchange currency in each country. Whenever we left a country, he gave me the leftover coins. Visiting family was very important as we had not seen our relatives for three years. When our leave was over, we flew to Hawaii, and back to the Philippines for two more years at the American School.

Bob: I could hardly wait for April 3, 1959 to roll around and board the SS President Cleveland and sail back to the USA. I vowed I would kiss the ground on arrival in San Francisco and I believe I did. One day away from Honolulu the ship picked up radio station KPOI and fed it into the cabins. Needless to say I was glued listening to the latest U.S. hits. Once in San Francisco we stayed at the St. Francis Hotel for a couple days, then on to St. Louis for a good week visiting dad's family. Our final destination was Akron, where we stayed with my grandmother in a big two-story house with two furnished rooms in the attic. I might add that my future wife just happened to live next door. Following the war in the late 40's we had lived at my grandmother's next door to Mary Ellen and we played as three and four year olds. Now as teenagers, she being the home town girl and I the world traveler, there began a connection that lasted. After a couple previous marriages for both of us, we connected again and have now been married for 39 years.

After a three month stay in the States we boarded the Cleveland again for our three-week sail back to the Philippines and my final two years at the American School.

These new classmates were now introduced to a new culture with new food and new customs and they gradually settled into life in Manila.

CHAPTER 8

᭰

Junior High: Grades Seven & Eight

Seventh Grade

One of Two Sections of the Seventh Grade Class
Terry Front Row Far Right, Mary 2nd Row Second from Right
Kleeman Family Archives

Mary: A total solar eclipse occurs when the Moon's apparent diameter is larger than the Sun's, blocking all direct sunlight, turning day into darkness. This historic event marked the first day of class when our group began Junior High on June 20, 1955. With a maximum duration of seven minutes, 7.74 seconds, it was the longest solar eclipse since the 11th century and until the 22nd century. It occurred near the Equator with Manila directly in its path.

Now that we were in junior high, we were eligible to attend the "convocations" that Headmaster Warfel frequently called together in the gymnasium. Sometimes they were nothing more than a pep rally for a game that was coming up, but usually they were to talk about something important, and what could be more important than a once in a lifetime eclipse? He explained what it was all about and dismissed us early. (He had sent letters home, so parents knew when to pick us up.) There was so much excitement in the air! Of all my years at the A.S., it's the only day where I can remember exactly what I wore: the popular circle skirt with three starched petticoats that made a crinkly sound when I sat down and a pastel halter top. It was a very hot day!

My physicist father would be home to explain everything in great detail and I knew that he had prepared smoky glass for all of us to look through. What was most memorable was that, despite being around noon, everything turned very dark and our chickens all went to sleep. Truly one of the most memorable days of my life!

I very much enjoyed U.S. Geography with Mrs. Peoples. One day she had an excellent lesson plan, given the fact that the members of her class had come to the Philippines from all over America, or so she thought. She had a large map of the U.S. in front of the room. She went up and down the rows, asking each person to get up, go to the map, point to their state and talk about it. Its natural resources, its mountains, lakes, rivers, national parks, weather patterns, in short, everything they knew and loved about their state. The rest of the class took notes and asked questions. I will never forget the sense of dread and panic in the pit of my stomach. I could not fake it, nor could I admit in front of everybody that I did not have a state. It would blow my cover. So I figured out approximately how much time people spent up front, and when it got to the third person ahead of me, I raised my hand and asked to go to the bathroom. I went down the hall and returned very slowly, peeking from behind the door to make sure that they had gone beyond my empty seat, hoping that they would just keep on going. Whew! They did. Disaster averted.

Sometimes when people hear such stories about my wanting to be seen as just another American kid, they don't get it. What was the big deal, they wonder. The big deal was that questions inevitably led to more questions. People were never satisfied with "I was born here". They always followed up with, "Oh? How come?" and in those days the Holocaust was a taboo subject. In fact, I don't think anybody even used the word. I certainly had never heard it back then. So the words I would have had to use were words like "refugee" and "Hitler" and I did not want to go there. Nor did I want to lie. That was my dilemma. And in those days I fit in at the American School; everyone just accepted me and I felt "Americanized."

One day when I was in high school I found my birth certificate and had a good laugh. It listed the address of the Manila hospital where I was born; it was on Vermont Street! I could now claim Vermont as my birthplace and it wouldn't be a lie. No, I never actually did that, fearing that the person I was talking to could be from Vermont!

Another distinct 7th grade memory involved P.E. class. I loved floor exercises and rhythmics, but not team sports. One day our Girls P.E. teacher, Lina Nepomuceno, said that she had a special treat for us: we were not going to have class in the gym, but outside on the soccer field. When we got there, she explained what the treat was. We were going to play baseball! All the other girls jumped up and down and yelled "Yeah!!", while my stomach was gripped by fear. Baseball?!? I shyly walked up to the teacher and said, "Excuse me, how do you play baseball?" She replied, "Oh, it's easy. It's just like softball." Well, THAT was a big help! In the meantime the girls were begging Lina to make them catcher, pitcher, whatever position they wanted to play. I pulled one of my friends aside and asked, "What should I ask for? What's a position where you don't have to do anything, because I don't know the first thing about baseball." She said, "Outfielder. Tell her you want to be outfielder. You just stand way out there and do nothing." I got my wish and thought to myself, "Great! This worked out! I'm good at standing and doing nothing." I stood there daydreaming, paying no attention, when suddenly I heard everybody screaming, "MARY! MARY! The BALL! Get the BALL!" It came hurtling at me, but I couldn't catch it, nor would I have known what to do with it. So I guess I let my team down. A most humiliating, embarrassing experience. To this day I tell that story when people ask me why I don't like baseball.

Aurora's 13th Birthday Party with Aurora, Dabney (not in book), Mary, Gloria and Tonya
Abrera Family Archives

The rest of Seventh Grade went by in a whirl. We had our own classroom, but a different teacher came in for each subject. In high school the students moved around, as we did not all have the same schedule, but in junior high the teachers came to us. We became involved in after-school activities, attended and cheered and screamed at the basketball games, went to parties on the week-end (some sanctioned, some not), had crushes on members of the opposite sex and, in short, behaved like the precocious pre-teens that we were.

Eighth Grade

Mary: We had finally made it to the top — Eighth Grade. It was to be a very special year with much to look forward to: the Sadie Hawkins race, the eighth grade play, eighth grade Skip Day, Sports, lots of parties, Graduation and Prom. The class consisted of three of us who had been there since first grade (Mary, Tonya and Karel). Ellen was here in first grade, but left and did not return until eighth grade. Gloria and Aurora joined in second grade. The seventh grade added Ray Domingo and Raymond Kim. Other classmates came and left. Terry joined in seventh grade. Bob and Nancy joined later in the eighth grade. Our eighth grade class included thirty-eight students, with Terry as our president.

The eighth grade classrooms were at one end of a wing of the American School Main Building, and, again, the students did not change classes, but the teachers did. We had Latin, English, Science, Philippine History, Recess, a rotation of Art, Music and PE, depending on the day, and Math. Our entire building was the junior and senior high school, with offices and the junior high on the first floor and the senior high and the library on the second floor.

There was a ticket window in the front office, where we could purchase "chit books," which were little tickets one could tear off and use in the canteen instead of paying there with cash. It made it easier for the two men who operated the canteen, Silvestre and Emilio, whom we got to know well over the years. They sold hot dogs, sweet buns with icing on top, but the best were the cinnamon rolls. Of course, there were sugary soft drinks as well. Coca-Cola, 7-Up, Tru-Orange, Bireley's Orange and Bireley's Grape. They also had popsicles. All in all, it was not the world's most nutritious menu, so a lot of us brought our own sandwiches from home.

This was the sixth year the eighth grade boys participated in Tri - colors. It consisted of soccer, basketball and a foul shot contest, in which participants were given a set number of shots to see who made the most.

October 27, 1956 marked the date of the Kanteen Karnival, In this carnival the eighth grade had one booth which was one of the most popular and made the most money of any single booth. We contributed 75 pesos (about $40) to the canteen fundraiser.

Sadie Hawkins Day, named after the Li'l Abner comic strip by Al Capp, was ingrained in American folklore in 1937 and was popular for close to forty years. By the 70s times had changed. The idea of girls chasing and grabbing boys, whose torsos were covered with lard, making for a slippery mess, seemed suddenly outdated. The seventh and eighth grades Sadie Hawkins's day race was held on December 1, 1956 on the grounds of the American school. Both classes went home with happy memories of a wonderful day.

The day began at 12 noon and ended at 5 PM. It started with a picnic style lunch, after which the traditional Sadie Hawkins race was held. It was great fun! Girls got to wear jeans to school and a large oversized white shirt, borrowed from their father or older brother. The boys took off their shirts and rubbed their torsos with Purico, the name of the local lard. That way they were harder to catch. However, girls could pull at their belts, which sometimes led to embarrassing moments. That evening was the high school Sadie Hawkins Dance, when the girls had to invite the boys and where Li'l Abner and Daisy Mae were crowned. Students had the opportunity to vote the entire week from a slate of nominees. It was great fun at the time, especially since we were allowed to participate in a high school event!

It was an American School tradition that every eighth grade class put on a three-act play. Ours was *There's One in Every Family*, a hilarious story about a social climbing mother who wants to marry her daughter off to a rich man. Grandma cleverly and successfully derails the attempt and the young lady, of course, ends up marrying the man she loves instead. Everyone in the class was somehow involved. There were twelve speaking roles, but others worked on Publicity, Stage Crew, and Scenery or were ushers or prompters. There was a matinee and an evening performance in January of 1957. We had rehearsals every day after school for weeks with our director/English teacher, Mrs. Valerie Newsome. We now realize that the purpose was, not only to teach us a little about theater, but also to give us a project to do together and bring us closer. If so, it worked, because when we get together, more than sixty years later, we still talk and laugh about it. Mrs. Newsome, who had some theater background, was a demanding English teacher. She assigned many essays and made a big point of not allowing us to use the word "got". She said it was vulgar, and, no matter what the circumstance, there was always a better word to use. Some of us still think about that to this day when we write. When the play was over the gym was cleared and we had our dance from 10 pm until midnight. Everyone was in high spirits because of the success of the play.

Nancy: Mrs. Newsome, our eighth grade English teacher, was only there about one year. She lived two doors down from us in Mandaluyong and, about a year before she started teaching, she invited me over a couple of times to spend the day, while her husband was traveling. We had filet mignon for lunch, and I was totally impressed, as I don't think I had ever had a steak before. She also served me coffee, which my parents would not have liked, had they known.

Mary and I did some crazy things that year. We liked to call one of our classmates and pretend to be part of a radio show. We told him that he had won a big prize and what he had to do to claim it. After a while we felt guilty about it, and confessed to him what we had done. He said that his father had gotten very excited about the prize and was very proud of him. We never did that again.

Mary: One day Nancy and I decided to call Mrs. Wolfe, our math teacher, and play loud Elvis music into her ear when she answered the phone. It just so happened that Mrs. Wolfe lived in the apartment building across from the school and the following day we decided to go there and ride the elevator up and down. I guess elevators were such a novelty to us at the time. At one point it landed on her floor, opened up, and there she was. She assumed we had come to visit her, which was the furthest thing from our minds, but we made up a story about wondering what the homework was, when, in fact, we had already done it. Then she invited us in, offered us cokes and had us sit down and chat. We just wanted to get out of there, but had to be polite. THAT's when she said, "You girls are SO nice! Not like some other kids, who called me yesterday and played loud music into the phone." We were mortified and tried to keep from laughing, SO thankful that we could bring our coke glasses to our mouths to disguise our discomfort, hoping that GUILT wasn't written all over our faces. And we didn't dare look at one another or we would have just lost it! We agreed how terribly rude and disrespectful that behavior was, while our stomachs were churning. We eventually thanked her for the cokes and the homework assignment and escaped down the elevator, howling and shrieking the whole way, as only thirteen-year-old girls can do. That was the last time we rode that elevator!

After we were done playing tricks on people, we turned to something much more interesting. A popular show in the U.S. at that time (1956) was "The $64,000 Question". Somehow we found out that a local radio station was starting a take-off on the show, to be called the P640 (peso) Question. The show was looking for contestants, and Nancy and I both filled out applications. For some reason they chose me and not Nancy, with no explanation. On the assigned date, Nancy's and my family sat in the audience, and I was called to the stage. It started with two general questions, one for P40 and, if answered correctly, one for P80. If one missed, one received some sort of health tonic, which I did NOT want. The P40 question was Eisenhower's nickname and Nixon's middle name. Whew! Ike and Milhous. Easy! The P80 question was "Who wrote *O Captain, My Captain* and whose death did it commemorate?" Thanks to our excellent American School education, I somehow knew that it was Walt Whitman, commemorating the death of Abraham Lincoln. So, I had made it to the next tier for the following week. The show had a short list of subjects and I had to choose one. I wasn't an expert on any of them, but the good news was that I could bring someone along for help. I decided to choose Philippine History from the list and asked Mrs. Grant to be my back-up.

Mrs. Grant

The following week, with Mrs. Grant at the microphone next to me, the moderator asked the P160 question: "What were the names of Magellan's five ships?" I knew Columbus' three, but not Magellan's five, so I hoped that Mrs. Grant knew. She rattled off the first four, the Trinidad, the San Antonio, the Concepción and the Victoria. Then she stopped to think as the seconds ticked by loudly. Tick tick tick. I was holding my breath, as was everyone in the audience. With one second to go, she called out "The Santiago!" The moderator and the audience went wild as Mrs. Grant and I hugged. P160! Even though that technically was $80, it was more like $160 in purchasing power. For me, a fortune! I had to return the following week and state whether I wanted to go for the P320 or take the money and run. Had it not been such a close call, I might have been tempted, but I was not going to push my luck. A definite P160 or a bottle of health tonic if we missed the next question. I still had to return with Mrs. Grant the following week, where I thanked them profusely for having given me this opportunity and grabbed the envelope. It was an amazing experience and I still can't believe I actually did that. Maybe that's why I enjoy "Jeopardy" so much. I was only sorry that my friend Nancy didn't get a chance to participate as well.

Bob: Besides the organized activities, there were many parties in students' homes, usually to celebrate a birthday. I remembers those 8th grade parties, all that great new music with the advent of Rock 'n Roll and all of that "dancing" which I tried to ignore. I remember trying to shuffle across the floor doing some step that eventually resembled the Mash.

A lady lived near the school and gave ballroom dance lessons once a week after school. Many of us attended and learned the rudiments of leading and following, plus the waltz, the swing and, our favorite, the boogie. We especially enjoyed dancing to Bill Haley and the Comets' *Rock Around the Clock* and *See You Later, Alligator*. It was the legendary fifties, an easy time of innocent crushes and "going steady." Just fun.

Terry: Junior High at the American School holds some of my best memories. Boys had their activities and girls theirs but we also got together on special projects like the eighth grade play, the Kanteen Karnival, Skip Day and more. This was an important time when we were beginning to do things with the girls and a wonderful time for me. It was all wholesome fun. Those two years were the highlight of my time at the American School. It was the perfect place to grow up.

Candelaria: Skip Day

Mary: An advantage to being an eighth grader is that we had a designated "Skip Day". It was a school day when everyone else envied us because we all piled into buses and went somewhere fun. The buses took us to the Paco train station at 6 am and from there we went to Candelaria. Nancy remembers it was a fun train ride, especially buying bread from vendors through the train window at one of the stops. But then one of the teachers warned us not to eat it because it could cause dysentery. The swimming pool and the giant inner tube were great. Ellen recalls, "I remember the trampoline as well as all the candy. I remember buying some green mango and bagoong (a pungent fish paste, made of fermented salted fish) to dip it in on the train." (Ugh, now)

Classmates on a Chaise by the Pool
Kleeman Family Archives

From Terry's mother who served as a chaperone for the trip: "Candelaria is a lovely spot, an oasis. The town itself is a scruffy little town like so many in the Philippines, but within a block of the railroad station is this lovely spot. It is a large tract of land owned by the Peter Paul candy factory. Part of the territory is covered by the factory and the remainder is beautifully arranged and landscaped for the four American families who live there in lovely modern houses. We were in two of the homes and they were furnished beautifully. The high spot was the recreational facilities. They had a nine-hole golf course, a swimming pool with a patio and barbecue pit at one end. There is a playground for the small children and a little red schoolhouse – all this within the compound. There are eight adults and twelve children living within the compound. We left Manila at 6 am and returned at 8 pm. It was a wonderful day and the kids had a grand time. They spent most of the time in the swimming pool. Then we made a tour of the candy plant. All they make are Coconettos and Choclettos. Needless to say, it was in the middle of a coconut plantation. Of course, the kids were sent home with all the free samples they could stuff into their pockets."

Graduation

Mary: Of course, the day we looked forward to the most was Graduation Day, followed that same evening by the Prom. In the Philippines girls didn't buy their graduation/prom dress in a department store. They looked through magazines to find the perfect design; then purchased the material, yards and yards of dreamy tulle; then took the design and the material to their dressmaker; had several fittings; and were ready for magic. No caps and gowns. We floated onto the stage in our gowns, a little wobbly on our high heels. Well, we did have a graduation in our finery. However, beloved President Magsaysay had just been killed in a plane crash. The entire nation was in mourning, so it would not have been right for us to party at that time. So, after graduation, on April Fool's Day 1957, instead of going to a prom, everyone went their separate ways.

I remember going out to dinner with my parents and some friends at the Bulakeña on Dewey Blvd., after which we saw *Oklahoma* at the Gaiety Theater.

A few months later, at the beginning of 9th grade, we finally had our "prom" at the Elks Club, right next to the Army Navy Club. It was okay, but it is impossible to put the spirit and the excitement on hold and expect to recapture it three months later. By then, some of our classmates had left, so it wasn't the same. What I recall was that girls sat on one side and boys on the other and teachers kept going around saying, "Why aren't you dancing?" Pretty much of a ho-hum evening. The very definition of "anticlimactic."

On a positive note I would like to return to the graduation ceremony itself. We were looking forward to receiving (not "getting"; thank you, Mrs. Newsome) our diplomas, but assumed that we would have to suffer through a boring speech in return. As it turned out, we were wrong. The speaker was the brilliant father of classmate Paul Hoshall, who used the popular Frank Sinatra song *Young at Heart* as his theme. Working with the lyrics, he described us as we were and as he hoped we would remain. The song begins:

Fairy tales can come true
It can happen to you
If you're young at heart . . .

CHAPTER 9

✑

Memories of High School
Finally! We made it to High School!

For us there was no new school to attend. We just kept going to our familiar Donada campus, the only difference being that our new classrooms were now upstairs in the same building where we had been for Junior High. There was a hallway going the length of the building with the library at one end and the chemistry/physics lab at the other. In the next four years our total class size would vary year by year between thirty-seven and fifty-four. That meant that actual classes were small and, while students arrived and left from year to year depending on their fathers' work assignments, we were a cohesive group; we all knew one another.

Our first day in High School was memorable. We now had to move from classroom to classroom for our different subjects. We were excited and a bit nervous to meet our new teachers.

The High School experience at the A.S. was a combination of serious academic study, the *Bamboo Telegraph* (school paper) the *Kawayan* (yearbook), Glee Club, Drama Club, Scholia (honor society), student government, student court, many clubs and committees and a variety of intramural and Varsity sports, of which basketball was king. We took cheerleading tryouts very seriously, and we had pep rallies on game days. All students knew the cheers and most attended the games at nearby Rizal Memorial Stadium. There were school-sponsored dances, such as the Sadie Hawkins Dance and the Christmas Formal, but there were often parties on the week-end, in homes or in clubs. Between classes and after school activities we enjoyed a never-ending whirlwind of learning and fun.

Academics

It was taken for granted that everyone would go to college in the U.S. We received an excellent college prep education, using the same books that were used in the States. We wrote many essays and learned how to write research papers. In twelfth grade we had to write a senior term paper, which was almost like a thesis, and defend it orally before a board, consisting of several teachers or administrators. When possible, it included someone from the community who was an expert on the subject of the paper. This was excellent preparation for college term papers because we had to learn how to use library research techniques. In those days the card catalog and the Dewey Decimal system were used to find reference materials and 3x5 note cards for our notes, which we arranged and rearranged to get the proper order for our paper.

Most of us were scared to death at the idea of having to defend our research paper before an intimidating group of educators who had read the paper and had prepared questions. But what a great preparation for our futures, an advantage of a small class and excellent teacher who took the time to go through this process! Having been a teacher myself, I realize what an effective tool this was for preventing plagiarism. One had to know what one was talking about or risk looking like a fool or worse.

The American School did not have any shop or home economics classes; it was a strictly academic college-prep school. We had the previously mentioned non-credit typing class in the summer, not part of our curriculum. We worked on the school newspaper and the yearbook as an after-school activity. The same was true of the Glee Club and the Drama Club. We did those activities for the pure enjoyment and camaraderie of singing and acting and being together. Little did we know that in the United States these are considered electives, for which students receive credit, even at highly academic schools. Would we have racked up the credits!

For each class we had two-hour final exams, which we took in the hot, cavernous gym. The desks were placed about 6 feet apart. Most of our tests were essay questions with occasional multiple choice and we often used blue books, those dreaded little books with a blue cover and intimidating empty pages that would stare at us until we collected our wits.

Every few years there would be a story about an "exam scandal" and, yes, in our junior year we had ours. Someone in our class, and we were all pretty sure who it was, cooked up a scheme. He or she (just to be gender neutral), had paid a janitor to take the mimeograph master of one of the exams out of the wastebasket. The student who masterminded the scheme then made copies, not sure how s/he reversed the print on the back of the mimeograph page, and sold or gave them to friends the day before the exam. None of the classmates in this book of course (Darn! Nobody ever offered to sell US advance tests!). That gave them time to look up answers and share them with one another. There was a lot of buzz outside the gym just before the exam was to be administered. We all took the test, but, needless to say, everyone had to take a new one a few days later. That way it was easy to spot who had been in on the scheme. Clever, these teachers. They weren't born yesterday. There was a number of students implicated in this scandal and a few suspensions.

Left to right: Noelle Ayres, Phyllis Roth, Gloria Chua, Mary Brings, Nancy Buerer, Priscilla Litwin, Joan Esther, and Holly Bernhart.

Members inducted in February were Geoff Brown, Jane Donnell, Christine Hamm, Jan Hamilton, and Gordon Lester.

Scholia, the Honor Society, From the Kawayan Archives

Our Honor Society was named Scholia. We began our Senior year with four of us who were carried over from having been inducted as Juniors, i.e. Mary, Nancy, Gloria and Priscilla. After the "exam scandal" we revised the Scholia constitution to raise the requirements and to make it possible to remove members for other than academic reasons. Membership was now based on integrity as well as scholarship.

The induction ceremony was a formal affair, held in the evening, so that parents could attend. Our favorite line in the induction script was, "The food of the scholar is bread, cheese and wine." And yes, every ceremony included all three, including a small glass of wine! Later that year four more girls were inducted, three juniors and one senior classmate, Noelle Ayres. That's right, no boys! At least not until the following February when two boys were inducted.

Teachers

Most of our teachers were from the U.S. although some came from other countries or were Philippine nationals. Some were American college-educated wives of men whose companies had assigned them to the Philippines. Most had U.S. teaching credentials and all were dedicated to their work.

The following are some of our most memorable teachers, whose names come up every time we get together.

Mr. Nestle: Our Math Teacher

The first thing that comes to mind is his pipe. Always in his mouth, always unlit. He made math fun, but sent "love notes" home when students did not do their homework. He stayed in his classroom, which he called "Siberia", after school to help students who had not done well on the weekly quizzes. However, he named his room in jest, as it was a very "warm", welcoming place and, for the most part, students came voluntarily. He wanted us to succeed and, as he could not tutor everyone personally, he arranged for the more advanced students to help those who were struggling. It was an honor to be chosen by him to be a student tutor.

Mrs. Doris Hourihan: Our Senior English Teacher

Each quarter Seniors were assigned four books to read, for a total of sixteen books a year. The selection included such books as *Crime and Punishment*, *The Prince*, *Madame Bovary*, *The Forsyte Saga*, *Brave New World*, *A Farewell to Arms* and *Anna Karenina*. Mrs. Hourihan had an ingenious plan. Rather than having each student write a traditional "book report", with all the plagiarism which that often involves, plus producing an inordinate pile of papers for her to grade, she did something very clever. Toward the end of each quarter, having (hopefully) read all four books, we came to class with nothing but paper and pen. Mrs. Hourihan walked up and down the rows, asking each student to reach into a bag and pull out a slip of paper. No second chances! On that slip of paper was a complex question relating to one of the four books. Unless you had read the book carefully and thoughtfully, it was impossible to deal with the question. If you were a gambler and read only one book and IF you happened to pick the question on THAT book, you were in luck. But every once in a while someone wailed, "Oh, no! That's the only one I didn't read!" Too bad.

Besides these sixteen books, we read, discussed and analyzed *MacBeth*. In addition to all of that we had a thick anthology of English literature. To test our comprehension of what we had just read, she would require a precis or a character sketch that always required some form of critical thinking. A precis, we learned, is a miniature of the original piece without being a summary. It requires very careful reading and analysis. She required weekly essays, having to do with what we read. The highest grade she gave was 95% and that was rare. After reading George Byron's *Apostrophe to the Ocean*, she not only explained iambic pentameter, but she also she made US write a poem in iambic pentameter. All of this on top of the dreaded senior term paper! That course was more demanding than many college English courses.

Mr. da Silva: Our Physics Teacher

He was of Portuguese descent.and received his masters degree at La Salle University in Manila where he taught several years before coming to the American School. At the American School he taught math, algebra and physics. Terry remembers: "Physics was my favorite high school class. Mr. da Silva made it so interesting, because in his class I began to really understand how things worked. I remember one eye opening lab experiment with a little toy cart on a hill, where we measured forces in several directions. It started me on the path of wanting to know how things work, awakening a curiosity that I still enjoy today.

Mrs Friman: Our Librarian and Typing teacher in the summer

Mrs. Hilda Friman was born in Shanghai but came to us from Hong Kong. She was very "proper" and had a heavy, clipped British accent that students liked to mimic. A voracious reader, she told us that she read five books a week — books of all kinds. She put up with no nonsense. She was well known for ousting students for talking in the library. Mary recollects: "One day I was in the library with Noelle and we were combing our hair. Mrs. Friman chastised us by saying loudly, 'This is NOT a ladies' boudoir!' " It worked; we never did that again.

Ellen remembers: "Mrs. Friman liked my sisters and me because we obviously liked books, but she was a source for all the gossip around the school. It always cracked me up, because she told us so much. We were out of the social circuit, so didn't ever talk about her stories to others. I liked her as a person—quite interesting herself."

Mrs. Friman taught us typewriting during the summers. We sat in the library with our hands hidden under wooden barriers that prevented us from looking at the keys. One day in summer school typing class, we had an assignment to type a restaurant menu. Being a naughty teenager, Terry typed a menu for Joe's Cathouse, complete with blondes and redheads. Bob made a similar menu and we all posted our menus on the board. Terry and Bob were kicked out of class for the rest of the summer. They just had a couple more typing classes to go, and Terry did not want his parents to find out what he had done. So each morning, his dad would drop him off at school on his way to work, Terry would hang around the school and then get picked up at the proper time. As far as he knew, his parents never found out, or at least they never mentioned it.

Mary remembers, "There is a story behind my Baguio trip with Judy Tye in the Summer of 1960, the summer before Senior Year, except that Judy would not be there. Her father had been reassigned back to the U.S.

My parents weren't wild about the idea of my going to Baguio alone with Judy, not because they didn't trust me, but because that was the summer I was scheduled to take Mrs. Friman's summer typing class in the library. The class schedule interfered with the availability of the Baguio cabin. So I made a deal with my parents. If I got myself a typing book and taught myself to touch-type accurately forty words per minute, would they let me go to Baguio with Judy on the train? They agreed. Of course they thought I wouldn't be able to do that, but of course they were wrong! So what could they say when I showed them how well I could type? Judy and I went to Baguio."

Señorita Martinez taught Spanish

Señorita, as everyone called her, was a legend. In fact, at the new, third generation of the school, now called International School, there is a plaque in her honor in one of the hallways. The current students and staff never knew her, but the legend lives on. Those of us who had known her and attended the Centennial reunion at the new International School in 2020 were moved to tears upon unexpectedly running across that plaque.

Priscilla Litwin remembers Señorita Martinez as being both firm and fair in her teaching: "She took us through the adventures of the little dog, *Fortuna*, as well as those of *Don Quixote*. I still can recite *La Vida es Sueño*. Señorita taught us grammar along with literature. Her sense of humor and love of teaching were always in evidence. One time when I came to her class after German class, I was asked to go to the board to write something in Spanish and without thinking wrote, 'Ich quiero un vaso de agua.' My classmates gasped, but, thank heavens, Señorita had a sense of humor, as she dramatically asked, 'ICH. ICH. ¿¿¿Qué es ICH???'. Later when I became a teacher for thirty-two years, I always remembered her example: to be firm, but fair and to keep a sense of humor".

Dorothy Batchelder & Ric Adonay taught Latin

Mary: Latin was one of my favorite subjects. Mrs. Batchelder was our 8th grade Latin teacher. Everybody took Latin because it was a requirement for 8th grade graduation. I had enjoyed the class and continued my Latin studies in high school. One day in my sophomore year I was sitting in a very large study hall, doing homework, when Mrs. Batchelder walked in. As she approached me, all I could think was, 'Uh-oh, what did I do? Am I in trouble?' She was a rather large lady with much jewelry dangling from her ears and around her neck, but she crouched down next to me and explained that a new boy had just entered the 8th grade class mid-year and had never had Latin before. He was worried that he would never catch up and would not be able to graduate. His parents called her and asked if, perchance, there might be an advanced student who could tutor him every day after school. They were willing to pay. ₱1.50 an hour, the minimum wage. To me it sounded like a fortune. ₱1.50 every day for months! Not only that, but it sounded like great fun, and I felt so honored that she had chosen ME! I met Johnny Fontaine the next day, a bright, motivated, thoroughly delightful boy. We worked until he was caught up with the class, which took almost the rest of the school year. Of course I attended the 8th grade graduation ceremony. My first student! As I went through the line to congratulate everyone, there was Johnny, beaming. He threw his arms around me and said what I remember so clearly, "I wouldn't be here if it weren't for you." That sealed it! I owe my 40 plus years as a language teacher to Mrs. Batchelder. I only wish she knew!

Out of all my high school classes, my Senior Latin class was by far the most fun. There were only about eight students in it, and it was taught by a Filipino ex-priest, Ric Adonay. He was young and he clearly enjoyed teaching us. We were smart, mature Juniors and Seniors who loved Latin. A teacher's dream class! He taught us Cicero's orations, and we even had an oratorical contest. Latin, of course, is known as a "dead" language because nobody speaks it anymore. But that didn't mean that WE couldn't. We asked Mr. Adonay if Fridays could be Latin conversation day and he thought it was a great idea. So every Friday, instead of doing translations, we conducted the class in Latin, speaking conversationally on a variety of topics. But our best idea was to organize a Roman festival! We put together an entire program and invited the underclassmen. It took place in the gym in the evening. We marched in two by two in our togas, led by two Junior boys, who played the trumpet. We wore long togas, while the younger students wore short ones and had to serve us. They brought us grape juice, representing wine, while we reclined languorously on cushions. Mr. Adonay had put together a full menu of appetizers, all with Latin names. The gym teacher, Lina, taught me a dance with a Grecian urn, which I performed on stage. We also put on a short skit, in Latin, from Ovid's *Metamorphosis*. It was *Pyramus and Thisbe*, the myth on which Romeo and Juliet was based. Was there ever again a fourth year Latin class like ours? Was there ever again a Roman festival? I wonder.

Bill Allison taught Government and Economics

Mary's other favorite teacher: "Mr. Allison was a tall, young, handsome biracial gentleman from Georgia. Just as I owe my language teaching career to Mrs. Batchelder, I owe my critical thinking skills and my political leanings to Mr. Allison's class. The first semester was Government, now called Civics, and it was my opportunity to learn how the American government and the Constitution worked. It was my fervent dream to come to the U.S., and I considered myself a 200% American. I had a utopian vision of America and wanted to learn everything about it. The class could have been dry, but in 1960 we had to throw ourselves into the Nixon vs. Kennedy election. To his credit, Mr. Allison never gave any indication of which candidate or which party he preferred. It was up to us. There was no Internet back then, but the library subscribed to Time, Newsweek and U.S. News and World Report. This course was my introduction to these periodicals, and I read them voraciously, studying and comparing the platforms of the two candidates. We had to write a paper on which candidate we preferred and give cogent arguments as to why. It didn't matter what Mr. Allison thought. It mattered what we thought and how well we could defend our opinion. I had to weigh all the information and decide which felt right to me. This decision has greatly influenced my life in so many ways. I chose JFK, of course."

Olga Ifland de Wit: Our Music Teacher

Mrs. de Wit was born in Melitopol', Zaporiz'ka province in southeastern Ukraine on 29 April 1909. Her parents were Rosa (Rachel) Moiseevna Tyshler (Jewish) & Joseph Kalmanovich Ifland (German heritage). She married Willem Jan Duyvene de Wit, a Dutchman she probably met in Manila, and her son Bill de Wit was born in the late 1930s. Olga and Willem divorced sometime before 1950.

Having attended the demanding Moscow Conservatory of Music, Mrs. de Wit easily found a job as music teacher. The fiery Russian redhead scared everyone at the American School to death, but she knew her music, she didn't take any nonsense from anyone, and she could teach! When her students performed, they sang in perfect harmony — nothing less would do. The scariest part of her class was test time, when each student had to approach her piano and sing a designated song to her accompaniment. Shy students tended to sing softly, but the softer they sang, the softer she played. You couldn't win! Clever, those teachers.

Memories from Sonya Rodolfo-Sioson, Mary's good friend, who studied under Mrs. de Wit for years and the two of them became close friends: "In June 1950, I was a Freshman majoring in chemistry at the University of the Philippines. I cross-registered to the U.P. Conservatory of Music for a piano course. To register I had to choose an instructor. I selected Olga Ifland (part time), knowing that Russian pianists are among the best on the planet. I deduced that Ms. Ifland's being 'part time' might indicate that her talents were also in demand elsewhere." (Mary adds, "The 'elsewhere', of course, was the American School.")

Sonya continues: "I reported for my first lesson. This fiery brown-eyed redhead was seated with thighs crossed, skirt hem three inches above her knees, a thermos of black coffee beside her. She instructed me to sight-read a simple piece. I was so nervous that I stumbled. She exclaimed: 'You are in 5th-year piano, but you have not learned to count. As you play, say, '1 AND 2 AND 3 AND 4'. As a green 17-yr-old, I was flustered, so I burst

into tears. She said: 'Come, come, I am not in the business of making little girls cry.'"
(Mary: "Which showed that she did have a soft side. More bark than bite.")

Sonya: "A year later, in April 1951, Olga Ifland's star pupil Alberto Mahinay Gutana, the first to complete the Soloist Course, was scheduled to rehearse his graduation recital program under her supervision. I accepted her invitation to sit in. Things went well until the final movement of Chopin's second piano concerto. It contains a cascading group of notes played *allegro vivace*. One note did not sound. In a fury, Olga shouted as she threw the score at him. He shouted back, as he repeatedly hit the offending key: 'This key does not work!' and threw the score back at her. I cowered, saying to myself: *When elephants dance, mice must take cover.*

As I continued to take lessons from her, we became friends. On several occasions, she had me over to her Pasay house for a lesson. On such days, Ricky, the first Doberman pinscher I ever saw, would bound over to me, stand up on hind legs, and put his fore paws on my shoulders, scaring me half out of my wits. Olga often said that a dog is more trustworthy than most humans. Sometimes she spoke about her time in prison camp. I recall her saying bitterly, 'The Japanese made us carry rocks from one stupid place to another stupid place.'

She mellowed in her old age, switching from a Doberman pinscher to a chocolate poodle named Laalee. She said, 'My most contented hours are with an exciting book and Laalee at my side at the end of the day.'

Sonya: After I married and had children, our friendship continued. Auntie Olga invited us to the marvelous old house she rented on Del Pan street in Pasay, near Roxas Blvd. She instructed my children to call her Oma, saying that is Dutch for grandmother.

She passed away in Manila on 28 June, 1985 at age 76 from an unknown cause".

Sonya and Mary agree that she was one of the most unforgettable characters they have ever met.

In addition to our regular music classes with the notorious Olga deWit, Dr. Zipper, the famous conductor who was introduced in Chapter One, made yearly trips from Chicago to the American School and other Manila schools as well. It was a homecoming for him as he had conducted the Manila Symphony for many years. What a special privilege for us! He brought members of the symphony to play for us kids, patiently explaining the music and the different sounds of the instruments. He was always friendly and funny—and interesting. How many schools have a famous conductor come 3000 miles to expose a small school to classical music?

A documentary, which received an Academy Award nomination in 2006, was made about his bringing music to the inner city schools in the U.S. It was entitled *Never Give Up, The Twentieth Century Odyssey of Herbert Zipper.* One of his greatest achievements in his effort to bring classical music to the Filipino people was to commission a Tagalog translation of *Carmen.* The setting was changed from Sevilla to Manila, which also had a tobacco factory. He made the tickets very affordable, so that the people who did not normally attend concerts would come and be exposed to this gorgeous opera, perhaps leading to a further interest in music.

Freshman Year

Back to us classmates. The first order of business for the Freshman Class was the election of class officers. As we couldn't remember the outcome after all these years, we looked it up in the yearbook. Imagine our surprise when we discovered that our two author/editors who put this book together were President and Vice President-Treasurer, Terry and Mary! We then remembered that at the class meeting where the votes were to be counted by a show of hands, the volunteers who counted the raised hands came up with different results every time they tried for accuracy. This proved to be both exasperating and hilarious, but the result was not in doubt.

In 1955 a new, much larger canteen was built, as was a new gymnasium that also served as an auditorium. The old canteen had been at the entrance of Heilbronn Hall and was nothing but a small room with a window. We had to line up along the elementary school hallway, place our order and pay with chits from our chit book. It became slow and cumbersome, so we were thrilled to have a new canteen that had tables and benches where we could eat lunch. It even had restrooms! The old canteen was turned into the nurse's room. A perfect use for such a small space. But what does this canteen have to do with our high school experience?

At the beginning of our Freshman year in 1957, suddenly there appeared a jukebox in our new canteen. It was red with flashing lights and had all the latest hits. We were overjoyed! To this day we don't know who was responsible for acquiring it; I guess we just never asked. Because of the new jukebox somebody decided that the canteen was now a good place to have a dance. Too small for the entire school, but perfect for the new Freshman Class, our class, as an introduction to high school and an opportunity to crown a Freshman Queen, who turned out to be lovely classmate Vicky Schultz.

The gym, Spruance Hall, was also built in 1955. It was named after Admiral Spruance, a United States Navy admiral during the Battle of the Philippine Sea during World War II. It was behind the canteen and backed onto Taft Avenue, a very busy street. It had a basketball court, and most of our gym classes were held there. The stage was on one side and chairs were set up on the basketball court when there was a play, musical event or assembly. We could fit the entire student body in the gym for assemblies. On one side of the stage were locker rooms where we could change and shower. On the other was the music room.

Sports

Kawayan Photo of Coach Rene Amabuyok

Neither Nancy nor Mary was very good at team sports; we preferred the floor exercises and the balance beams. I, Mary, always smile with recognition when I hear the line in Janis Ian's song *At Seventeen*, where she sings *And those whose names were never called when choosing sides for basketball*. However, we didn't want PE to keep us off the honor roll or off the Straight-A list. Naturally, we figured out a way around the dilemma. If you were a member of a team, any athletic team, you got a double perk. You did not have to go to PE class and got a Study Hall instead. What's more, as long as you were an active, participating team member, you got an automatic A in PE. Perfect. But what was a team sport where we could try out without total humiliation? The swimming team! Coach Rene Amabuyok said that if we could swim 50 meters in under a minute, we were on the team. It took some practice, but we did it! (You can see our swim team on the Title Page of this book, Nancy standing on the far left, Mary on the far right.)

The American School belonged to MAASS (Manila Athletic Association for Secondary Schools), competing with other Manila public schools in volleyball, basketball, tennis, softball, badminton, and swimming. But not having a swimming pool or track, the school sent its students to the Rizal Memorial Stadium.

Rizal Memorial Stadium
In the Public Domain

The following schools were members of MAASS: Adamson University, American School, Philippine Chinese High School, Polytechnic Colleges of the Philippines, Rizal Central College, and Union High School. But don't be misled! Philippine students continue from high school to college in the same school. Therefore, although some schools have the name of college or university, we only played against the high school students.

The local schools had the advantage of a large student body from which the teams could select their players. We did not, which meant that almost anybody who wanted to play on a team could do so. Our students were generally taller, however, which could be an advantage in basketball.

In our Freshman year the Boys Varsity swimming team, including our own Ray Domingo, won the title of National Secondary Champions. Both the Girls' and Boys' Volleyball Teams won first place in the MAASS League.

In our Sophomore year all teams played well and displayed excellent sportsmanship, but only the Class A Boys Swimming Team and the Girls' Varsity Volleyball Team emerged as champions in the MAASS League.

In our Junior year classmates Kaye Fisher, Priscilla Litwin and Leata Thomas played Girls' Softball and won the first place trophy. Even though the Varsity Basketball team did not win the League Championship, they fought hard and played well. In one tight game The *Manila Bulletin* reported that Rizal Central won by 61-60 over the American School Indians after the latter had tied the game 54-all on a foul toss by Terry Kleeman.

In our Senior year Art Zurhorst was top scorer on the Boys' Varsity Basketball team. Art was chosen as the most athletic boy of the year. He received a plaque for being the captain of the Varsity Softball team and a member of the Varsity Basketball, Soccer and Track and Field teams. Our outstanding cheerleaders, including Classmates Linda Pratico, Noonie Neely and Leata Thomas, succeeded in giving a fighting spirit, not only to the team, but to the huge cheering section in the stands.

A.S. Girls Perform Moro Dances
Litwin Family Archives

In 1960 for the first time our girls performed a Moro dance from Mindanao for the MAASS Folk Dance competition and happily won second place. Classmates Priscilla Litwin and Noonie Neely were among them.

What was wonderful about our school was that, despite its small size, there were so many opportunities to be active in some type of physical activity. We were all given the chance to participate, and most of us could find something that we truly enjoyed. Headmaster Warfel felt that physical activity was part of a well-rounded education and began the tradition long ago of seeing to it that something active was available for almost everybody. His motto was: *Mens sana in corpore sano.*

Art Zurhorst will never forget the first basketball game he played at Rizal Coliseum. He had arrived in the Philippines only a few weeks earlier and he was so happy that Coach put him on the starting five. It was our first game and the Philippine Olympic team was playing after our game. The place was packed to the rafters with people who came to watch the Olympians play. Very early in the game Art grabbed a rebound and started dribbling up the middle of the court. Paul Hoshall had gotten a head start, and by the time Art was at half court, Paul was down court cutting toward the basket. Art grabbed the ball while on a dead run and started to pass it to Paul, so he could make an easy layup. Just before Art let go of the ball, he saw a player from the other team cutting between Paul and him, so he hung on to the ball. His forward momentum made him fall forward while tucking the ball to his stomach. He hit the floor and, like a flat rock thrown across a pond, he skipped on his side along the floor still clutching the ball. The whole crowd of about 18,000 burst out laughing. To this day, it remains his most embarrassing moment. However what Art cherished most were two things: What gracious people the Filipinos are! As a result of what must have been "group embarrassment", the entire crowd roared anytime he did something good the rest of the game. He said, "They responded to every basket I made like it was a last second shot that won a championship. The rest of my years most of the Filipinos lived up to that first impression of natural graciousness. The other thing that struck me was that immediately after it happened all of my teammates told me not to worry, it was ok. It was then that I knew how quickly I had been accepted into an exceptional group of people who had already been together for a long time."

We had pep rallies in the gym before basketball games, where the cheerleaders appeared on the stage. They performed their well-practiced cheers and taught them to the spirited student body. One of our classmates, Noonie Neely, was a cheerleader and she described the camaraderie among the squad. "Our senior cheerleading team was the best. I cannot recall any conflicts and I learned the value of teamwork on that squad."

Now that the student body was all pumped up with school spirit, we were ready to walk over to the game at Rizal Memorial and yell ourselves hoarse. Most of us still remember those cheers. One example was:

Two bits, four bits, six bits, a dollar.
All for the Indians stand up and holler.

At one point in the early fifties, the cheerleaders felt that, since we were in the Philippines, we should add a verse using the Philippine peso. From then on, the above cheer was followed by:

Two bits, four bits, six bits, a peso.
All for the Indians stand up and say so.

It was important that girls had their sports teams as well. Classmate Kaye Fisher gives us her recollections: "When I started reflecting on the girls' sports program at the American School, I remembered that we actually had competitions between other schools including Clark Air Force Base. What is notable about this is that particularly in the States and most other countries this was definitely not a trait that was encouraged in young girls at that time. High schools in the U.S. offered gym classes that consisted primarily of jumping jacks, throwing a ball around and ugly uniforms. There were no team sports, no competition. At the American School I played softball and volleyball. Not only was it social and fun, but the self confidence it gave me has been invaluable. It's important to realize that this was years before the feminist movement, and decades before Title 9. I shall be forever grateful that I had an opportunity to attend a school that was ahead of its time."

Our School Neighborhood
Safety Patrol on Donada Street

Safety Patrol on Donada Street
Courtesy of Warren Gerig

Because Donada Street was very narrow and many cars dropped off and picked up students, there were enough accidents that in 1959 the school set up a student-led Safety Patrol. Our classmate Warren Gerig was among the first patrolmen and he describes how it was: "Upperclassman Jackie Rodriguez was the Lieutenant, I was the Sergeant and we had six patrolmen. The accidents stopped!"

The school decided we needed to look more professional, so a young Captain from the Philippine Army came to school one day to drill the Safety Patrol and that person turned out to be the future President Ramos. Mrs. Ramos, his wife, was Warren's home room teacher at the time. She was also a counselor and continued working until 2020!

Sari-Sari Store

As the American School was a gated school with guards to keep would-be intruders out, the students couldn't normally leave during school hours. But there was a sari-sari store right on the corner of Donada and Menlo Streets, a stone's throw away from the gate. Needless to say, we figured out how to get our essential chewing gum and champuy, the dried salted plums in the little box. There is always a way!

DiMarks Pizza sign
Courtesy of Warren Gerig

DiMark's Pizza

Since the canteen did not serve lunch, just hot dogs and cinnamon buns, we needed a place where we could hang out together and get some good food, either before, after or instead of an afternoon activity. Di Mark's Pizza around the corner on Menlo St. was just the ticket! Less than a five minute walk, great atmosphere, great food, great camaraderie and, looking back at it, wonderful memories.

The Bamboo Telegraph and the Kawayan

Bamboo Telegraph Masthead
From Bamboo Telegraph Archives

Our prize-winning newspaper was the *Bamboo Telegraph*, which came out every two weeks. It was sold very inexpensively, but was financed primarily by advertising. Many parents purchased ads as their way of supporting the newspaper. Each year an editor-in-chief was selected, who then chose the other editors, such as Copy Editor, News Editor, Features Editor, Sports Editor and Lower Grades & Junior High Editor. A varying number of reporters was assigned to each page by the respective editors and each reporter was responsible for his or her "beat".

The crew got together biweekly afternoons-into-the-evening at the print shop downtown, laying out the paper, proofreading, getting the photographs made into the metal plates which were mounted on wood blocks and getting the articles to the linotypist. We had a lot of fun doing it. It seems amazing now that we could accomplish so much in one afternoon. Of course we couldn't leave until it was done, so we often got home quite late in the evening, but exhilarated by the experience of working as a team to put together a first-class school newspaper.

Classmate Priscilla Litwin recalled a funny story about waiting for a jeepney on Dewey Boulevard with a friend so that they could go downtown to the *Bamboo Telegraph* printers. Priscilla was a Junior at the time; her friend Candace Gibbs, a Senior.

Priscilla: Candace asked me if I wanted to play a game while we waited. "Sure," I said, whereupon she opened her purse and whipped out her balisong. With a few intricate flips of her wrist she had the knife opened and locked. I had seen switch blades in pictures, but never anything like this, especially with the elaborate presentation by Candace. The game, she explained, was to toss the balisong and have it stick in the ground within six inches of the outside of the opponent's foot. Placing one's foot where the knife hit, it was the other person's turn to toss the knife back within a foot of the first tosser. The game continued like this, back and forth until someone fell over. So there we were on Dewey Blvd., in our crinoline skirts, tossing a balisong back and forth, our legs getting wider and wider with each throw. (No wonder passing cars were honking!) Happily, our jeepney came before we were doing complete splits and falling down. Candace put her balisong back into her purse and we were on or way to our next activity. Just another special afternoon in Manila playing our unique version of Twister.

Balisong
In the Public Domain

Balisong knives have handles that rotate around the tang of the knife and conceal the blade when they're closed. (The tang extends from the blade to run into the handle of the knife.)

The Tagalog word for bamboo is *kawayan*; hence our yearbook was the Kawayan, another huge student-run project with some guidance from Activities Counselor, everybody's mom, Margaret Woodrich. It required photos of all the students, faculty and staff and spreads of every club, every committee, every activity, every sports team with detailed descriptions, plus every special event and pages of candid shots. Our school year began in June. By August the Kawayan staff was well underway. They worked tirelessly on all the little details, such as the captions under the pictures and making sure all the names were correct. We had to learn layout pretty much on our own by literally cutting and pasting, long before computers did it for us. Someone had to think of all the cute phrases and quotes that went under the senior pictures. Wilma Braat, our class artist, drew cartoons of each senior, depicting them doing what she thought they might be doing in the future; some of them tongue-in-cheek, others quite accurate. Again, the ads paid the bills. By the end of the school year the following April, they were bound and, for those students who wished it, they could have their names embossed in gold on the front cover. The many hours spent in putting it all together paid off. The book was quite a professional looking product for such a small school. Then came that bittersweet ritual, the signing of the yearbook, which ranged from "Lots of luck to a nice kid" to long series of "Remember when . . .."

Student Court and Forum

Student Court in Action Including Classmates Terry & Priscilla
From Kleeman Family Archives

We had not only a Student Council with the requisite elected officers, but also a Student Court, which tried violations of the Student Handbook. The attorneys and judges who served on the court took their jobs very seriously, and the "defendants" respected the fact that they were being judged by their peers. In our Senior year all the cases were minor, but the previous year when we were Juniors, a spectacular case made the Manila newspapers. Seniors took on most of the roles, but two classmates (Juniors at the time) served as Associate Judge (Priscilla Litwin) and Alternate Judge (Terry Kleeman).

Terry lays out the case: "The accused was charged with bringing a firearm, a pistol, to a school party. The police were called and they confiscated the weapon. Bill Dunkum was the prosecuting attorney. Bill presented a strong case, including witnesses and photographs of the weapon he had obtained from the local police. The judges found the accused guilty and recommended a brief suspension from school".

Priscilla paints the picture: "I remember the notorious student court case. Bill Dunkum was right out of an episode of Perry Mason. He had a bulletin board which he dramatically flipped around to display photos of the gun in question. "Is this the gun you brought to the party??" Yipes! Case closed. It really struck home how serious our roles were. The following year when I served as student council president I remember taking very seriously the appointment of judges, even though we never had a case like that again!"

Another group unique to the American School was The Forum, organized by Mr. Allison for the purpose of getting students interested in the world around them — its problems and achievements. It eventually became an interscholastic organization through panel discussions, debates and, just before the 1960 Presidential election, a mock debate between Juniors Eric "Jack Kennedy" Harrington and Bill "Dick Nixon" Hand. At their last of many programs during the 1960-61 school year, The Forum sponsored a mock session of the United Nations with students representing all of the U.N. members, similar to Model United Nations, now an activity at many U.S. high schools.

Fun and Games with Cars and a Guard-Monkey

In the U.S. teenagers can't wait to turn 16 and get a car. Very few of us had cars. We used the jeepneys and buses, or cars driven by one of our parents or our drivers. One has to be eighteen years old to get a driver's license in the Philippines.

However, Mary wanted to learn how to drive before leaving for the States, where she knew it would be a necessity. She still laughs about what happened: "One day, while I was at school shortly before graduation, my mother went down to the local equivalent of the DMV to pick up a Learner's Permit for me. When the clerk saw my birthdate, he did the calculation and said, 'Oh, I see that she is not yet eighteen.' My mother wasn't aware of the requirement and started to leave when the clerk called her back and said, 'No problem. We'll just change 1943 to 1942. Now she's old enough.' I saved that perfectly legal 'fake ID' for years, but never dared use it a year early in the U.S."

Bob's car story: "It's true most of our families had drivers. Goodrich hired them and allotted them to us and we paid them. We were also provided with an automobile which was either a Chevy or Ford. Our driver Carlos was so young, in his twenties. I learned to drive in Manila and took lessons on the Luneta Park from a recommended instructor. I was probably 15 at the time and liked the idea that it was a stick shift. In later years Skip Haven and I got a hold of a '38 Chrysler Royal that belonged to the Victor Lopez family and had been sitting in storage for years. We got it running and drove it a while till it conked out on Highway 54. I remember just leaving it on the side of the highway and each time we went by there would be a little bit more missing from it. It finally disappeared altogether. Years later Victor only said good-naturedly that he always wondered what happened to it, thereby letting us down easy."

Another car story from Art Zurhorst: "The Hamm family used to live on the same street I lived in San Lorenzo, Melantic St. I happened to look out my window one sweltering afternoon when I saw Bobby Hamm and a couple of other guys from school pushing his '41 Ford down the street towards his house. Apparently it had just conked out. So I ran out to help. Bobby was maybe my height and all of 110 lbs. Well, he decided that working smarter was better than working harder, so he jumped in the car while we were pushing, figuring someone had to drive the beast while all of us expended the energy. The thing was, we all started giggling and laughing so hard, we didn't have the wherewithal to push that dang car down the road. A stream of expletives escaped from Bobby's mouth as we pushed, making us laugh even harder. We had a great time and the memories are still vivid to this day."

Terry also remembers a group of us with Bobby Hamm as he was driving that old car through Forbes Park, Makati's oldest and most elegant gated community. The car had no muffler: We were chased by a security guard on a bike. When we went to leave the area, the guard had set up a barricade and was standing there with his gun drawn. We were all taken to the security office. Someone made a phone call, pulled some strings and we all went home. In retrospect we are not proud of this escapade.

Many of us lived in Makati's gated communities and interacted with one another as neighbors, almost as family, not just as schoolmates. Classmates spent time in one another's homes on a regular basis and enjoyed the idiosyncrasies that some homes, such as Priscilla's, displayed. Which just made for more fun!

Of course, Priscilla remembers it well: "Signs on other people's lawns might read *Beware of the Dog*, but the sign on the lawn in front of our house in San Lorenzo Village read *Beware of the Monkey*. The object of the warning was a large, full grown Macaque monkey named Dennis. My father brought him home one day from work where one of the men assured him that Dennis would be a better guard for our house and his car than any dog. My sister and I, being typical image-conscious teenagers, were mortified. In spite of our protestations, (how could we face our friends again), my father installed Dennis on a perch in the carport and set him to work. Dennis took his job as guard monkey very seriously and promptly bit anyone who came near. He lured people into the carport with a welcoming grin, then launched himself through the air on his 8 foot tether. He even bit Dr. Winters (Tonya and Carol's dad) when he thought Dennis wanted to be petted. Anyone feeding Dennis knew to slide his bowl to him from a distance, then retreat as quickly as possible. As Dennis' reputation grew, so did the number of boys from school who came to harass him. Dik Bartlett loved to dance in front of Dennis, making hooting and grunting noises, while pretending to scratch under his arms. Dennis would go ballistic with Dik's antics until my mother would finally come out and ask Dik to stop teasing 'poor Dennis'. 'Poor Dennis' was with us for years, and when it was time to leave Manila my parents donated him to a local zoo. They said, when they visited him, he was so forlorn and unhappy.

When I heard this, I actually felt sorry for Dennis. He had been a devoted guard monkey, a member of our family, always on duty. A menace to many, but in the end he was our menace and we loved him."

Rock and Roll

Rock and Roll was definitely a presence during our time in Manila. Elvis was king and all the girls were crazy about him. Some boys imitated his slicked back hairdo, and Lou Gopal did his Elvis impersonation with the canteen jukebox to a surprised Bob Howell, another Elvis impersonator!

New arrivals from the States were welcomed with the questions ,"Did you bring any records?" and "What are the new dances?" The 45 and 78 rpm records were eventually available in little stores downtown. They were "pirated" copies with unknown labels made in the Philippines or Hong Kong, but we didn't care.

Manila was on the overseas circuit for a lot of American rock stars, and we actually were able to spend time with some of them. Terry recalls when Little Richard did a show in Manila. "Several of us saw him outside after show at the Araneta Coliseum. He was smoking a cigarette. He could not believe everyone in the Philippines did not have a car." Terry still has his autograph. He also remembers that Neil Sedaka came to town and arranged for some of the girls to "rush" him at the show. "I'll never forget the thrill when some of us spent an afternoon with him at the Polo Club pool."

Terry's Copy of Little Richard's Autograph
Kleeman Family Archives

Harry Belafonte, Johnny Mathis and the Everly Brothers gave memorable Manila performances as well. Bob also remembers being at one of Dik Bartlett's parties and seeing Johnny Preston (*Running Bear*) and Paul Evans (*Seven Little Girls*) who were guests. We kept waiting for Elvis to come, but his manager, "Col." Tom Parker kept a tight rein on him and it never happened.

On February 3, 1959, rock and roll musicians Buddy Holly, Ritchie Valens and "The Big Bopper", J.P. Richardson were killed in a plane crash near Clear Lake, Iowa during their midwestern tour. We were Sophomores at the time and were devastated by the news, now often referred to as "The Day the Music Died" from the 1971 song *American Pie*. Terry still remembers exactly where he was when he heard the news.

Of course, we had our own homegrown talent as well. Ray Domingo used drumsticks on the guitar strings, playing *Little Darlin'*, Danny Marquez was a whiz on the piano, but the only song we can remember him playing was *Plantation Boogie*. But he played it well and extremely fast.

Every year we had a talent show called the February Frolics when in February or the Musical Cavalcade when not, where students and teachers went on stage to perform. Some acts were hilarious, such as Dik Bartlett's version of *The Dying Swan*, some involved lip synching, rather than actual singing, such as the group of guys organized by Bob Liese to do *I'm Not a Juvenile Delinquent*. There were serious numbers, beautifully done, such as Señorita's Spanish students in Valencian costumes singing *Valencia*. Teachers got involved, too! Miss Lind danced the Charleston with Dudley Babb and Mr. Adonay, Mr. Krane and Headmaster Mr. Sandoe pinned cheerleader uniforms to their shirts and made a spectacle of themselves attempting some of the routines.

However, we saved the best for last. Everyone was taken aback by the amazing performance of schoolmate Jerry Kaukonen on the guitar, playing and singing Jimmie Rodgers and Ricky Nelson songs. You may know him better by his real name, Jorma Kaukonen of *Jefferson Airplane* and *Hot Tuna* fame. He still tours nationwide and American School alums who attend his annual concerts enjoy chatting with him backstage about the good old A.S., which he remembers fondly.

Jorma, known in high school as Jerry

Backstage with Jorma 2019

Party Time

Formal Dance
From Lou Gopal's Manila Nostalgia, Photo by Charlie Jones

We had many different opportunities to socialize in Manila. There were formal parties with invitations on cards, where the girls would wear pretty dresses and the boys, their white dinner jackets or barongs.

Not all parties were that formal. When American School guys and Spanish guys from LaSalle were at the same party, occasionally fights did break out, usually over a girl, and one or both ended up bloody. Once one of the upperclassmen, showing off his machismo, put a needle and thread through his cheeks. Just boys being boys with raging hormones and the need to show off! Pretty tame by today's standards. While beer might have been involved, there were no drugs. Not until years later, long after we were gone.

Then there were the parties with those magic words "open house" where anyone and everyone could attend. Great parties at classmates' Makati homes.

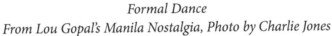

Guérnica's sign, Courtesy of Warren Gerig

Since there were no restrictions on drinking age, we were able to party at the local night clubs. One could be served a Singapore Sling under the stars at Casa Marcos, or the sultry Embers Club or even dance on the tables at the lively Guérnica's, while listening to the band playing *Trio los Panchos* favorites, such as *El Reloj*. Those were magical evenings, and we felt so grown up. Under age? No problem!!

However, Priscilla's parents got the Polo Club to set aside a room for a teen canteen, where we could play our records and dance and play liars dice. So much fun. Finally, some school dances had a theme, such as Hernando's Hideaway or Sadie Hawkins. Priscilla remembers after one dance Warren offered to drive chaperone Mrs. Hourihan home. "We all piled into his car with Mrs. H in the back seat. We got her home after a little detour to an abandoned air strip to see if Warren's car could go 110mph. (It could.) When we finally got to her house, Mr. H was at the door with a very angry face. From the back seat came a little voice, 'Hi, honey.' We think she had some 'splaining' to do!"

A different type of party was the "slumber party". The girls enjoyed getting together at each other's houses, where staying up as late as possible was the norm and talking (usually about boys), laughing and even singing until all hours until everyone finally collapsed in a heap on the floor.

Classmate Noonie and her mother lived at the Manila Hotel for two years. Noonie recalls: "The truth is I hated living there. I wanted to live in a house or apartment like everyone else. So I liked spending time at other people's homes. In reverse, of course, the other girls liked spending time with me at the hotel. We had a lot of hotel adventures. Jane Donnell said I reminded her of the children's book *Eloise at the Plaza*. Jane and Steve Malchow were a couple then. One weekend Jane was spending the night with me. I did not know that she had a very strict and early curfew. At curfew time her mother called to check up on her. No Jane in yet. She was never allowed to spend the night with me again!"

Another slumber party story from Priscilla: "What started as a slumber party at JUSMAG (Joint U.S. Military Advisory Group) ended up as a 'junior delinquent' incident when one of the girls climbed up a ladder to Gene Cepeda's room and planted a balut in his bed. When Gene came to the window to see what was going on, he landed right on the egg which resulted in the Great Balut Fight. Gene got all the boys together and everyone was throwing eggs. I remember racing through a back yard and yelling to the guard who had his rifle shouldered, 'Don't shoot! We're just playing!' Later, Keith Claxton said he had to bury his clothes. I would have to say we were one lucky group of kids!"

Sadie Hawkins Guys Preparing for the Chase
From Bamboo Telegraph Archives

Another lighthearted tradition at the American School that we looked forward to every year was Sadie Hawkins Day. It was an American folk event and pseudo-holiday originated by Al Capp's classic hillbilly comic strip *Li'l Abner*. This inspired real-world Sadie Hawkins events, the premise of which is that women ask men for a date or a dance.

144

The way it was practiced at the American School was that the girls lined up on one side of our athletic field and the boys on the other. The girls would then chase down the boys and when a boy was chased by a girl he liked he let her catch him. Not easy, because the boys were shirtless and had smeared themselves with lard. There was a lot of mischief in the voting for who would be Daisy Mae and who would be Li'l Abner for the dance. There was also a wedding booth, where, for a few pesos, a couple could get "hitched."

Senior Year

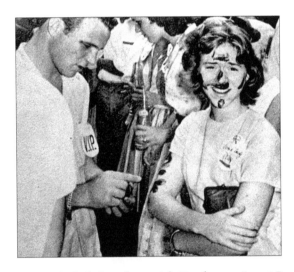

Senior VIP Dik Bartlett with Freshman Janet Lee
Caption from Kawayan: "Freshmen begin with "suffering . . ."

We remember how our Senior year started. We as Seniors, some of us wearing homemade VIP buttons, carried out the tradition of lighthearted rites of passage as we teasingly welcomed the Freshmen into our fold. One day was designated, with faculty approval, where Seniors would smear lipstick (or shoe polish in a few cases!) on Freshmen's faces or ask them to carry our books. The Freshmen seemed to enjoy the attention!

We asked our classmates if they could remember any embarrassing moments. We are sure there were many, but there were only two responses. The irony is that, by complete coincidence, both involve Mr. Allison. In today's teenage jargon we would have called him "awesome," which made the embarrassment that much more painful.

One came from Noonie Neely, an active, popular Classmate: "I was in Mr. Allison's Economics class and one day he was discussing new business products. He cited that the first diet drink had just come on the market, but he could not remember the name. I immediately piped up 'Yes, Metrecal by Mead and Johnson'. The whole class laughed, and I was totally embarrassed."

(Metrecal was a brand of diet foods introduced in the early 1960s. Though its products were criticized for their taste, it attained a niche in the popular culture of the time.)

The second one is from Mary and it occurred on Senior Skip Day, our chaperoned school day at the beach: "It was time for our buffet lunch. We sat on a low concrete wall surrounding the lunch area near the beach. I happened to be sitting next to Mr. Allison. We were engrossed in conversation when I took a big bite out of my luscious ripe tomato. Of course, it squirted all over his shirt. If ever I wanted a big hole to open up under me, that was the moment, but he was most gracious about it."

Senior Skip Day on Matabungkay Beach photo from Kawayan's last page with the caption:
"... but as Seniors celebrate".
Mary 3d from left; Priscilla 2nd from right; Noonie on her left next to Leata

Priscilla Litwin remembers the day well: "Senior Skip day was a special event for Seniors where we were allowed a day for fun away from school. All of us Seniors piled into a bus at 7:00 a.m. and headed for Matabungkay Beach. It was a long trip coming and going, but the weather was perfect, and we had all the revved up hormones of teenagers playing hooky. Kathy Stolberg kept Noonie and me laughing all the way with funny stories like singing her first song while still in a crib: *You've got to accent the positive*. Then we started with *Hundred Bottles of Beer on the Wall*. That took a while. Of course, we weren't totally on our own, as there were chaperones, but happily they were settled in under the palms and we were left to roam the beach and frolic in the water. For me, a scary moment was when a group of us were way out in an over-loaded banca. I happened to look down into that clear water and saw a huge shark way below us. I said loudly, but firmly, 'Let's go back in', without ever saying why. Sure enough, when we were close to shore we capsized, and everyone tumbled into the water, but no harm done. We had escaped a *Jaws* moment. The chaperones fixed a beach supper, but Karel, Kaye and I climbed up into a tree house and stayed there until dark, laughing and telling stories until the adults made us come down. Some boys put rocks in front of the bus in hopes that we wouldn't have to leave, but of course, it just caused a small delay. We left at 9 p.m. and returned to our waiting cars at midnight. We were happy and content and were much too exhausted to even sing one more bottle of beer off the wall. It had been a wonderful, memorable Senior Skip Day."

Graduation photo with Mary speaking and Nancy on far left
From Brings Family Archives

Our graduation ceremony was held outdoors on April 4, 1961. Ironically, Mary's last American School activity began in what had been her Kindergarten room (now Art Room) in 1948 when it all began. This room was the staging area for the processional out across the lawn where the proud parents were sitting, up the stairs to the makeshift stage. We were dressed in caps and gowns, ready for the speeches and the diplomas.

Those of us in the Glee Club sang the famous Latin student song *Gaudeamus Igitur*, followed by a song from *Aida* and, finally, the poignant *Moments to Remember*. We had changed the lyrics to reflect our own "moments," but the chorus remained:

> *Though summer*
> *Turns to winter and*
> *The present disappears*
> *The laughter we*
> *Were glad to share will*
> *Echo through the years*
> *When other nights*
> *And other days*
> *May find us gone*
> *Our separate ways*
> *We will have these*
> *Moments to remember*

Of course, the final party, the Senior Prom, was the culminating event of our entire American School experience, whether it was one year or thirteen (counting Kindergarten). After the graduation ceremony we returned home and changed for the gala event. The girls all wore fabulous dresses. Some were made of dreamy tulle; Priscilla's was a pale peach, hand beaded by her mother; Mary decided to be different and wore a black gown, short in front, long in the back, with an appliquéd rose embroidered on it diagonally. Our dates picked us up with the requisite corsage in hand and off we went for an evening of feasting and dancing. It was held at the Wack Wack Golf and Country Club on their upstairs porch and balcony, which had been converted into a twilight terrace. A combo provided the dance music. It began at 9:00 p.m., with a sit-down dinner at 10:30. It ended at 2:00 a.m., after which many of us left for a last visit to Casa Marcos on Dewey Boulevard.

At 4:00 a.m. we drove to Dik Bartlett's, who lived near the Polo Field. (Good thing we had drivers!) His parents had laid out badly needed breakfast food and strong coffee! Then everyone filtered over to the Polo Club, which was just opening for the day. We were fading fast in our finery and were taken home for much-needed sleep.

The current year is 2021, the 60th anniversary of the Class of 1961. We editors wanted one girl and one boy from our class to sum up briefly what our shared time at the American School was all about. Priscilla and Art were not main characters, but you have met them through their contributions to this chapter.

Priscilla Litwin: There were those great parties, school dances, beautiful sunsets, killer sports competitions, senior skip day at the beach, field trip to Corregidor, the Moro folk dancing contest wearing long metal nails, the jeepney rides downtown to work on the *Bamboo Telegraph*, the teen canteen, sitting on the terrace at the Polo Club to watch practice, hoping no one would yell "fire" in those packed movie theaters, seeing teen headliners at the Araneta Coliseum, watching the ground roll in a tremor, playing a Jet in a scene from *Westside Story*, plastering the school with posters for *Pris for Pres*, slumber parties, taking flamenco dancing classes, asking my parents to adopt triplets from the orphanage (they said no!), terrific teachers and friends—well it just goes on and on.

Art Zurhorst: There were so many wonderful memories from the time I spent at the American School. Watching the sun rise the morning after senior prom, doing the clown diving thing at Army Navy Club, all of the wonderful parties, my 18th birthday party that made my house overflow with all my friends, the night Typhoon Dading hit, cruising Taft Avenue in my little white Standard 10 car. I will always remember my only year at A.S. (senior year) as one of the best of my life.

CHAPTER 10

℘

We All Go Our Separate Ways

Some of us left the American School before high school graduation, but soon we all went our separate ways. We each found our path, some planned and some just reacting to opportunities. But our life experiences continued and we each share our story.

Terry
The Boy from Iowa

After our family left the Philippines we moved to Milwaukee and I entered as a Senior at Dominican High School. I played basketball at the American School so I tried out for the varsity basketball team at Dominican High School. I found that the style of play was much different. At the American School we played a fast paced game, but at my new school it was much slower. I made the first cuts and thought I had a good chance to make the team, and then I could show what I could do. However, my enthusiasm got the best of me. At one practice the coach decided to do a scrimmage. He decided to play and I ended up guarding him. I wanted to show him what I could do, so I played my best defense. Twice I blocked his shots. I am not saying it had anything to do with that scrimmage, but I was soon cut from the team. I was learning about life.

I started gathering information about colleges my junior year at the American School. I wanted to study engineering and selected Purdue University, one of the best in the country. I applied, was accepted and was off to Indiana the fall of 1961. I loved Purdue, the classes, the Big Ten school spirit, the giant 400-member marching band and my dorm that had its own "sweet shop," radio station, cafeteria, laundry and much more. I looked at fraternities, but when they showed me the "make out" room where boys took girls, I was not impressed. These were not the values I had learned.

During my freshman year I developed severe pain in my lower back. I had to drop out of school. I spent a lot of time seeing different doctors and getting a lot of tests. Eventually, I was on crutches. Finally, my father said "enough is enough" and he took me to the Mayo Clinic in Rochester, Minnesota. For those of us from the Midwest, Mayo was the "holy grail" of medicine. Right away their doctors diagnosed my problem as ankylosing spondylitis. This is basically arthritis of the vertebral joints and is very painful. The cause was largely unknown and there was no cure. I was put on a large regimen of aspirin for pain and as an anti-inflammatory. Much better drugs are now available. After my diagnosis I was sent to an "arthritis group" education program, mostly of old ladies who asked questions like, "Will I still be able to knit?" I was devastated and left the session in tears. I had my whole life ahead of me. I still remember my father trying to console me.

I suffered a lot of pain for almost thirty years and was on anti-inflammatory drugs, which caused me to develop esophageal problems. I also got eye problems. The arthritis stopped all my sports activities, even golf. The good news today is the arthritis seems to have kind of "burnt" itself out and I am off the anti-inflammatory drugs and am doing well, but the vertebrae in my back have fused from the inflammation, causing me to bend forward. I got old fast, but never lost that spirit for life and continued to strive for achievement. One good outcome from my condition is having learned real empathy for others as I saw first hand that things happen that are beyond one's control. We all need help sooner or later. And with all the "biology" I experienced during my testing and diagnosis, my interests changed. I moved from engineering to biological science. I regret this a bit. Although I had a good career, I think I should have stayed in engineering, as I am always wanting to design and build things.

At the time of my diagnosis, I had to drop out of school. We were living in Milwaukee, so I went to Marquette University for a year while getting medical treatment. Then I transferred back to Purdue, where I graduated in 1965. During my junior year my parents were transferred from Milwaukee to Paris, France, where I spent two summer vacations and toured around Europe with my brothers. One summer my younger brother John and I took French for Foreigners at the Sorbonne. My brother was very diligent, but I was not so much. The teacher was an attractive young woman and I liked to talk to her, so we became friends. When the grades came out, John got a B and I got an A. Another life lesson learned!

Since the French do not take kindly to Americans butchering their language, we were reticent to practice our French in our everyday activities. To continue our education, we found that the ladies in Pigalle, famous for its red-light district, were happy to talk to young American boys, so we found ourselves practicing our school work in Pigalle. Of course, being good Iowa Catholic boys, improving our language skills was the extent of the education we received from those ladies that summer.

During my senior year at Purdue, I interviewed for jobs with drug companies. I related my aspirations, and was told I needed to go to graduate school. I had not thought about that. In 1965 I was off to Oregon State University, where about thirty graduate students were in the microbiology department. It was during the Vietnam War, and the graduate schools were full. I started as a teaching assistant while taking advanced microbiology courses. After my first year I was offered a National Institute of Health fellowship which funded my PhD so I did not do a master's degree.

While I was in graduate school, my parents were transferred to South Africa during the period of apartheid. I spent a month visiting them. I asked my father to take me to a gold mine, a diamond mine, a farm and a wildlife park. I was always a sports car fan, and as a bonus Dad took me to the South African Grand Prix. He did a lot of work with the tire manufacturers, so we got a "pit pass." I met and got a picture with Dan Gurney, my favorite driver.

The gold mine was very deep and we took a fast crude industrial elevator down, which took forever. When we got to the bottom, we felt very hot, being a bit closer to the earth's core, we were told. In the gold mine we learned about mining and also about the African workers. We learned that most were not from South Africa, but were from other African locations. They could come to the mines and earn enough money to go back home and buy land and cattle. We also learned that they would select the best workers to be in charge and would give them watches. The best workers would keep track of time, and this gave them stature. I am sure our guides wanted to make a good impression with what they showed us.

My trip to a South African farm and its workers interested me. I saw rows of small but very well kept houses, each with a small fenced yard that was completely taken over by growing gardens.

I met my wife Edwina while in graduate school. We both had the same professor in our major subject. She completed her master's degree and moved to Vermont to work in public health. We corresponded, and I proposed by mail.

After graduation, I took a faculty position at Fresno State in California, where I taught for five years, Virology, Microbiology and Electron Microscopy in the Premed, Medical Technology, and Nursing programs. I spent my first summer off at the School of Public Health at U.C. Berkeley, getting specialized training in diagnostic virology.

I loved teaching, but it was very difficult work. It required a great deal of study and researching current journals to keep up with the science. And campus politics was difficult for me. I always pushed to provide our students with the most up-to-date and best education possible. I visited the local hospital and talked with the pathologists and asked how our university programs could be improved. I shared this information with our department faculty, again trying to improve our curriculum, but my suggestions were not well received. Another life lesson! While in Fresno, Edwina and I learned that we were not able to have children.

Somewhat disillusioned with academic life, I took a job with the New Mexico State Public Health Laboratory as head of the Virology/Serology section. I worked on the diagnosis of infectious diseases with John Mann, who later became head of the World

Health AIDS program and who was killed in a tragic plane crash in Africa. I did a great deal of diagnostic and epidemiology testing. One epidemiology program for New Mexico was to do surveillance for equine encephalitis, which can also infect humans. We monitored for the presence of the virus across the state. If the virus was in the area, mosquitos would bite chickens so we put out flocks around the state. The local folks would then draw blood from the chickens and we would test it. We started with 25 chickens in a flock and there were fewer and fewer as time went on. I wondered if some folks had fried chicken on the state. I got immunized to do rabies testing, The first weekend I was on duty, a New Mexico state patrolman came in with a large plastic bag. This patrolman had on high black boots and a belt full of bullets. I opened the bag to find seven dog heads. It seems a pack of dogs had attacked an individual and we needed to know if any of them had rabies. I had to open the skulls and do the testing on the brains. What a change from teaching at the university! But I liked the work and felt I was making an important contribution.

In 1977, an opportunity opened up at a larger state laboratory and I went to work for the North Carolina State Lab, also as head of Virology/Serology. Again, I did extensive infectious disease testing. I was also involved with several research projects. In collaboration with a professor at Duke University, we did studies on Rocky Mountain Spotted Fever, a significant problem in the state, and we published that work.

In 1983, I was recruited by the pathologists at our local hospital who doubled my salary, and I accepted the job as Director of Clinical Microbiology at Rex Hospital, a 400-bed community hospital in Raleigh. At Rex I was actually part of the pathology group and we contracted with the hospital to provide professional laboratory management. I also became an adjunct professor at North Carolina State University and provided microbiology majors and pre-med students with special studies at the hospital. When a professor at the University of North Carolina at Chapel Hill had a heart attack, I was recruited to take over his virology class in the School of Public Health.

I was on call 24/7 and carried a pager. Remember those? I was called in when a special case required my assistance. One late night, for example, when a pediatrician had to deal with a baby with encephalitis, I ran a test for Herpes.

While working at the hospital, a decision was made to remodel the laboratory. I was asked to collect information and work with the architects. Ah, my chance to do some engineering, sort of. I knew the details of lab operations, took out my drawing equipment from Purdue and drew up a set of plans. The hospital decided they did not need the architects.

By the late 90s, our group had to accept a new contract from the hospital that eliminated funds for my position. Our group wanted to keep me, so I began doing less microbiology and more health care administration.

In spite of the challenges I experienced over my career, I feel privileged to have had the opportunity to help educate students and then motivate them toward a career. In my clinical work, I was able to improve the health of thousands of individuals and to have, no doubt, saved many lives through testing programs and consultations.

After retirement, Edwina and I moved to Bellingham, Washington, and I started a railroad museum. I served on Boards as a patient advocate at our local hospital and have authored several railroad history books.

I have always been somewhat active in politics. I was raised a Republican, but after my back problems, I developed a strong social conscience and have leaned Democratic ever since. I have been active in advocating for universal healthcare.

~

Aurora
Spanish Heritage

I attended the American School until seventh grade, and then I went on to Maryknoll College in Quezon City, Philippines. Maryknoll College did not have an eighth grade in their curriculum, so I went directly from seventh grade at the American School to ninth grade at Maryknoll College. The classmates I left behind at the American School continued to the eighth grade. Thus, my classmates at the American School were dubbed the "High School Class of 1961." At Maryknoll, I was a member of the "High School Graduating Class of 1960."

There was no question in our family that after graduating from high school, one went straight to college. In the Philippines, particularly for the boys, that was the only option for anyone to have a career and a decent salary. Without a college degree, a young person with a high school diploma or less could remain stagnant in a low-paying clerical position for many years or stay at a manual labor position forever. Young girls like me had another option. They could end their studies after high school graduation and get married. The girls who had no intention of getting married and/or wanted to wait for a few years, opted to attend college or else stay home with their parents until they got married.

Since my father and other members of my family had attended and graduated from the University of the Philippines, U.P. was, by tradition, my only choice. The question that followed was the degree I needed to pursue. When the time came for me to register at the university, I had to make some quick decisions. What did I want to do with my life? I knew that I enjoyed socializing, traveling and meeting people. After a short review of my degree options, I settled on pursuing Foreign Service. I know now, however, that I was not mature enough to take the choice seriously. A year later I shifted to English Literature when I discovered I wanted to spend more time reading stories. I had no real desire then to have a career; rather, I attended school just to say that I had graduated with a degree, but actually planned to eventually get married, have children, and become a stay-at-home mom.

College to me then was one great adventure to learn more, make more friends, and indulge in numerous fun activities. Nevertheless, as the months went by, college life gave me more than I expected. The classes grew on me, and I began to appreciate the knowledge I was drawing from the various courses. I started making friends, not only from the different provinces of the Philippines, but also from around the world and the personal decisions I had to make introduced me to a very different and grown-up world.

My interest in helping people grew in college. I became involved in a social service organization that I had started in senior high school with a friend. It was called the Philippine Band of Mercy. After visiting the Band's headquarters and meeting the patients there, I was impressed by the hard work being done by the organization and the numerous and very poor people they helped. It did not take us very long to get organized and plan activities to raise funds. We were able to raise funds through rummage sales, fashion shows, bingo games, and raffles. These funds enabled our group to purchase and present medicine, prosthetics, hospital furniture, medical devices and hospital appliances to the patients and their doctors. When I graduated after four years with a BA degree in English, I had turned into a more serious person shaped by the courses, the activities and the experiences of university life.

Immediately after my UP graduation and not yet knowing what else to do with my life, I found a job at the boys' college near my high school alma mater, the Ateneo de Manila. It was an Administrative Assistant/Secretarial position in closed circuit television under Father Leo Larkin, S.J. This job was brand new, and so was the building I walked into. Everyone I met there was excited about the new curriculum and TV productions that were being created in it. I was thrilled to be working for the first time and earning my own keep, meeting new people, learning how to file and label documents, putting them in order, answering phones, and running errands. It was fun to watch the TV productions being shot behind a large glass window. I was also fascinated by the fact that during those "modern times," the Jesuits had constructed a hidden level between two floors of the building that was accessible through a trap door. It struck me as rather strange to have such a medieval concept built into such a "modern" building. I didn't understand why they built it, unless the Jesuits had such a history of rebelling against political forces everywhere they lived that, in order to have the ability to hide from government authorities and be safe, they made the secret floor part of their construction plans everywhere in the world, including the Philippines!

That summer as I worked, my parents encouraged me to apply to schools abroad for graduate school. My father urged me to apply to the University of Pittsburgh, situated in the "steel town." I headed to the United States in the fall of 1964, still quite naïve, but ready for a new adventure in a place I had never seen before.

The first "adventure" I experienced started early on. In 1964, I was in mid-flight over the Pacific, headed to Los Angeles when my father discovered that I was booked to arrive at Philadelphia instead of Pittsburgh. The travel agent had mistakenly sent me to the wrong city! My usually calm father was quite upset when he informed the travel agent about the error. She frantically rebooked the flight before I arrived in L.A. Completely innocent of the proceedings, I was directed by the loudspeaker in L.A. to another flight (Pittsburgh) that was already preparing to take off and parked much farther than where I was originally supposed to embark. Overdressed in a tight skirt and very high heels, as people dressed up for flights in those days, I sprinted to the new gate that seemed miles away in that huge airport. As I was running, someone called to me, and I looked back. I was frightened to see a man in a suit chasing after me. This spurred me to run even faster and as far away from him as possible. I felt I was in deep trouble and needed to escape from this stranger. Nevertheless, the stranger caught up with me. He had my airplane slippers in hand, which I had apparently dropped from my hand carry. He handed them over to me, breathing and perspiring heavily, but happy to have caught up with me to hand me the slippers. I felt sheepish for having thought of him so badly, but grateful for having gotten the slippers back!

Graduate school in Pittsburgh was like nothing I had experienced before. I was living thousands of miles away from home and managing my existence in a dormitory all by myself for the very first time. I was assigned a dorm room in "Tower B" at Pitt. The best part of living there was the daily maid service for all the rooms. Very quickly I felt much at home, surrounded by students from all over the world, just as I had experienced at the American School. The campus was beautiful, situated in the heart of the city, with the main building appropriately called "The Cathedral of Learning" because it was designed and looked exactly like a cathedral. Even more interesting was the fact that the classrooms on one floor inside it represented different countries, complete with the furniture and ambiance of the country. The builders and designers of the rooms also came from the countries they represented. Thus, during my studies there, I attended a class in the "Polish Room" and the "English Room." Initially, entering an ethnically designated classroom was exciting, but once a class started, everything was "back-to-the-books-normal!" One of the newest additions to the classrooms today is the "Philippine Room" funded by a large fund-raising drive by the Filipino residents of Pittsburgh.

Perhaps some of the most memorable events of my life began in Pittsburgh. For example, shortly after I began my graduate studies at Pitt, I attended a special gathering of the university students attending college and graduate school at the University of Pittsburgh, Carnegie Tech, Duquesne University and Chatham College. There were many international students attending, among whom I was one. Organizers of the event asked the international students to come dressed in their national costumes that evening. I chose to wear a beautiful colorful costume worn by the Muslim ladies of the island of Mindanao in the Philippines. In the course of the evening, representatives of different countries wearing their national costumes were asked to introduce themselves to the large crowd. To my complete surprise, awards were given out, and my name was called out as the winner of the "Miss International" title. Rather bewildered and befuddled by all the fuss, I accepted the fanfare, put on the sash, savored the title, and enjoyed the evening's fun. It was memorable because I was never involved in any kind of activity that focused on myself as a winner of anything marching in front of hundreds of people. I enjoyed my one and only "fifteen minutes of fame" that evening!

Pittsburgh is the city where I met and married my first husband, Jules Somerstein. It is also the city where my first child, Joseph Aaron, was born. He was followed a few years later, by two more children, Sandra and Marc. Years after my divorce, I met and married Jim Campbell from Texas. Throughout the subsequent years, I have had the opportunity to live and work in New York, Thailand, the Philippines, Venezuela, and Texas.

I moved to New York where I started a daycare center that expanded into three locations in the space of 30 years. When I moved to Dallas, Texas in 1997, I was asked to start childcare centers run by church groups. At one time I managed all five schools in two states at the same time. I flew between New York and Texas on a weekly basis. It was hectic but very rewarding. I discovered that my world in Texas was different from my New York world, so working out of both states made life really challenging and interesting. The schools I owned in New York were in Westchester County and were comprised of an international group of students whose parents worked in Wall Street and high-tech corporations. On the other hand, one church school in Dallas was composed of Mexican-American children needing to be helped in Spanish and English; the other church school was focused on personal behavior/character and religious subjects. The diversity in the different schools stimulated my imagination and enriched my working days and hours.

I also enjoyed a fifteen-year stint in television. It was not a career, just a fun hobby, but I treated it seriously and with great enthusiasm. I had always wanted to be in radio and it was a dream of mine throughout my growing-up years. When I was thirteen years old and being driven home from school one day, I was listening to Manila Station DZMB when I heard there was a contest to find a one-afternoon radio host for the station. I became very excited and as soon as I got home, I immediately called the station to sign up. To make a long story short, I went for an audition at the studio and was chosen out of a group of ten, to be the host for an afternoon. I was only thirteen, but the studio people must have thought I was older! They allowed me to go on air, and I emceed the show without any problems! It was a memorable experience and the media bug hit me from that time on. Years later, I finally got the opportunity to start a TV show of my own when a local TV station opened a studio in Westchester County where I lived. The studio was required to make their station accessible to residents who wanted to get involved in television, and there, my opportunity arrived. Once again, I attended introductory TV classes and then auditioned with other interested individuals in front of cameras. Shortly afterwards, I was called and given the go-signal to start my own show. I knew the rich cultural heritage of my community and the abundance of well-known residents living there. I was convinced the show would be successful. Thus, once I started featuring the talented and popular residents living around me, the show took off. The popularity of the show grew and individuals and corporations, such as the Starbucks Corporation, started writing and calling the television station requesting that they be featured in my show, entitled "Peekskill Profiles." The show was broadcast throughout Westchester and Rockland counties, and had a viewership of 150,000. For a small-town show, this Cable feature hosted several well known guests, such as composer Aaron Copland, *Life* editor Ed Thompson and writer Ben Cheever.

While I was married and living and working in New York, my father died suddenly of a heart attack. After traveling from New York to assist at my father's funeral in Manila, I had to fly back to the U.S. to rejoin my husband and little son. I brought my mother and youngest sister with me back to the U.S. knowing that immigration issues are never easy. It took time to get that done—gathering letters from friends, speaking to U.S. immigration officials, so many bureaucratic details. I spent many sleepless nights wondering what I would do if that request were denied.

This was also difficult, because my mother had just had a stroke and could hardly walk. She also had heart disease and diabetes. My youngest sister had been adopted by my mother as an infant, and at the time of my father's death was only a pre-schooler. How would U.S. Immigration allow them to live with me in the U.S.? My parents' friends came to the rescue when I mentioned the challenges I faced from U.S. Immigration. Our friends immediately wrote letters explaining the circumstances that our family faced, and, from Manila, I quickly sent their letters to the U.S. Immigration authorities in the U.S. My time was limited because I was a few months' pregnant with my daughter at that time, and had to be back in the U.S. in order to give birth. I was overwhelmed by anxiety, wondering what would happen and how fast I would hear from the authorities. By some miracle, the letters from our friends touched the people from the U.S. Immigration office. Shortly afterwards, my mother and sister were granted visas to travel to the U.S. with me and to live permanently in the United States with me and my family

The tragedy of my youngest son's fatal car accident in Upstate New York in 2001 left me devastated and stressed while I continued to commute and run the daycare centers between New York and Texas. I felt a lot of guilt and questioned my decision to send him to college in snowy New York rather than to attend college in warm-weather Texas.

Eventually, dividing my time between two states became too complicated and stressful for me, so I decided to make Texas my permanent home. I consolidated the three schools in New York into one entity and sold it to a wonderful Swiss couple who wanted to expand their daycare business. My school fit perfectly into their daycare philosophy, and so the deal was made!

Once I was in Dallas, Texas, I returned to college teaching. Teaching English Literature and Grammar at the University of Pittsburgh had been my first job during my graduate school years, and I was delighted to resume teaching at that level at Tarrant County College. I actively taught there from 2001 through 2018. Finally, in 2018, I decided to take a leave of absence from my teaching career. My husband Jim underwent hip surgery, followed by a second one four weeks later after falling and breaking his femur in four places. I opted to be with him and to see him through his recovery. I finally decided to retire from teaching in 2020. Shortly before I ended my college teaching career, the administrators presented me with the *Outstanding Adjunct Faculty Award*. After teaching various subjects at various levels, I can sincerely say that I enjoyed teaching to the utmost!

I have been blessed to teach fifty-five years at all grade levels in different schools and countries around the world. My own experiences traveling and studying in different places were an asset to my career. Exposure to different people, I believe, made me more understanding and respectful of people and their cultures.

~

Gloria
Chinese Classmate

I always knew that I would be going to the United States for college. It was my father's unspoken goal for me; he thought that his children would have the best quality of life here, as well as the most successful. The A.S. had prepared me well academically; I knew American history and government; and I had been exposed to American lifestyles and points of view from my many years at the American School. I thought I could adjust easily to life in America.

But I had never set foot in the U.S., and was a little shocked when I landed in Ohio, in the little college town of Oberlin, seemingly in the middle of nowhere. In fact, I asked the taxi driver transporting me from airport to campus how far away we were from my destination and he said, "You're here." It was not quite what I had expected.

In my first months at college in Ohio, I realized these things about myself: I am a city person and I hate cold weather. The first time I went to Cleveland, the big city closest to Oberlin, I thought, why did I not choose a school here or at another city?

When the temperature dropped to 50 degrees F, I thought I was going to freeze to death, and I knew that the worst was yet to come. Getting the hang of winter clothing was hard; I was very unacquainted with hats, scarves, mittens, coats, snow boots, etc., etc., etc. I also despised having to wear hats and gloves to church, but solved that problem by joining the church choir.

I had an excellent college education, but it was a grind. After freshman year, I needed eyeglasses; I could no longer read the subscripts in the Chemistry equations written on the board.

After Oberlin, I was accepted to graduate school at UCLA—big city, sunny weather —and was about to head there until I realized that I wouldn't know how to maneuver around L.A. I had lived a very protected life in my first four years in the U.S. with dormitories, dining rooms, bikes and no cars. I had become a small-town girl. Could I fend for myself in L.A.?

So, back to Manila for a re-think. I ended up teaching English at the A.S. Principal DiVirgilio heard I was back home and asked me to teach 7th and 8th grade English. The A.S. would only hire native speakers to teach English, so the school was always searching for English teachers. It was desperate enough to consider me, an alumna, a native speaker (my third native language!)

I had a very good teaching experience. The students were great. I never had a disciplinary problem; everyone came ready and prepared to learn. My seventh graders were particularly enthusiastic students. I fondly remember their performance one day in class when we had an unexpected visitor, a parent newly arrived in Manila who was intending to enroll her child at the American School and wanted to observe one of the classes. I was a little dismayed when I discovered her presence in my classroom that day, because it was the day that we were to start the poetry section of the literature textbook. I wasn't entirely sure how the kids were going to take to the poetry.

To my great surprise they took to it! They "got" the language and structure of the little poem under discussion. And then, proud of themselves, they began a thrilling poetry discussion to show off to the visitor!

Later in the day in the school office, the staff reported what a great review the class had received from our visitor. Whew!

My eighth-graders were more of a challenge: they gave me my first-ever headaches! But one couldn't blame them. This class was the last period of the day, ending at half past noon. The kids were tired, hot, and hungry.

During this year, I also had a part-time job in the English division of a Chinese newspaper company. I was investigating another potential career path.

I returned to the United States, this time to California, to earn a master's degree in English Literature at the University of California, Santa Barbara. There, I had a completely different academic experience from my undergraduate school. I was in a beautiful place, with perfect weather (72 degrees just about year-round), and having great fun. In truth, in the 1960s, Santa Barbara was pretty much a party school.

At my first class, I had as classmates a former bartender and a former cocktail waitress (with whom I would become very good friends). My graduate professors were much looser types than the ones I had in undergraduate school, though they were eminent and widely published scholars. One professor, visiting from a prominent Eastern college, was not just a well-known scholar of Romantic poetry, BUT also a great party person. She lived in a wonderful house with well-stocked liquor cabinets alongside bookshelves filled with many books she'd authored. She had parties there, handily helped by her bartending students!

Later, when I was a doctoral student, I had a professor, a published poet, who insisted on holding doctoral seminars at night at his house in Montecito. The first thing he'd ask when we students arrived was, "What would you like to drink?"

Then there was the advising professor I had when I was a Teaching Assistant for English 1A and 1B. He loved having people over for dinner or going out to dine. I remember cooking a big adobo dinner for him and fellow students.

I completed my M.A. in one year, making all my deadlines for required courses and passed an oral exam. I went back home to Manila to teach 12th-grade English at the A.S. An intense teaching year. As my fellow alumni might remember, senior English had many stringent requirements: Shakespeare, poetry through the ages, major novels. I assigned an essay a week, a book-report a month, and a major term paper each semester. It was a tough curriculum put in place by previous senior teachers (including our A.S. classmate Carol Naylor). The senior term paper that had been required of our class of '61, which had to be explicated and defended before a board of teachers, no longer existed. I have never decided whether to be sorry about its disappearance.

I missed the Santa Barbara way of life, so I went back to UCSB for doctoral studies. As I was going through all the requirements of the PhD program, I also began working part-time in publishing companies: John Wiley & Sons opened a branch office in Santa Barbara and I worked there to learn about textbook acquisition and production. The office was located in a Spanish-style mall in downtown Santa Barbara, in a space that had been a chapel and locale of Clark Gable's wedding to Carole Lombard.

Ultimately, I realized that I was not a serious enough scholar to be a professor, and there were hardly any teaching jobs, anyway, so it was time for another re-think. I took a leave of absence from school, went up to Berkeley, and never left. I met Mike, my future husband, at a geothermal consulting firm where I was putative editor-in-chief of the company's scientific reports (more like a typist-in-chief, putting together large reports with the help of the new IBM Mag-card typewriters, the precursor to computer keyboards).

My experience there led to a career in technical editing and writing. I worked for Kaiser Engineers in a marketing/business development department that put together multi-million-dollar proposals to build transportation systems, highways, high-security government facilities. I found out that Kaiser had been part of the engineering consortium that built Boulder Dam—the dam I had chosen to research for a project in Mrs. Gaffney's 7th grade class. The Boulder construction site was located in the middle of nowhere, so Henry Kaiser, visionary and compassionate employer, decided to organize medical and health care for his employees there. It was the beginning of the Kaiser Hospitals system, and ironically the sole survivor of the multitude of Kaiser companies (including Aerospace, Aluminum, Cement, Steel).

I worked for both of the scientific laboratories founded/named after E.O. Lawrence, Nobel Laureate radiation physicist and inventor of the cyclotron. At Lawrence Berkeley Laboratory's Technical Information Department, I had a pretty ideal job editing scientific reports and books. It was fun to work at a site in the Berkeley hills, above the UC campus, amidst seven Nobel Laureates.

I ended my work life at Lawrence Livermore Laboratory, a national security lab with the mission of ensuring the safety and security of the nuclear stockpile. The lab's employees must be U.S. citizens and have Secret (Q) clearances. The lab is located on a one-acre site that is secured by guards, guns, and gates. To enter the work site, I had to go through a checkpoint and have the guard literally touch my security badge. I wore that badge at all times on site, but never off site. My final assignment at this lab was to write articles for its science magazine, in effect translating the jargon of scientific reports to a "story" that an interested audience (e.g., Congressional funders) could understand.

Along the way, I had married Mike and we had a daughter, Kathy. Also during this period Mike went back to graduate school at UC Berkeley, completed his PhD and went to work at Livermore Lab, from where he was recruited to a geophysical research company formed by Berkeley colleagues. A few years later, that Berkeley company was acquired by a French technology company which, after a few years, assigned Mike to their Middle East technology center in Abu Dhabi.

I had retired from work by that time, so had no problem transferring with Mike, although I had hoped the foreign assignment would be in Paris. But as a non-French speaker, it was probably easier to adapt to life in Abu Dhabi. It was a pretty upscale life: an apartment larger than our Walnut Creek house, complete with servants' quarters; generous travel and entertainment allowances.

From our perch in Abu Dhabi, it seemed like we were often taking off for somewhere in Europe or Asia. One of our most memorable trips during that time was a golf vacation in Spain.

We had been pondering a vacation destination. I mused, "It might be nice to go someplace where we don't have to deal with call-to-prayer five times a day," and Mike, a golf-fanatic, immediately found a golf vacation deal in Malaga, Spain.

We had a great time in Spain. My golf game? So-so. I was a golf neophyte. I had learned to play late in life (after retirement). But I did have some solid golf lessons in Abu Dhabi from excellent teaching pros. There, I also got to practice and play with other women beginners, a very good way to improve. The truth is that golf is just not a talent I have. So, I try to confine myself to easier golf courses and nine holes of play. And take credit for playing bad golf all over the world.

We entered the next stage of family life upon our return from Abu Dhabi. Our daughter brought us a son-in-law, and then, a granddaughter and a grandson. We also inherited a large and interesting in-law family.

That family enlargement added busy-ness, energy, and activity to our lives. Then came Covid lockdown. Life for me became a series of dog walks, occasional grocery shopping, cooking and cleaning, cooking, and more cooking. In contrast, Mike, who is supposed to be retired but has never stopped working on projects, actually got quite busy with consulting requests.

We are both looking forward to normality. We want to bust out of our Covid cages, go to shows and concerts, travel far and wide. In this new time, I am hoping that we will regain a measure of rationality, logic, and truth to our way of thinking.

Nancy
Missionary Family

I left the Philippines for college in August of 1961 and have not been back. I graduated from Cedarville College (now Cedarville University) in Ohio in 1965 with a degree in biology. I was married right afterwards.

We lived in Baltimore, Maryland for six years. My husband was an elementary school teacher for three years and then went to U. of Maryland full time where he eventually got his PhD in 1972. I worked as an Environmental Health Specialist in Baltimore County. In 1971 we moved to Chambersburg, as my husband took a position teaching for Shippensburg State College (now Shippensburg University). Our two daughters were born in 1972 and 1974. In 1973 I began an MBA program at Shippensburg, which I somehow miraculously finished in 1978. Our marriage started deteriorating about 1973, and in early 1976 we were divorced. In 1975 I got a position as manager of a Joann Fabrics store that was opening here. I worked there for a year and then had an opportunity to join an intern program for Computer Programming with the Federal government.

The internship required 4 months of training in Rock Island, Illinois. My sister Peggy had just moved to Iowa, and she offered to keep the girls so I could go to school. That worked out for a while until she got pneumonia and I had to take the kids with me. However, it all worked out, and I was guaranteed a job back in Chambersburg at Letterkenny Army Depot, where I stayed for 28 years until I retired in 2004.

I had several different positions at the depot, programmer, supply systems analyst, and a supervisor. I worked in supply, quality assurance, equipment management, and the data bank.

When I got to Letterkenny, I met a coworker named Bill Jones, and 2 1/2 years later we were married. He had 2 children also, a boy and a girl. They all lived with us. We had a few difficult times with the merging of the families, but now we are all very close, and we love to get together. My yearbook picture (a frazzled mother with 4 children) did come true in a way.

I am forever grateful for the opportunity to work for the Federal Government. We enjoyed wonderful benefits which I still have in retirement. I am still friends with many of my coworkers and their families.

In 1990 I traveled to Israel and Jordan with a group from Cedarville University and took my eldest daughter. Needless to say, I was bitten by the travel bug (which was planted at the age of 3, when I went to Africa with my missionary parents). Travel is now a passion of mine, and I have been to many places in the Middle East, North Africa, Europe, Cuba, and Costa Rica, as well as within the U. S. I also enjoy music (finally realizing a dream to sing in choruses as well as solos, duets, etc.), gardening (I am a Penn State Master Gardener), reading, scrapbooking, and family stuff. We have eight grandchildren and one great grandson. Active in our church in the music program, I have taught Sunday School and been a deacon and church librarian.

I have slowed down somewhat, but I am still busy and enjoy my life very much. I thank God every day for the wonderful life He has given me.

～

Mary
The Girl whose Parents were from Austria

I left Manila on the S.S.President Hoover with my mother on May 21, 1961, Immigration visa in hand, wondering when and if I would ever see Manila again. Our first stop was beautiful Hong Kong. At that point I had never been out of the Philippines! In those days rickshaws were plentiful and we took one to our YWCA Hotel. Hong Kong was still a British colony, so the money and the stamps all had pictures of the relatively new (1953) young and pretty Queen Elizabeth. The instructions from my college as to what to bring included something called a "car coat". I had no idea what that was, but we found one on Nathan Road! It was short, navy blue, with a quilted brushed nylon outer fabric lined with an acrylic pile. I agreed to let my mother buy it for me just to humor her because I frankly couldn't believe I would ever be able to stand wearing anything that warm. I was so wrong and so thankful to have it, as that coat saw me through many California winters. We spent a few days sightseeing, then boarded the "Asia" of the Lloyd-Triestino line, which was going to take us to many fascinating ports on the way to Naples, from where we traversed Europe by train.

What a grand adventure! It was my mom's first trip back to Vienna since she was forced to escape in 1939. Of course, it was very emotional for her. She had a hard time looking at people of a certain age, wondering how they had behaved during the Nazi era. She would say, "My mountains are still here. I came back to see my mountains." On the other hand, she never held a grudge against the young Germans and Austrians, saying that they should not be held accountable for what happened before they were born. I loved Europe, especially Austria and Italy, and I have returned many times.

From New York we took the Greyhound cross-country, making many stops along the way to see friends and relatives. Our final destination was Fresno, CA, where I would be attending California State University, Fresno. From the 1st grade on I knew that I would be attending college in the U.S. Our American School classes were based on the

U.S. curriculum with exactly the same textbooks. As I always loved languages, my dream was to attend Middlebury College in Vermont. One day some American friends were at our house and asked me where I was going to college. When I mentioned Middlebury as my first choice, they said, "It gets cold there!" I looked at them wide-eyed and asked, "You mean I'll need a sweater?" They roared with laughter and said, "You'll need a lot more than a sweater in Vermont!" So I reconsidered and decided that California was a better choice and learned that Fresno State was one of the best teacher preparation schools in the country. I majored in German and minored in Spanish with the intention of becoming a high school language teacher. It was my goal then, and I never deviated from that goal. I received my B.A. and M.A. there and taught lower division courses as a T.A. I met my first husband there and stayed married for 15 years. After I received my teaching credential and my M.A., I took a high school job in San Francisco, teaching German and Spanish at an excellent comprehensive high school, George Washington High.

After being single for seven years I met and married Peter Farquhar, geographer, retired college prof, expert on Asia and rice, photographer, climber, Peace Corps volunteer, Renaissance man. He had three children, all grown, so I'm a step mom. I never had any kids of my own, but have always loved animals. In the Philippines we had both dogs and cats. Since living in the U.S., after being done with dorm life, I have never been without a cat or two. At the moment we have a rescue Russian Blue named Dante.

My father died in 1973, but my mother continued to live in the house with the two house girls until her death in 2001. Whenever I went back, which I frequently did over the years, I was really going "home" to the house where I had lived from 1956 until I left in 1961. After my mother died it was up to me as an only child to sell the house, dispose of her belongings, have some of them shipped to San Francisco, and make sure the pets and house girls were taken care of. All of this in the wake of 9/11, which occurred while I was there. The neighbors across the street expressed interest in purchasing the house, so, since my time was limited, and I had so much to take care of, I sold it to them reluctantly, fearing that they would tear it down. Of course, they did and replaced it with an eyesore. On my subsequent visits home, I would always arrange to meet my dear neighbor, Mrs. Dy, elsewhere, never in the old neighborhood where I could not avoid seeing that industrial-looking house with no garden. So, although the two "houses" I lived in are no longer there, Manila is still my "home".

In 1991 I transferred within the same school district to a magnet school that is considered to be one of the ten best public schools in the country, Lowell High School. Their AP German teacher had just retired and I was offered the job. The students were wonderful and, despite the fact that it was a highly stressful place to work, due to the competitive atmosphere and the helicopter parents, it was also exhilarating and rewarding.

My students won national awards and trips to Germany, and they were among the highest scorers on the German AP exam nationwide. We published a monthly German newspaper, and we had an email partner school in Germany back when email was something new and exciting. Needless to say, I was busy. In 1996 I was named one of four Outstanding High School teachers of German in the U.S. by the American Association of Teachers of German. My mother, who lived to see this, could not stop laughing about the fact that the child who never wanted to speak a word of German at home was now an "outstanding German teacher." One of life's little ironies!

People ask me how I can teach German, the language of my family's oppressors. For one thing, in my advanced classes I did teach a unit in German on the Holocaust. But I also loved teaching the logical structure of the language, not to mention the literature. I introduced students to the music and the art as well. Teaching language includes teaching culture and German is a language with such a rich culture. This is what makes it so difficult to comprehend how the land of Goethe and Beethoven could have succumbed to committing such unbelievable atrocities. All of it comes down to stereotyping, profiling and discrimination. During the last few years we have certainly seen these tendencies across the world, even here in the USA. Teaching high school German also allowed me to have a successful exchange program with a school in Austria. In my opinion, having kids live in each other's homes and become part of each other's' families is the best way to promote friendship and erase those stereotypes, prejudices and misunderstandings between cultures one step at a time. I am certain that this strong conviction is rooted in my cross-cultural experience all those years ago at the American School.

After I retired, I spent a few years as a consultant for the San Francisco Unified school district. What gave me the greatest joy, however, was private tutoring. People who, for some reason, wanted to learn or improve their German somehow found me by word of mouth. These students were generally adults who were willing to come to my house. They were highly motivated and, in some cases, they became good friends.

Peter, my geographer husband, and I love traveling. When we're not homebound due to a pandemic, we take at least one big trip a year. We also go to our cabin in the Sierra, which his family has owned since the 1940s. We love Mexico and own two timeshares in Mazatlán. Many aspects of Mazatlán remind me of Manila in the 50s, especially the wide boulevard with waves crashing against the seawall and vendors walking up and down selling street food. Since I speak Spanish, I feel very much at home there.

I left the Philippines at 17, but my parents stayed on in the home they built, thanks to my father's foresight to retain Philippine citizenship. He died in 1973 at the young age of 68, but my mother kept going until 2001. She was the last of the Quezon/Frieder refugees given a home in the Philippines. My mother died at age 96, having lived and worked in the Philippines happily for 62 years, tending her beautiful garden, and being cared for by her two loyal house girls, who were like family. I am still in touch with them and their extended families.

With some regularity, both in Manila and in San Francisco, when I am at a social event attended by Filipinos around my age, someone will shriek, "What!? You are the daughter of Dr. Brings (or Mrs. Brings?) My favorite teacher!" My parents definitely left their mark on their adopted country.

When I occasionally go back to Manila for American School reunions, I look out of the airplane window and see the Pasig River. Even though I have called California home for decades, I still choke up at the sight, and I think to myself, "I'm home."

$$\approx$$

Bob
The Boy from Ohio

I graduated in '61 and headed back for college. A Goodrich Corporation family in Australia had a son bound for college also and our parents had the idea that we could travel back together. So we hit Hong Kong, Bangkok, New Delhi, Tehran, Rome, Paris and London. We arrived back in the USA which was then Idyllwild airport and took a cab to LaGuardia. Then it was home to Akron and off to Miami University, which is not in Miami, but in Oxford, Ohio.

Following my first year at Miami of Ohio, I joined my family headquartered in Florida for their second home leave. We have family there and the rest came South and joined us. I returned to Manila with them in July '62 aboard the President Cleveland. Because I had many U.S. government and military friends, I visited Subic Naval Base a couple times, but we mostly went to Clark Air Force Base. We would stay at the officers BOQ which had a machine that dispensed beer for 25 cents. Once my friend went to visit a girl he knew, so I was on my own for a while. I sauntered over to the officer's club and relaxed poolside. I was ordering U.S. beers and looked pretty young for 19, so I was finally ushered out. Another incident happened at the Clark AFB main gate. It was a good jaunt to the main highway to catch the Philippine Rabbit bus for Manila, so we piled into a jeepney. When we reached the highway, the driver wanted two pesos apiece which the Airmen probably paid regularly. Being Manila boys and used to the ten centavo fare, we told him to get lost in no uncertain terms. He removed the gear shift and went after us as we ran and caught the bus. My friend who knew martial arts turned around, gave the driver a swift kick, and tossed a few coins his way to cover what was reasonable. Boy, those were the days!

I attended the University of the Philippines (UP) and carpooled with Tonya Winters and a Spanish fellow who was a friend of hers. Around August '63 I returned to the States, having enrolled in a small Lutheran college in Mankato, Minnesota. Together with a few others I rented a house off campus and threw parties until the school heads caught on and expelled some of us. Not surprisingly, the school sports team members were not asked to leave. Probably it would not have been considered an infraction at a typical university.

Being of Draft age and with the Vietnam War heating up, I chose to beat my 1-A classification, which arrived only days after I had enlisted. I was sent to a Communications Technical school in Biloxi, Mississippi in August '64, where there were still reminders of segregation. In fact, when we received our orders for Biloxi, there were some very upset Blacks. Following training as a Ground Radio Operator, I filled out my "Dream Sheet" for my next assignment choice. Naturally I chose the Philippines or Japan, only to find out I was going to Greenland. I was told there'd be a girl behind every tree; only there are no trees in Greenland. My class dedicated the song *I'm Sitting On Top Of The World* to me. The silver lining to that was a return State-side guaranteed to the area of one's choice after a remote tour. So I chose Southern California and wound up in Riverside. March AFB in Riverside was a SAC (Strategic Air Command) base and brimming with B-52 bombers painted black for operating in Vietnam. I soon volunteered for the Intelligence School at Lowery AFB in Denver, CO and became a Photo Interpreter. I had to obtain a Top Secret clearance once back at the March Reconnaissance Squadron. With that you might imagine what we were doing for the Vietnam effort. I knew that I could not be sent anywhere else for a year and by then I would be discharged.

After four years of active duty in the Air Force, I decided to stay in Southern California and headed for the San Fernando Valley, where I graduated from Cal State University (Northridge). I spent 16 years in the San Fernando Valley working for a subsidiary of Avco Financial Services before relocating to my birthplace, Akron, Ohio in 1982. I am always asked why I ever came back. No reason other than to marry someone I had known practically all of my life, my childhood sweetheart, Mary Ellen. I inherited three children who are all grown and now have a 2yr. old grandson! In Ohio I worked for Kent State University in the area of purchasing and contract administration. I retired at age 60 with a state pension (PERS). Mary Ellen, an elementary school teacher, retired after thirty-one years, also with a state pension (STRS). She felt that she had put in enough time with all the new requirements and restrictions.

Today I'm a fairly laid back and conservative individual. I am thankful for my good upbringing and must say that my stint in the Service did not hurt me, either. The Hippie era with its drugs and psychedelic music went right on by me. I was too into the "oldies" music and busy finishing school, anyway!

Warren
The Viking from New Jersey

For college, I selected the University of Arizona because of its warm climate. My career choice was "Engineering" because that's all I knew, since my father and his friends were engineers. I made a big mistake, as I couldn't get used to all the formulas I had to remember and the need for advanced math. This was not a favored subject, I realized. Right away I wished I had given my major more thought. However, I learned a fantastic lesson, that is, whatever you do in life "Be Prepared," the true lesson of the Boy Scouts. So then I switched to "Business Administration," much more to my liking and a natural for my lazy brain.

I worked at Safeway, stocking shelves at night to make ends meet and went hunting every chance I got. On holidays I visited Las Vegas, where nobody cared in those days how old I was. My parents always taught me to be a charitable person and if I couldn't give money, then I should give of my time and service. So in college I joined Pima County Search and Rescue. It gave me something exciting to do. Several of us members were given Northeast of Tucson as a search area. It involved a large land mass (East of the Interstate through the Catalinas into Sabino Canyon). We would have to look for the lost at night at least once every three months.

One day while in class someone entered the room and asked for me; I was told in front of the class that the Dean's Office wanted to see me. There were a few laughs, and I even wondered what I might have done. As soon as we left the room I was told the Dean's Office had excused me from class to attend an immediate emergency in progress downtown, and he handed me an address. It was the Supreme Cleaners on Stone Ave, March 1963 and that was all he said. I drove to the location, listening to the radio about an explosion at the cleaners. On arrival at the scene I saw devastation; the concrete building was totally gone, and a fire was raging. Immediately I knew this was no rescue; it was a recovery. I watched with others of my squad while firemen put out the fire. Then we went into the smoldering wreckage to recover the dead and charred bodies. Back then nobody provided counseling; we just "sucked it up." It took a couple of weeks to harden myself to death and gruesome sights, but it helped me from then on; I could deal with anything. A few years ago, I stumbled on the official report of the incident on the internet, and I am pictured looking at the fire just before recovery.

After college I needed to move to a cooler climate with green grass and trees. I found my first real job working for Saint Regis Paper Company in Rockland County, NY. I was a research worker in the new products department. It was a good job and I was able to buy a new Chevy. I also joined the New City Volunteer Fire Department and became a fireman.

Vietnam was getting a lot of headlines in local papers, and I wondered if I could do anything to help. I didn't need to worry about being drafted because I had a deferment due to my being a research worker. But I could not have lived with myself if I had not joined up, so I went to see an Army Recruiter. I figured if I died in the Army there would be something left of me to bury, while nothing would be left of my body in the Navy or Air Force. Go figure! My first choice was to join U.S. Army Special Forces as a Green Beret. I learned quickly that the recruiter couldn't help me. In fact he thought I was "Nuts". With all the tests I took and education I had, I could do almost anything I wanted, even go into OCS (Officer Candidate School) after Basic. He said I would have to earn a spot in Special Forces and the best way to get in was as an enlisted man.

I asked what I should do to be an enlisted man. He said, "Go into Airborne Infantry." I said, "Put me down for Airborne Infantry." His response was, "Now I **know** you are nuts". Off I went to the Induction Station in New York and then to Fort Dix.

I spent many hours developing my strength. I started running and actually began to like it. By the time I graduated Basic, I was in excellent shape, the best condition I have ever been in. In fact, it went downhill from there. Just as I was graduating from Heavy Weapons School, a Special Forces (SF) Recruiter came through and I applied. They gave me seven hours of constant tests —some of the hardest tests I have ever seen. I was accepted but was told that they only needed Medical Specialists. I wanted to be a weapons man. The Sgt. Major said, "Do you know who we are? We are the U.S. Army and we have weapons people coming out of our tail! What we need is a Medical Specialist, and your score says you can do it." So that's what I was going to do. I spent two intense years studying medicine, diagnosis, treatment and surgery. I did an amputation and treated a lot of Gun Shot & Bouncing Betty wounds (landmines). I graduated in the top eleven out of fifty-seven candidates. Actually I loved medicine. I was to act in the capacity of a doctor whenever a doctor wasn't present. Wow! Cool!

My time in the service was spent doing medicine for the 3rd Special Forces GROUP Airborne at Fort Bragg, NC. I found myself in between the Army and a dermatologist at Fort Jackson, SC during 12 weeks of on-the-job training and became an extremely valued witness in an Army Court Martial. Now, I'm not to be put in harm's way, just like my Dad. I waited forever to witness in this Court Martial (Capt. Howard B Levey), which upset me, because Special Forces was returning home and the war was winding down. The case turned out to be far more important than I thought. It was reviewed by the Supreme Court, and it is now Case Law in trials for war criminals. At the time I considered it a waste of time. Wow! Who would have thought?

I spent some time as a Police Officer and worked for United Airlines (UA) in JFK, Chicago, Denver, and back to NewYork City, while I was living in New Jersey. The commute was long and tiring, but it all was inside, so weather was not an issue. Once boarding the train in Summit, New Jersey, I remained inside or underground for the rest of the trip right into the basement of "30 Rock," then up the elevator to the 29th Floor. While in New Jersey, I was a High Adventure Scout Master and I led scouts to the Seabase in the Florida Keys, where they would learn about sailing and scuba diving.

My travels around the world gave me a taste for working with people and kids, just like my father. He was successful because he was more like an ambassador than a businessman. He took his time discussing ideas and engineering with his Filipino partners. His example helped me to understand people and how they want to be treated. This not only helped me gain in military rank faster than others, but I also moved quickly in management when working in the airline business. Then my personal goal was to help kids become better leaders.

Eventually United asked me if I would go to the Philippines to fix some serious issues and to handle a job that could be dangerous. I could not believe it could be dangerous, having played baseball and soccer with the kids who were now running their fathers' businesses and were some of the most powerful people in the Philippines. So off Noria and I went! As soon as United's PR person announced my arrival in Manila the phone started ringing, asking, "Are you the Warren Gerig who went to American School in the 1950s?" It was as though I was returning from a two week vacation. Guess who was still Mayor of Pasay City: Pablo Cuneta, 32 years later. We made immediate contact with the Mayor. At last the individual who was considered by United to be dangerous became a puppy when he found out whom I knew. As I was the third male in my family to live and work in the Philippines the assignment was fairly easy. However, the country was still in economic trouble because of President Marcos' policies of Martial Law. We only had power for 8-10 hours a day. Any decent restaurant and hotel searched everybody without exception for guns & weapons. People were now less tolerant of our apparent wealth and expensive living. I chalked some of this up to Marcos and his grip on the country. Many people, even the previously privileged and wealthy, suffered under Marcos' tyranny.

I met the U.S. Ambassador and there was a Special Forces Association Chapter in Angeles City outside of Clark Air Force Base. I saw then President Ramos at a function and reminded him of when he taught us how to be efficient Safety Patrol members. He looked at me, and we had a good laugh. He turned out to be a good friend. Even when we were in Thailand, whenever he visited, he invited Noria and me to have dinner with him. He wasn't smoking anymore, but he always had an unlit cigar in his hand.

This time I lived in a compound inside a compound in Forbes Park. There was absolutely no trouble here; it was as safe as Ft. Knox. We had our own electricity generator to do the full house, including air conditioning. We were suffering with only 8-10 hours a day with power. We lived just three doors down from the JUSMAG Commander Col. Nick Rowe, whom I met when we were both in U.S. Army Special Forces during the Viet

Nam era. Then again in 1980 or 1982 at Fort Bragg at an anniversary celebration. A fantastic, extremely bright individual, he was one of 30-some to escape from the VC bamboo tiger cages in the jungle. He was a West Point graduate. He wrote the Survival Evasion Resistance Escape Manual for the Army and ran the training operation. He was killed in 1989 in Quezon City by a unit of the New People's Army in the Philippines called the Alex Boncayao Brigade. I met the Special Agent in charge of the FBI who investigated his assassination. He said they fired over 200 hundred rounds at his bullet proof car, hit the car 24 times and one bullet hit the joint where the glass of the window connects to the metal frame. He was on the floor when that one bullet went into the vehicle and hit him in the head, killing him.

During this second venture in the Philippines I met and enjoyed being with many dedicated business men and women. They were just like any other business people in the world, trying hard to make their operation successful. The small businesses were constantly trying to make economic ends meet. I remember having lunch with four Filipina ladies who owned different commercial enterprises. They brought up the need to pay "baksheesh" or political bribes for anything and everything, such as licenses, building permits, employment inspections, customs brokers, facilitators, influence-peddlers and many other operations involving business. They stated they never knew how much from a budget point of view bribes would cost in a particular year, so planning expenses was extremely difficult. I said, "It's also wrong". One of the ladies said, "It's our culture; we must pay." I never looked at this problem as a cultural issue, but it explained why bribing is rampant in the Philippines. These Filipino business women saw the "baksheesh" as a way of life. As do many other Asian countries. Luckily, American firms in business could fall back on the Foreign Corrupt Practice Act of 1977, which had huge fines and imprisonment if American Companies were caught paying bribes to foreign politicians or individuals working for foreign governments and organizations. I did not have a problem with paying baksheesh in the business world because the bribe-takers understood my position; however, as an individual doing personal business a bribe was expected.

Clark Air Base was a mess in those days because when the Air Force left the Philippines, the surrounding communities looted anything left behind and totally destroyed the buildings. This was in strict contrast to Subic Bay Naval Base, which, when it closed down, was protected by the Mayor's Police Department; thus it became a new, thriving economic zone. Clark and Angeles City also were pretty much destroyed by the 1991 Mount Pinatubo eruption. When driving through the area we saw a church completely covered with volcanic ash; only the cross on the roof could be seen. A new super highway to Clark and North is a sharp contrast to the narrow two lane road to Clark we used in high school to go up to the base "Teen Room." One night while returning from Clark late at night my friends and I were shot at by bandits while running their road block. We were lucky they were bad shots that completely missed us. Our hearts were thumping in our chests.

There was a good relationship between myself and headquarters, that considered me a person who did the job without causing more issues. That's why I was shipped off to Taiwan. United needed to reduce personnel as they planned to reduce the hub in Taipei for more gates in Tokyo. We needed to cut staff legally and reduce flights quickly; fortunately, most staff could be protected in other cities in Asia where United flew. While we were in Taiwan (1995-96), the Chinese started "rattling their sabers" and firing missiles over Taiwan. Many feared the Chinese would attack the island because the DPP (Democratic Progressive Party) publicly announced its plan to separate from China and no longer be a renegade province of China. The one-China policy agreement between the USA, Taiwan, and China meant there was no U.S. Embassy in Taiwan. However, the American Institute of Taiwan (AIT) handled American affairs. The AIT Regional Security Officer (RSO) and I decided to recommend we "hunker down" if attacked since there were a number of insurmountable issues to evacuating American citizens.

I did what my father did in India: set up an escape plan to Goa (Portuguese Colony in India) and onward. However, I was planning to go to the Philippines in a fishing trawler out of a small fishing village on the Eastern part of the Island with the help of friends from the KMT. The Kuomintang Party, or Chinese Nationalist Party, is a major political party in Taiwan. Luckily it was not needed. China was always the problem; even today the Chinese are still threatening India and Taiwan. China has just seized land belonging to India, and it is bullying Taiwan in 2020.

Taiwan was in strong need of leadership, so I spent much time working with their legislative and government think tanks regarding airline and airport issues. I spent many hours explaining why certain airline procedures were important. I went to many meetings where I didn't understand the language. They thought I knew Mandarin, but I just couldn't speak the language. In reality I had not planned on what happened next.

One day after things started to settle down, I received an early morning call from a high ranking official at Manila International Airport. He said he could not discuss the issue on the phone and I needed to get to Manila ASAP. This person never minced words and sounded very serious, so within an hour I was on a flight to the Philippines.

What I found out when I arrived stunned me. I could not speak, just stood there and stared. When I finally got my wits about me, the aforementioned official and I went over what was going on in the Philippines. A man by the name of Ramzi Yousef was arrested in an apartment complex after a bomb went off in the apartment. I knew the name from my last posting in Manhattan, New York City for United. He was the individual who was responsible for the truck bombing of the World Trade Center in NYC, but he escaped and disappeared. There was a Red Letter Warrant by Interpol for his arrest for the bombing of the World Trade Center (WTC), that caused six deaths.

I was in New York when he was planning the World Trade center bombing and in the Philippines when he was planning bombings of aircraft. What was the urgent news that brought me to the Philippines? A laptop in the apartment was picked up by the National Bureau of Investigation (NBI, the Philippine FBI). They eventually got Ramzi Yousef's laptop deciphered and translated into English. Ramzi Yousef and his Uncle Khalid Shaikh Mohammed of water boarding fame were planning three terrorist actions called the Bojinka. Plan 1 was to Assassinate President Clinton and/or the Pope on their visits to Manila. Plan 2 was to blow up eleven 747 Airplanes in the Pacific in one night, killing over 3-4000 people. Plan 3 was to fly airplanes into buildings. Yes, this is 1993-4, long before 9/11 in 2001. So much for connecting the dots!

What was important about their activities in the blown up apartment? They were assembling the bombs for the eleven airplanes. Ramzi Yousef had already tested the bomb twice: once in the Greenbelt Theater in Makati, killing one person siting in the seat where the bomb was planted; the second time was on a Philippine Airlines airplane going from Cebu, Philippines to Japan via Manila. This was a test to see if Ramzi Yousef could sneak the ingredients of the bomb on the plane and build the bomb in the lavatory, place it under a seat and get off in Manila. This bomb was not meant to bring the plane down, but just to see if the plan would work. It killed the person in the seat with the bomb underneath. As it was on a non American airplane, the incident did not raise suspicion. It worked!

From this point on, we looked carefully for anyone trying to put a bomb on our flights out of Asia. There were many sleepless nights. The first "do not fly list" came out with two names on it; now it has over 60,000 names. The list started to grow and planes from Thailand started to drop into Taipei in the middle of the night with the Security Department of the FAA (Federal Aviation Administration) requiring a full search of passengers and cargo. After the third flight UA sent me to Bangkok to check and verify that our operation was operating effectively. I was there for eight years because it was considered the viable airport to place a bomb on an airliner. After a while we were advised that the FBI arrested Ramzi Yousef in Pakistan. He now resides within 60 Miles from our house in Colorado; it's called "Super Max" where he is serving a life sentence. This prison, truly escape proof, is for the worst of the worst.

On July 1, 1997, Hong Kong was peaceably handed over to China in a ceremony attended by numerous Chinese, British, and international dignitaries. Noria and I planned to be in Hong Kong on what was known as the hand-over day. We stayed in a hotel United used right on the Harbor looking over Prince Charles Barracks. The Chinese troops arrived with angry looks on their faces and rifles at the ready. It looked grim for the territory. Although we had fun celebrating, we were sad the British were leaving because we always knew the Chinese would never honor the treaty. It rained in the afternoon and evening. The Chinese thought this was a blessing, and the British thought this was an ominous sign. East meets West—go figure! Something interesting happened in the morning. A Royal Marine went to remove the British flag from the flagpole and a terrific gust of wind came along and blew up his kilt. We finally had our answer to the age-old question: Do men wearing kilts wear underwear underneath? Answer: NO! The next day his bare ass was on the front page of all the Hong Kong papers.

I was recognized in October 2005 by His Holiness Pope John II as a Knight Commander of the Equestrian Order of Saint Gregory, the Great. This was in recognition for work with a number of fund raisers and support of Father Joe Maier of the Kwong Toey Rescue Mission and Mercy Centre, as well as other deeds for the Catholic Church. Because I was not Catholic, the Apostolic Papal Nuncio (Papal Ambassador) awarded me my Diploma instead of the Pope at the Vatican.

However, this was not my first experience with His Holiness Pope John Paul II. One day in Manhattan a coworker asked me if I minded having the Pope pray for me. My first thoughts were I was becoming the butt of an office joke. He sounded serious, so I decided to play along. My question to him was why he would be seeing the Pope. He said he was a member of a previous Pope's family and knew this Pope personally. United had asked him to go see the Pope and explain what we would do for him during his visit to the United States. The next question was, "Why would you ask him to pray for me?" He then reverted back to what I learned in the Philippines working for my mother and the Women's Clubs she belonged to in order to help the poor. This stuck to me and I carried it on in the New York City Area. He knew of my working with the Boy Scouts and my being a Deacon and then an Elder in my church in New Jersey. He also was aware that I was trying to convince United to dedicate a Boeing 727 with Flight & Cabin Crew for a "Make a Wish come True" for terminally ill kids to fly from New York and Northern New Jersey to Disney World in Orlando, Florida. This dream came true two years later after much coordination to accomplish this idea. I told him I was honored to have the prayer said for me. When he returned, he said the Pope and he, for twenty minutes, kneeled and prayed in the Pope's study. It was an Apostolic Prayer.

We retired in Colorado, where we always wanted to live. Now I'm a private investigator getting ready to retire at 78 years. I work for several churches, keeping them aware of "Threat/Risk Intelligence," and I serve on a church of 3500 members on the Life Safety Team. I'm a member of an FBI Program called "InfraGard" that provides infrastructure protection after 9/11, and TripWIRE, a DHS organization that provides Terrorist Information and Explosive Intelligence. I also work with the Colorado Springs

Police Department, Gold Hill Division, as part of its Civilian Advisory Committee, representing my church.

For 15 years I have served in a large Kiwanis Club, which has relations with seven schools (K-12) in Northwestern El Paso County, CO and generates over $80,000 per year for our Monument Hill Foundation to distribute to needy organizations working with children in the area.

One of the most rewarding things I do in retirement is work for a military organization for eight years, training young adults from high schools up and down the front range of Colorado on Leadership. It's called Rocky Mountain Youth Leadership Conference and takes place at a local college for one week every summer.

I am now standing down after nine years as President Emeritus of the Colorado Chapter of the "Association of Former Intelligence Officers;" however I will remain on the Board. We are trying to stay safe, healthy and content.

We began to move in different directions. But as we look back on our lives, we see that many of us chose professions in public service, reflecting the values we learned in and out of the classroom at the American School in Manila.

CHAPTER 11

❧

Reflections
Who We Are Today

Terry
The Boy from Iowa

During my years living in the Philippines and attending the American School, I lived in a bubble largely created by the founders of the school to provide an academic program in preparation for college in the U.S. Today at the age of 78, I am again living in a bubble created by a viral pandemic, COVID 19. Though these are very different bubbles sixty years apart, my interactions are now limited, although in a different way.

Reflecting, I was very active in school activities, especially sports. I did not have any friends in the Philippines outside the American School. So, we classmates did everything together. And when we had family trips and vacations, we went to places like Baguio and played with our school friends who were there as well. We also went to a wonderful beach on the South China Sea with a group of my parents' friends, all Americans. I now regret that I missed the opportunity to be immersed in and to learn the Filipino culture. What can I say, I was a teenager!

My studies were always a bit of a struggle for me. It is interesting to note that later in life I felt I had trouble focusing, especially when driving, and at the age of seventy I was diagnosed with ADHD. I don't think it was ever acute, but I suspect it played a role in my struggling a bit in school. Nevertheless, I still got satisfactory grades and persevered through graduate school.

I was always a sensitive kid; I still am as an adult. I was a bit shy, but soon grew out of that. I was driven to achieve, especially in sports. I was never a big star, but generally held my own. We classmates, girls and boys, did things as a group, rather than pairing up. It was a wonderful time with great memories. By the time I reached my junior year, things began to change. I joined the trend of the time and decided to "go steady." For me this just meant we did not date other girls. I was still "the naive boy from Iowa" and did not really fit into teenage awakening sexuality.

Also during my junior year a few male students started getting a bit rough and mean with what seemed to me to be aggressive behavior. Instead of being able to fully enjoy parties with friends, some drank too much, and, in at least one instance, a fight occurred. This behavior was probably typical for high school, but not my cup of tea. When someone I had never seen before tried to pick a fight with me during basketball practice, it really bothered me. I suspected some of my "friends" set this up. With events such as these, although it was difficult not being able to spend my senior year at the American School, I was pretty much ready to leave at the end of my Junior year.

When looking back at my time at the American School, I consider two main things that have impacted my life. First, I learned tolerance and that racial and religious differences were not important in interacting with classmates. Second, I learned to always strive for the best. Our eighth grade motto was, "Nil Nisi Optimum," Nothing but the Best.

When our family moved to the Philippines, we entered a different world. As I look back, I really did not know anything about the background of my classmates other than some had been born there and many had moved there, mostly from the United States. My good friend Raymond Kim was from Korea. Some were white; others had darker skin. None of that seemed to make any difference. Only later did I fully appreciate the wonderful diversity we enjoyed. At that time it all just seemed normal. When I contrast that with the world we live in today, I believe something innate in children causes them to treat others without prejudice. The environment at the American School allowed each of us to interact with all classmates in the same manner without even thinking about it. Today, as our world's youth, who are now more connected than ever, take control of things, might we hope that they will grow up to show the same tolerance we saw at the American School in the 1950s.

Another important factor that influenced me were the high standards that the American School set, not only in the classroom, but also in our extracurricular activities. Most classmates were involved in sports. I was in a play, was a class officer, and was on the student court. We had a school newspaper, with reporters, articles and commercial printing that was sold to recover costs. Our wonderful yearbook had our teachers. It also had individual student photos with lists of our activities, including sports. There were candid pictures and a section with advertising to defer some costs. This environment of high standards eventually helped me in my career, but also at times made life difficult. In my healthcare field, I always tried to provide the very best for the patient. That meant that I insisted on the best and most accurate laboratory procedures and the best computer systems to provide rapid laboratory results for the physicians. In North Carolina I was an active member of a group that included the "Heads of Microbiology" for several hospitals, and I met monthly with my counterparts, including those from University of North Carolina and Duke Medical School. This helped me to always stay up to date and to constantly update testing procedures in our laboratory. Often people did not deal well with constant change, but that was the nature of the medical field I chose. On occasion, staff members showed resistance. I always tried to be considerate of their concerns, but I did not compromise when it came to what I felt were my responsibilities. This extended to other areas of my life, not always easy.

As I progressed through my higher education, I came to understand that many factors make us who we are, including genetics that we receive from our ancestors, our parents' influence, our early childhood experience, our schools and teachers, our careers, our social interactions and sometimes lifelong health issues. What follows are some thoughts of how my education and the rest of life's experiences influenced who I am today.

I recognize that genetic variation and natural selection produced the world we live in. This principle also applies to human evolution. Tribalism is deeply embedded in our heritage. An aggressive tribe would wipe out neighboring tribes and then gain the opportunity to produce more offspring. So, we need to recognize this basic tribalism in our heritage. But we must suppress this in the realization that if we want a peaceful world without discrimination, tribalism is counterproductive.

I respect all animals and abhor cruelty to them. But I recognize predation is an integral part of our natural world. Humans evolved as predators and remain so, but raising animals and processing for food must always be done humanely. I firmly believe that animals are part of earth's family. I have always developed a close relationship with my dogs, in many ways the ultimate "man's best friend."

My defining health issue was the development of ankylosing spondylitis when I was a freshman in college, a painful arthritis in the joints of my neck and back. This changed many aspects of my life and added significant challenges. It also made me very empathetic toward others and their challenges.

I have made a good living, and I was able to retire comfortably at age 60. I strongly believe that everyone should have equal opportunity, but that everyone should also have the opportunity to choose their own path. All of us are different, and we need to respect those differences. A kind and valued laborer or a kind, highly compensated physician should both be shown equal respect.

I have become a social liberal to some extent as I believe in helping people to help themselves, but not taking over their lives. I believe strongly in tolerance and find that ethnic and religious diversity enriches our lives. I have a strong spiritual nature, but do not belong to any church. I believe in enjoying life as it is (always a bit hard for me), and, especially, I believe in good and caring friends.

And even though I do not have children, I believe that we should fully protect our environment for ourselves and those who come after us. Greed cannot be allowed to "Trump" our responsibilities to our mother Earth.

Finally, I would add, "Love thy neighbor as thyself." We can and must strive for this, but as humans we share a "built in" drive for self-preservation and we share conditioned prejudices that we must overcome.

At 78, life has been good, but, as with everyone, not always easy. I have been fortunate with supportive parents, mostly good teachers, comfortable living free from economic stresses, and good medical care when I needed it. On the other hand, I have experienced health and other challenging issues that have taught me that in the end, besides achievement, understanding and caring for others is key to our human existence.

Warren
The Viking from New Jersey

Our education at the American School in Manila was much better than what I had encountered in the USA. What do I mean? In the Philippines we had a small class of about thirty-eight students. It was easier to study with a small class, unlike in the USA, where classes where I lived were much larger and learning was different. The American School had more intimate-size classrooms, where one knew everybody and wasn't afraid to ask questions. Teachers were hand picked by a Board of business people and paid a higher salary than many U.S. teachers. They were also stricter about learning and I believe they truly cared for our welfare and learning experience . So when it came time to select a college, it wasn't as hard to get into the school of our choice because we had a better preparation than most U.S. kids. Colleges also knew that American Schools Overseas had students who were from highly educated families or very smart entrepreneurs. Yes, it was an excellent school and it is still growing. Today the student body consists of students from all over the world in new quarters. It is now called the "International School" because it has over 50% foreign versus American students and it encourages Filipino students to enroll in their "scholars program." It is considered one of the best schools in Asia. So, what did it do for me?

Personally, I learned about leadership and how to be an example for others. When I left the nest, I was acutely aware of the lessons learned in high school, studying with and playing sports with other nationalities and races. I feel this is why I have integrated and function well with those of color in America. As I look back on the overseas experience, there were lessons learned without even realizing it. I am truly grateful to have had the opportunity to live overseas. It has served me well in all my endeavors since then. I only wish that I had understood life better at the time because I was a little rambunctious back then. My time at the American School served me well in all my careers and will allow me to meet my maker with joy in my heart for everything that gave me a good life with my partner in love.

There are still some issues I'm concerned about, and I pray we start to understand what we are doing as a nation. I'm politically a Fiscal Conservative and we are looking at some serious monetary issues coming our way. The national debt is growing at an alarming rate and we as a country are living way beyond our means. At some point inflation will erase the value of our money and we will have to pay the piper, which will be extremely painful. Citizens will be carrying around thousand dollar bills and possibly hundreds of thousand dollar notes to buy groceries and clothes. Unless we change our ways, the IMF and the WTO will demand that we clean up our act and pay our bills. They may also take away the dollar as the world's currency, which China would covet, as their currency would rule. Meanwhile, our Treasury Notes would be worthless. We cannot continue to print money without backing it up.I probably will have passed on by then, but predict that the new "World Power" will be China. This has always been their goal.

My faith is everything, God will prevail and I believe we will wake up to what we are doing to ourselves. Only then can we stabilize the situation and repair what is broken.

Aurora
Spanish Heritage

In life there are many highs and lows, and mine has had many of both. The highs in my life include having the pleasure of having made many wonderful, admirable friends and keeping in touch with them through the years. On occasions when life was low—stressful or difficult—my friends provided me with advice, comfort, and support when I needed them. Events like the sudden death of my father of a heart attack in 1972, the death of my mother after complications from surgery in 1994, and the unexpected death of my eighteen-year-old son in a car accident in 2001 were tremendous losses that could have easily taken me down into a deep emotional abyss; however, the presence of good friends helped give me strength and courage to overcome my profound sorrow on these occasions.

The most important element of life is time, and we must give it wholeheartedly and to the best of our ability to those we love and cherish the most. I look back at the many years I worked, ran a business and raised a family, and I remember how little time I thought I had to accomplish all that I wanted to do. Thus, I was always rushing from one event to another, staying up late to finish tasks and assignments, and trying to squeeze a lot of work into twenty-four hours of the day. Of course, there was never enough time, and oftentimes I would find myself exhausted and frustrated. If I were to do it over again, I would leave much more to chance and the universe and would spend more time and vacations with my loved ones more than anything else.

I also realize now that I presumed many things about life that were not true. Not everyone thinks and feels the way you do. The first time I realized this was quite early when I was about fifteen years old. I was at home playing with a cousin's daughter when the child was visiting our family. We both had a wonderful time playing together. When her father, my cousin, came home, he became very angry at me, completely upset with me for spending time with his daughter. What I thought was a wonderful afternoon spent playing with my little niece was apparently very displeasing to my cousin. He grabbed her from me and took her back to their home in a huff. I found out much later that my cousin had issues with my parents and did not want his family to bond with us. I was shocked and saddened that people bear grudges and misunderstandings throughout their lives and because of a lack of communication between the parties, never resolve the issues. I promised myself as an adult that I would try to understand and communicate with people more, so that I could avoid unpleasant and even unnecessary situations like that again.

We should treat animals lovingly and humanely. I never appreciated animals as much as I do now. Our family always had animals in our home. In fact, some of them were quite exotic. We got the animals through adoption or as gifts from friends and relatives. As I look back, we had quite a variety of pets at different times. Pigs, monkeys, cats and dogs, goats, doves, and horses were with us from the time I was born. In the Philippines, animals were cared for by maids and houseboys. Only when I was much older and started taking care of them myself did I grow to love and appreciate them. My husband Jim and I had just bought our home in Southlake, Texas in 2000 when Jim decided to adopt a Bassett Hound. He had adopted one years before when he lived in Corpus Christi and missed having a pet at home. Thus, we started with one Bassett Hound. That grew into two and three: Dexter, Dudley and Roscoe. We also had cats: Tiger, Phoenix, Bonito and Sweetie. All sweet animals, they gave us unconditional love. Much to my dismay, I have come to realize that although animals are loved, many are also cruelly maltreated by many people around the world. It is unfathomable to me that people can be so cruel. I pray and hope that this situation changes.

I value a good education. My parents were great believers in education, and they never let their children forget how important it is. They practiced what they preached. They reminded us that, although they were not wealthy and could not guarantee an inheritance, they would work hard to pay for our college educations. To them, that was our passport to success.

Now that I have had opportunities to live and travel to different countries around the world, I see the difference education makes in people and their lives. I have realized that people who have had a form of structured education throughout their lives, or who have tried to educate themselves through reading and practical learning, have had greater opportunities to be happy and to have fuller and richer experiences as they have grown older.

Bob
The Boy from Ohio

Spending a few years living in 1950s Havana, Cuba and being aware of its aftermath leaves me very fearful of the course our country is currently taking. Already we appear to be losing some of our basic freedoms as we are being led down that path by a demented puppet. Democracy has always been tenuous, and I observed this while living all those years in the Philippines.

When I arrived in Manila, I noticed that it had a way to go before having some semblance to the U.S.A. But when I left in 1963, Ayala Boulevard was beginning to resemble Park Avenue in New York. Gone was the old airport with its lonely tower surrounded by overgrown fields! In its place were the brand new developments, Urdaneta Village and Bel Air Village, complete with the new American School. Even the fairly new Rizal Theater was surrounded by a new mini mall, which was the gateway to San Lorenzo Village. North Forbes Park to the South of Highway 54 was well on its way to being built. I sometimes wonder what our house in Urdaneta Village would be like, sitting in the shadows of the skyscrapers along Ayala Boulevard.

Each time I departed Akron for Manila following a home leave, my future wife, Mary Ellen, told me I had no roots. So I came full circle to Akron and married her in 1982. I'll no doubt spend the rest of my days here in my birthplace after all my traveling. I never thought I'd get California out of my system, as the first year it was hard to get used to the Ohio weather. But viewing California today, I feel I left at the right time. Akron is not too big and not too small, to where one can drive across town in less than a half hour. There is no rush hour to speak of and everything needed is close by. The biggest plus is having the entire family and grandchildren in the area.

Thanks to the Veterans Administration, I quickly received my Covid shots. I have to say that the Covid scare has been pretty smooth, living in Akron. No lockdowns at all. We are just required to wear a mask while inside somewhere. Thanks to our governor, all golf courses remained open. I do the so-called "Romeo" breakfast twice a week now with my league golfers and we are all looking forward to the "new normal."

Nancy
Missionary Family

Attending the American School was a huge influence in my life as it taught me more about other people and more about myself. One of the greatest things I learned was to try to be the best version of myself. My classmates and schoolmates, as well as the faculty and administration, came from high achieving families, or they would not have been in the Philippines in the first place. I truly admire people who work hard and try to accomplish all they are capable of. We had some amazing teachers, who did not let us slough off, and who expected the best of us.

It is not easy to remember how I was in the late 50s and early 60s because I feel as though I have changed a lot, as have we all. I started at the American School in eighth grade after two years of correspondence school, and I was also very shy as I had not been around many people for a while. I think that is why my parents wanted to send me and my siblings to a "real" school, and I appreciate their wisdom in doing so. I also appreciate the quick and good friendship of Mary, Gloria and Wilma; especially since they had been in the school for years and I was new. It would have been easy for them to be cliquish, but they took me in. From the beginning I tried to excel in school. It never occurred to me not to try to get as good grades as possible, so I always wanted to study. I was in several activities: Council of Ten (similar to a Student Council) in 8th grade and swimming team in 8th, 9th, and 11th, but for some reason, when I got to 12th, I was in many different activities. I say this only because my senior year was a turning point for me, and I realized that I could really make a contribution rather than always being on the outside looking in. That realization has influenced me to this day.

I did not have as active a social life as that of many of my classmates; my parents believed that participating in movies, dancing, and the contemporary music were wrong. I respect them greatly for living according to their beliefs. However, I now believe that much is worthwhile and beautiful in our culture, and that I can selectively enjoy it while still honoring God through it.

I didn't date anyone until the summer between our junior and senior years. That summer I dated two different guys (not classmates and not at the same time!), and then sometime during our senior year, I started dating Geoff Brown. He was even shyer than I was, so it never really went beyond the Platonic stage, but it was fun and a good experience.

Today, I see myself as basically conservative (not in today's politics, however), fairly social, but still preferring to work individually. I enjoy the fine things that life has to offer, but realize that they are just things and that family, people, and service are what are really important and lasting. I have a deep faith in God and in what He has done through Christ in this world, but I do not consider it so much a religion as an understanding of His love for mankind and His plan for the world.

I have become more adventurous; I am not as afraid of new experiences as I was. In fact, I would think nothing of getting on a plane and going anywhere!

I have tried to do various service projects, such as playing the piano and to a lesser extent the organ in church, teaching Sunday School and Vacation Bible School—no talent in either of those—being a deacon and elder, and most of all, singing in the church choir and community choruses. I am currently a member of The Towne Singers, a chorus that has been in existence for 55 years. I am looking forward to starting it again when the "new normal" returns.

I enjoy taking care of my garden and find it very relaxing and therapeutic, as well as creating beauty in the landscape. I like having people over and sharing our home with friends. I love to travel and enjoy books. I can seldom come out of a bookstore without a new acquisition.

Most of all, I love being with my family. I was married in 1965, and had two beautiful daughters, but I was divorced in 1976. I went to Rock Island, Illinois, to participate in an intern program to learn Information Technology and to take a position at Letterkenny Army Depot here in Chambersburg, where I have lived since 1971. At my new workplace, I met Bill Jones, who also had two children and was a single parent. We married in November 1978, built a new house, and became full-time parents to all four children. We now have eight wonderful grandchildren and one precious great-grandson. It is wonderful when we can all get together.

Gloria
Chinese Classmate

I have had three citizenships. Born Chinese, I became Filipino at the age of ten (following my naturalized father in his new citizenship), and I am now an American. My American citizenship has been held longest, and I believe it is my final one.

The truth is, I have been American at heart long before I was a citizen and even before I had set foot in the United States. How come? In civics classes at the American School of Manila, I was introduced to the ideas of freedom and democracy delineated in the United States Constitution. Growing up in a restrictive family and rule-bound religion, I was hooked on Americanism.

But I am not wholly separated from my other citizen-identities. I will always be Chinese, for, as we Chinese say, you will forever look Chinese. I accept this sentiment, but only metaphorically. After all, think of all the blonde Asians you can encounter with pale, pale skin and round, round eyes.

I am more relaxed when amidst other Chinese. That was one of the attractions of California—lots of Chinese in San Francisco! But that wasn't 100% ideal because back in the 1960s, San Francisco Chinese were mostly Cantonese, and I am Fukienese, speaking a completely different dialect.

We Chinese differentiate from each other down to the provincial level. We also discriminate against each other. Canton and Fujian were poor, lowly provinces, but nevertheless, each thought itself superior to the other. Thus it was that my Aunt Margaret from Canton, who was a famous Manila socialite, mahjjong champion, Asian women's golf champion, married to No. 2 son—a highly prestigious position in a wealthy family—and lived to the age of 105, was always referred to by my mother and her siblings as "that Cantonese." I heard a superiority of tone in their voices but nevertheless was afraid/in awe of my Aunt Margaret.

I have a Filipino identity because the Philippines was my first home, and our family house still exists there. Wherever I go in the world, if there are Filipinos around, I seek them out. They identify with me and understand exactly who/what I am. I am a Chinoy (Filipino of Chinese origin) to their Pinoy.

When my husband and I were living in Abu Dhabi, I often found myself being chased around the shopping malls by Emiratis in dishdashes (white robes, red checkered headdress). They just assumed that I, a Chinese woman, must be a prostitute. In the absolute social stratification in place in the Emirates as well as in many other countries, you are what your race is. I'm a Chinese woman, and therefore a prostitute. That premise is also a comment on Xi Zinping's economy. The certainty that I was a prostitute was even higher when I was seen walking alongside my Caucasian American husband! It was infuriating and frustrating. But lo and behold, a Filipino shopkeeper in the mall would beckon me into the store and shield me until the dishdash went away.

Today, I am satisfactorily retired in Walnut Creek, California, living within walking distance (not easy, uphill) of my daughter, son-in-law, and their two kids. My grandchildren are one-quarter Chinese, a fact that my daughter reminds me of when I look (pretty much in vain) for signs of Chinese blood in them. Nevertheless, they are, in my biased view, beautiful kids.

My hope and aspiration for them is that they will be good people and good citizens. I think their chances to become so are pretty good, based on my daughter's experience growing up in this town.

When it was time for high school, our daughter had two high schools to choose from, one in our neighborhood and one in a wealthy neighboring town populated with high-powered professionals. That school had the highest academic test scores in the district. Kathy chose the first school because all her friends were going there. It was a choice I accepted but was disappointed by.

Over the course of four years, I came to appreciate her choice. My daughter's classmates were academic achievers, generous community supporters, good to each other, and protective of each other. Impressed by them, I wondered whether they were the exception in the school and that my daughter had been lucky to be among them. The principal's son was one of her classmates, so I wondered if this spurred more attentiveness on the academic achievements and behavior of this class.

In the meantime, all kinds of negative stories periodically emerged from the other high school. The one I was most disturbed and shocked by was the stabbing death of one girl by another over a spot on the cheerleading team. I gathered that because of all the high pressure at that school for academic achievement and social status, the kids got a bit confused about their values.

I have to say that in general, I have had a lucky, privileged life. I attended the American School, which led to a U.S. college education and U.S. citizenship. I have had a long chain of luck in my life; because of my education at the American School, I was accepted at a prestigious U.S. college. Oberlin was not easy to get into: I discovered that a majority of my freshman dorm-mates had graduated as valedictorians or salutatorians from high school classes of thousands of students. I was neither the first nor the second place graduate from my class of thirty-seven students. But Oberlin figured I could handle the academics since the A.S. was a strong school. They liked the fact that I could provide diversity—my Ohio classmates didn't seem to know where the Philippines was (next to Puerto Rico?)—and I did not need financial aid. All this I figured out years afterwards. The lucky chain continued. Because I had an Oberlin degree, I easily obtained a work visa and then also a generous fellowship for graduate school.

I was on the route to obtaining U.S. citizenship, which has never been an easy accomplishment. I had all the advantages which allowed me to navigate the citizenship route myself without the help of immigration lawyers. It still took a long time for the paperwork to morph into a permanent resident visa, then five years of residency, before I could formally apply for citizenship. I don't remember how long that paperwork wended its way through the bureaucracy, but I became a citizen after my daughter was born.

My final piece of luck—so far, anyway—is being a part of this group of friends and classmates who have, over so many, many years, managed to track each other and continue to share friendship and life experiences. You are my "internationalist" friends, even though most of you are American, because you have lived all over the world and have been exposed to different systems of government and different ways of life. In doing so, I believe you have come to understand and really appreciate our democratic system of government; and in being exposed to different cultures and lifestyles, you have come to appreciate, rather than be threatened by, the differences.

Mary
The Girl whose Parents were from Austria

While trying to gather my thoughts in December 2020 for this all important chapter, I received a Christmas card from an old family friend named Christy. Remember the name; it will come up again later. As I read her first paragraph, I was dumbfounded because all the thoughts that had been percolating in my brain for this chapter were right there. Down to the metaphor of using 2020 as a strict teacher! To try and paraphrase it would have been futile, as she had done such a beautiful, painstaking job. So I called her, told her about this project, and asked for her permission to use it as an intro to this final chapter. She was flattered and utterly delighted!

> We are all watching 2020 slip away, knowing it will be a year to remember, a marker in our lives. There have been silver linings, but there also have been hard lessons. 2020 has been that very strict teacher you can never forget and, like it or not, we have been her humble students. None of us signed up for this class, it came as a requirement. She relentlessly reminded us of how little we control beyond our own attitudes and actions. The patience lesson has been a doozy, we are not very good at it. We have witnessed loss of life, devastation of personal lives, and natural disasters all at a scale that tests our ability to comprehend. We knew we were fortunate, but seeing how really fortunate has been humbling. The silver linings are real, time together, sometimes too much time together, watching butterflies land on flowers, bees collect and hummingbirds dive. The slowdown of life has brought into even sharper focus the value of good health, family, friends, neighbors, community and the beauty and importance of the natural world. Our country has work to do to build and rebuild trust and to mend lives. We can do it. That's what we're being called to do, individually and collectively.
> —Christy Holloway

As Christy suggested, this strict teacher, 2020, taught me gratitude. Gratitude for all the things I have, tangible and intangible. I have a home in one of the most beautiful, cosmopolitan cities in the world. And, unlike many of my friends, I am not alone during this painful stay-at-home period. I have a wonderful supportive husband and quarantining at home has brought us closer than ever. We take delight in our cat, Dante, who brings us great joy. Every day he reminds us of life's simple pleasures.

But 2020 also reinforced my empathy for all those who have lost so much. So many lives lost. We can't allow the ever-increasing deaths on the TV to become just a number. As Joe Biden always reminds us, each number is someone who will not be at the dinner table tonight and whose family is grieving. I personally lost a dear friend to Covid, a Philippine icon, Benito Legarda, with whom I had just had lunch when I was in Manila for the Centennial Celebration of the American School.

So many small businesses, so many restaurants, so many shops that make up the fabric of San Francisco, gone. I feel deeply for those who have lost homes, jobs, opportunities, and this year I found myself giving far more in donations than ever before. Where did this feeling of compassion for the underdog come from? Partly, of course, from my parents, who fled the Nazis in Austria in 1939 and arrived in Manila with almost nothing. They had a strong social conscience and, while not wealthy, they were always generous to those with far less. But how does this tie in with the American School?

In the Junior High chapter I mentioned our revered Headmaster, Herbert E. Warfel, who called the junior high and high school classes together to the auditorium for an assembly whenever he had something important to say. You may recall that it was the total eclipse on June 20, 1955. Mr. Warfel called these assemblies convocations, which literally means "calling together." The eclipse experience stayed with me my whole life, but another one a few months later, which was for a very different reason, did so as well. I knew nothing about baseball. Basketball was the national sport in the Philippines, with soccer in second place, but no baseball. However, on September 8, 1955 far away in New York something phenomenal had just occurred. It was the World Series between two New York teams. The confident, sure-to-win New York Yankees were playing the scruffy, raggle taggle, no-chance-in-hell Brooklyn Dodgers. It was the seventh game. Everyone "knew" the Yankees would win, but no, somehow the Brooklyn Dodgers amazingly won the series.

After all these years in the U.S. I still don't understand baseball and am not a fan, but I have tears in my eyes right now, because I can still see and hear Mr. Warfel talking about the importance of this phenomenon and saying words to the effect of: "When the rich and powerful think that they are entitled to win, that's when you root for the underdog." That view has shaped my political leaning which was reinforced by my Government teacher, Bill Allison, who taught us critical thinking skills when we were Seniors and had to form and defend our position in the 1960 presidential election.

As a teacher myself I was active in the union, the American Federation of Teachers, and participated in all the strikes, rallies and marches, protesting cuts that affected our ability to teach and students' ability to learn. I certainly did not go into teaching for the money. It's one of the hardest, least understood and appreciated jobs, but the satisfaction of seeing those faces light up makes it worthwhile. Although I knew from the first grade on that I wanted to become a teacher, it was the day at the A.S. that Mrs. Batchelder asked me to tutor Johnny Fontaine that cinched it. Although rather quiet and shy by nature, my personality changes when I am in front of a class. It's like being on stage and putting on five shows a day, no matter how lousy you feel or what drama is going on in your personal life. You're on and you do it and you love it. I feel that most kids at the A.S. didn't really know me. They thought of me as quiet and studious, but on more than one occasion I had people tell me they were surprised how different I was when they got to know me better.

The beauty of the natural world is very important to me. I am a spiritual person and am overwhelmed by the wonder of the universe at the ocean or in the mountains. I love all animals; domestic pets, those found in the wild and those raised for food. I deplore any cruelty towards animals and donate generously to bonafide animal and environmental causes. As a result, my mailbox is filled daily with heartbreaking appeals. I wish I could respond to them all!

To maintain my health and vitality I enjoy daily physical exercise and keep a healthy pescatarian diet. During the 2020 lockdown I have made it a point to take daily walks. My exercise classes are right there on Zoom, so I have no excuse not to show up. My interest in nature and fitness goes back to my parents, who were climbers and skiers in Austria and who taught me to hike in Baguio and swim in the ocean at an early age. Zoom and FaceTime make it easy to connect with friends and family. I think about the people in the 1918 pandemic who did not have the luxury of our technology.

Hoping to reward myself for my 60th birthday I wanted to go to a fitness spa. At a social gathering I saw the aforementioned Christy and she was glowing. When I mentioned how great she looked, she said that she had just returned from Rancho la Puerta, her favorite spa in Mexico with early morning hikes, swimming, fitness, lectures, food from the organic garden. She mailed me some information a few days later, which I tucked away. It looked great, but was expensive. A month later I attended an American School reunion for all classes in San Jose. I asked an old friend, Doris Kaufmann, what she would be doing that summer. She said that she and her daughter were going to her favorite spa with mountain hikes, food from their organic garden, every kind of fitness and dance class plus yoga, meditation and lectures in the evening. Not to mention facials, massages and three pools. I asked her for the name and, of course, she said Rancho la Puerta. Like Christy, she raved about how life-changing it was for the body, the soul and the spirit. So I told myself that I would splurge that one time for my 60th birthday, but could never afford to go again. Well, life-changing it was and I attribute the ease with which I am handling this stay-at-home time to what I have learned there. With my Zoom classes I can pretend I am at the Ranch. Much of my cooking is Ranch-inspired, and I also learned to meditate. Needless to say, after that experience I couldn't afford NOT to go back. I saved up all my tutoring money each year and used that to pay for much of it. Of course, I was forced to cancel 2020, but was able to rebook for 2021.

Over a year has passed since our Covid lockdown began. Besides exercising and working on this book, much of my attention was unfortunately spent on the frightening political situation in our country. The American School turned me into a very patriotic American. In fact, when it came time for the National Sojourners annual essay contest on Democracy in Action, I was one of six winners. Their stated purpose was "to stimulate students' thinking about the function of democracy in the U.S." I wonder what they would have thought had they known that one of their winning essays had been written by an immigrant kid who had never set foot in America.

I couldn't wait to become naturalized. One of the questions on the oral exam was to not only name all the cabinet positions, but to name the men (no women at that time!) who were serving in those positions. I breathed a little thank you to Bill Allison as I rattled them off. I take voting very seriously and as soon as I retired, I volunteered to become a poll worker. I do all I can for my carefully chosen candidates, not only by donating, but by phone banking and writing postcards to 18-year olds, inviting them to the thrill of their first election.

That is why these past four years have been so profoundly painful. Everything I loved about America, everything I believed to be true about America was being systematically and cruelly dismantled. What made it even more painful is that this situation allowed people with a similar hate-filled ideology to come out into the open, ending with one of the most horrendous days in our history, a day I never thought could be possible in my beloved adopted home, January 6, 2021. I am inspired by a quotation by Tom Lantos, the only Holocaust survivor to ever serve in the U.S. Congress. He was a member of the U.S House of Representatives from California from 1981 to 2008 and he said, "The veneer of civilization is paper thin. We are its guardians and we can never rest."

I am optimistic about our new year and I trust that we are entering an era filled with empathy, justice and healing. We still have daily challenges facing us and our fragile democracy, but may we return yet again to "all that is beautiful and good".

I would like to close my portion of this book with a quotation by Mexican author Miguel Ruiz, "If you can see yourself as an artist, and you can see that your life is your own creation, then why not create the most beautiful story for yourself?"
I hope that is what we classmates have done, because the only way to understand the story is to tell the story.

CHAPTER 12

❧

Until We Meet Again
Reunions

The First Reunion, Chicago, Spring 2000
by the Editors Mary and Terry

The members of the Class of 1961 were spread out all over the country, with two living in Europe. We had lost touch with most of our classmates. Letters were slow, phone calls were expensive, it was all just too complicated and impractical. Some of us stayed on each other's Christmas card lists, but that was the extent of it. But suddenly there was this newfangled wonder called the Internet, more specifically email! Terry thought of the marvelous idea of forming an email group for our class, and we somehow came up with twelve email addresses. And so we got reacquainted, with Terry, the Listserv Master, capturing and disseminating all of the responses to the questions he sent out. Questions were mostly about our backgrounds, how we ended up in the Philippines, our memories about the school, the teachers, our thoughts and feelings. And we wrote. A lot! It was fun! It was freeing! It took us back to those special days. After a while we couldn't stand it! It had been almost forty years, and writing emails simply wasn't enough. We needed to see each other. Noonie and Tonya made the arrangements and we finally met in the flesh just before Spring Break 2000 in Chicago, a central location. We were nine people (plus spouses), most of whom hadn't seen each other since high school, but who had shared a special place and time in history. We picked up right where we had left off in 1961 (or earlier) and lunched on *pancit* and *adobo* at a Filipino restaurant. From among the seven main characters, Mary, Terry, Aurora, Bob and Nancy attended. From among the "other classmates", whom you will meet in Chapter 13, Ellen, Noonie, Steve and Tonya attended.

The following day we toured the city, visited museums, admired the architecture and received a special tour of the University of Chicago from our classmate Steve Gunders, who had done graduate work there. He was the boy in second grade who announced that his family had received their visa for the U.S. and shortly afterwards they departed. He discovered through a mutual friend that his A.S. class was conducting an email exchange and signed on out of curiosity. The only person in the group that he knew was Mary, but that was good enough. He was In! At the end of the week-end, we vowed not only to stay in touch, but to do our best to find more classmates and enlarge our group. Which we did!

Terry kept those email responses, compiled them, added pictures, made a 62 page book entitled *War Babies & Fifties Classmates* and put them in a three-ring binder for each of us, hinting that someday those responses in which we poured out our hearts on this new device called a computer, someday maybe they could be expanded into a book. We all agreed that it was a great idea, but it sounded like a lot of work, and we were busy people. Until Covid, and here we are.

Chicago, Spring 2000 Reunion
Classmates Ellen, Terry, Bob, Nancy, Mary, Steve, Tonya, Noonie, Aurora
with spouses Martin, Edwina, Bill, Maddy, Larry
Photo by Peter Farquhar

San Francisco & Echo Lake
July 27-31, 2001

The next year, 2001, was our fortieth anniversary, so of course we had to celebrate! Since Mary lives in San Francisco, a city that offers so much, that was the chosen spot, and she planned a busy few days for the group in late July. An enticing add-on was the possibility of spending a few days with Peter and Mary at the Farquhar cabin in the Sierra for those who could spare the extra time. Not everybody was retired yet!

The plan was set, the reservations were made, everyone was excitedly purchasing their plane tickets, but what nobody could foresee was that Mary's 96-year-old mother passed away in her sleep on the night of July 17, with her faithful house girls sleeping on the floor beside her. Mary dropped what she was doing, flew to Manila and, as an only child, took care of everything and made arrangements for the funeral. Through former

American School friends who lived in Manila she found a lawyer and a realtor and made plans to return to Manila in September. Several classmates suggested postponing the reunion, but Mary wouldn't hear of it. It was a difficult time and she needed their love and support.

After a little over a week in Manila, she returned on Friday, July 27 and took a cab from the airport, dropped off her luggage and met her classmates at nearby Café Kati for a scrumptious fusion dinner. Seeing her oldest friends after everything she had just been through was the best possible medicine. Hugs and tears and happy memories, followed by a whirlwind of San Francisco activities all day Saturday until late in the evening.

On Sunday morning those who had a few extra days woke up early to carpool to the cabin at Echo Lake in the Sierra. Peter's family has owned it since the 1940s and it is "rustic." While the structure is owned by the family, the land is owned by the forest service, so there was no indoor plumbing or electricity. Thanks to solar heating, there is warm water, however, and even a shower! It took several trips across the lake in the Farquhar motor boat to get all of us plus our luggage and food to the cabin. The lake was lined by granite hills on all sides. Wherever there was space in the rock one found cedar, juniper and pine. The entire scene was framed with a beautiful blue sky. The cabin was at the end of the lake, a couple hundred feet upslope, with a glistening granite "beach". The water was crystal clear and cold.

The first order of business was for everyone to choose a place to sleep. No, there are no bedrooms. Some chose the deck, others the "caboose" (an enclosed, protected area off the deck), others a tent on the rocks, or the main room, or the bunk room. Everyone put their sleeping bag on their chosen spot. Peter explained the cabin rules and how to use the high tech electromatic toilet up the hill. It was a bit of a climb, so one needed to plan ahead. There was also a small porta-potty in the bathroom for times when scrambling up the rocks in the pitch black night did not sound safe or fun. As you probably know, flashlights never work when you need them!

We shared a couple of days of relaxation and conversation. What wonderful conversations! Over and over again we marveled at the diversity of the group and the rich experiences each had to relate. How rare it is when a group can share and discuss such complex issues. This was not just a reunion, but a gathering of international classmates and spouses who share that special part of humanity. On Monday evening, our last, somebody picked up the guitar that resides at the cabin and Steve's wife, Maddy, an excellent singer, led us through all the old songs we knew so well. Meanwhile Peter fired up the grill and barbecued the lamb that had been marinating for hours. It was accompanied by grilled zucchini, rice pilaf, and salad, along with homemade wine, which Mike and Gloria brought along. They had their own label, Browndog, named after, yes, their beloved brown dog. For dessert, Mary brought mango sorbet with mixed fresh berries followed by coffee or tea. It doesn't get much better, especially in the mountains, where all the flavors are heightened, and in the company of our oldest friends who shared memories that "if you weren't there, you just won't get it."

Subsequent Reunions

You can tell we like each other's company, because three years later, in 2004, Tonya, who lived in Miami, organized a cruise to the Bahamas. The advantage of a cruise is that the only planning required is to decide which cruise to take. Everything else is arranged and available. Once on board we only made decisions on what to order for dinner and how much to gamble—if at all!

In 2005, just one year later, it was back to San Francisco, to take advantage of the fabulous food, entertainment, walks and shopping. Mary lives in the heart of Japantown, from where one can walk to the Marina or downtown Union Square. There are also four excellent museums, easily accessible by public transportation. On Sunday Steve and Maddy treated us to brunch in their gorgeous home with a view of the Golden Gate Bridge—Steve's #1 priority in buying a San Francisco home.

Our Fiftieth Reunion
Aurora, Steve, Tonya, Kaye, Noelle, Nancy, Noonie, Ellen,
Sylvia, Warren, Gloria, Mary, Carol, Ray, Bob, Karel

198

Believe it or not, we then took a fairly long hiatus, because the next one was the big one: 2011! Fifty years since graduation! Since Mary seemed to be the designated reunion planner at that point and since there is a large, elegant Filipino restaurant just south of San Francisco with a party room for rent, it was a done deal. So Retired Teacher Mary ordered the menu, collected the money, asked the American (now International) School to send banners and streamers and goodie bags and prizes for the games. Yes, she also came up with games that tested people's American School memory. We had a professional photographer and a professional Filipino singer. A playlist of 50s tunes during dinner—a bash for the ages! The following day Aurora's husband Jim arranged for a bus to take us to the wine country. We thoroughly enjoyed our winery tours and our tastings. On Sunday we once again went to Steve and Maddy's for brunch and did more reminiscing on the deck. It was October, San Francisco's Indian Summer. The perfect weather simply added to what was already perfection.

Before we knew it, it was 2016. Well, we knew what that meant. Our 55th! Can't let that go to waste. Mary insisted that we pick a different place. Please! Not San Francisco again! So it was Santa Fe instead, another lovely spot with much to do and see. There were two events that made this reunion special. One had been planned, the other had not (not by us, anyway.) One of our classmates had been on our email list for a while, however had never attended a reunion. Nobody had seen Paul since 1961, but suddenly he announced that he would be attending and that he would be bringing a guest, whom he did not name. While the rest of us were gathering in the hotel lobby, catching up on the last five years and getting ready to go to dinner, here comes Paul down the stairs with a lovely lady at his side, flashing a beautiful sparkling engagement ring. He had not seen us in fifty-five years, but we were the ones with whom he wanted to share this beautiful romantic moment. We were the first to officially meet the future Mrs. Hoshall. If reading our book up to this point hasn't already convinced you that we were a pretty special group with a very special bond, THAT should have done it. Two of our guys went to the bar and purchased bottles of champagne. And so our reunion began with glowing toasts to Paul and Mary Ellen. What a lovely way to begin! The other grand event was a train ride on our last day that had been recommended by Ellen's husband, Martin, who had done it once before. We had purchased tickets in advance, drove about 45 minutes to the station, and enjoyed the softly undulating Chama to Osier narrow gauge train trip through the mountains of New Mexico.

The 2020 Centennial Celebration
by Mary Brings Farquhar

The American School was founded in 1920, so 2020 was the year of the Centennial, a truly grand affair in Manila that had been planned for two years. There was a perfect balance between planned activities and free time for reminiscing and making new friends, even though many of them were born long after I graduated. Despite the fact that the name has been changed (now International School), the mascot has been changed (from Indians to Bearcats), and our modest school is now a state of the art 75,000 square foot suburban campus, the heart and soul of the school have remained the same. The oldest attendee happened to be a friend of mine, Margot Cassel Pins from the Class of 1949, who flew back to Manila from Israel, accompanied by her grown children. The youngest alumni had just graduated in 2019, exactly seventy years later! They attended very different versions of the same school, but the special love for that school was palpable through the decades. My only regret was that none of my classmates made the long trip, but I was happy and proud to represent our class at this unforgettable celebration where no expense had been spared to make it truly special.

David Nigel (Class of 1957) and I were asked to submit a recording of the old school anthem and fight song from the days when we were still the American School Indians. We submitted a film clip, assuming that they were planning to show it at some point, only to find out that it was actually an audition tape for the big Centennial show! We were on: the first act of the big show. A blast from the past, as those songs had been replaced after the demise of the Indians, and so they were unfamiliar to the younger alums. But with our encouragement, they sang along, as the lyrics were posted on two large screens on either side of the stage. We were a hit!

Mary in her Jusi(Pineapple Fiber) Kimona & David in his Barong Tagalog
On Stage Singing the American School Song and the Fight Song
From the ISM Archives

That they began the show with the old American School anthem and fight song was emblematic of the fact that they made an effort to include the entire history of the school, despite the fact that most of the alums present were from the 70s, 80s and 90s. They honored Margot, the oldest alumna, with a huge bouquet and interviewed her on stage. The mistress of ceremonies was a beautiful Swiss/Filipina alumna who has her own TV show in Singapore. The question to Margot that brought down the house was "Who was your boyfriend?" Without missing a beat she named him and added, "But he went to LaSalle!" (the exclusive boys' school down the street) Because she couldn't take the flowers back to Israel on the plane and couldn't bear to throw them away, she decided to go to the Jewish Cemetery the next day and scatter them among the graves of people she had known, including my parents.

The show was like a Broadway revue with singing, dancing, skits, jokes and, at one point, cheerleading. The organizers brought out from the archives the cheerleading outfits through the decades, with the current IS cheerleaders performing the current cheers. I immediately recognized ours from the fifties, a little the worse for wear, but they brought back memories of the basketball games, where we yelled ourselves hoarse.

The reunion committee organized a series of city tours with various choices. One choice included the part of town where our old school was located. It is still there, now a law school, and arrangements had been made for interested alums to tour the old campus without disturbing classes. For those of us who had attended the old school, myself and about seven students from the 50s, this was probably the most emotional part of the reunion because from the outside the buildings looked the same. The soccer field, where we held our Sadie Hawkins races, was paved over, but we couldn't stop looking at the unchanged buildings, especially Heilbronn Hall, with the letters carefully chiseled into the stone. Until somebody noticed something different and yelled out, "Hey! No fair! Look! They have air conditioners!"

Heilbronn Hall Plaster Replica at Entrance to Farewell Party
From the ISM Archives

The farewell party was held at the Polo Club with decorations that reflected all the years and all the changes that had occurred in one hundred years. The organizers were diligent in making sure that all decades were represented. I had tears in my eyes when, upon entering the party, the first thing I saw was a carefully crafted plaster facade of our Heilbronn Hall where I began as a Kindergartner.

CHAPTER 13

꼃

Other Classmates, Other Stories

In this final chapter we introduce you to some additional classmates whose stories continue to reflect a wide variety of backgrounds and experiences. Despite the diversity among us, our post-war time together in the Philippines created a remarkable bond that has lasted over sixty years. As Kaye Fisher Hautem explains below, it was truly "a special time in a special place."

Art Zurhorst
Memphis boy

My unusual last name has been traced back to the 14th century in Germany, where our ancestors were called "tor horst" meaning "from the pine covered hill". In the late 1800s, my grandmother came to the U.S when only six years old with her family who emigrated from "Das Musterland" area of her homeland. My grandfather at age sixteen with his fourteen year old brother had struck out on their own from Germany a few years later. My grandparents met in Memphis, where my grandfather worked for the railroad as a brakeman his entire life, while my grandmother stayed a *Hausfrau* her entire life.

My mother was of mixed descent: English, Irish, and Cherokee Indian. Her father was a local county sheriff in the early 1900s and was the last in the area to patrol on horseback and to carry holstered colt 45s. She was the only one in her family to get a college degree and became a teacher.

My father graduated valedictorian of his high school class in Memphis, and therefore was offered the only full scholarship to the University of Michigan in electrical engineering. Although he wanted to become a mechanical engineer, this was his only way to go to college, so he accepted the offer. His interest in mechanical engineering with his degrees in electrical engineering would propel him up the "engineering" ladder at Firestone Tire and Rubber Company. He graduated valedictorian and Summa cum Laude from Michigan, and then during his first years with Firestone attained his Masters from the University of Tennessee. Besides his work with Firestone in the early years in Memphis, he also taught night master's program classes in engineering.

We came to Manila when he was offered a position as the chief engineer for the Firestone Plant there. Later he became plant CEO in Manila, and then went on to Rome to design and build the first radial plant in that country. Seven years after my mother passed away, he married Pering Lim, a Filipina who was a fashion designer for Mrs. Marcos, Mamie Eisenhower, Jackie Kennedy, and a few more well known ladies.

As for myself, I was a frail child with very poor eyesight and judged at an early age to be unusually bright. Fearing I would become a "cerebral recluse," my mother introduced me to sports. Anyway, that gave me the outgoing, people-oriented personality I have to this day. I was also very mature for my age at almost every stage of development, so my first high school years were spent at a boarding school in Missouri with a strong academic base. That is why I was not behind when I arrived at the American School, which was also academically strong.

I am grateful for the wonderful times I spent at the American School, and the couple of years at the University of the Philippines that allowed me to spend additional time with some classmates. I can truthfully say that my time in the Philippines was the best I could have ever wished for.

After getting my liberal arts degree preparatory to the seminary, I realized that the Lutheran Ministry was not really for me. I continued going to school trying to find my niche in life, not realizing I was a "scanner" and would never be satisfied with an "in-depth" education leading to a specific profession. I was drafted and spent two years in the Army, finally winding up working in the Pentagon Liaison Office at Fort Dix N.J. where I helped troops with hardship discharges, medical problems, compassionate reassignments, and the like.

After the service I went back to the University of Memphis to find my "professional" self, and continued in the tradition of a "scanner" and picked up a degree in Biology to go along with my Liberal Arts and Psychology studies. One semester into a master's in Psychology I realized I would never find a profession that would satisfy my eclectic interests, so I moved to San Diego and went to work.

From there my life has been a complete roller coaster. I met my wife in California, and we had one son. When he was only five months old, we lost his mother in an accident and I suddenly became a single parent. The rest of the years were spent mostly in retail management and dedicated to raising my son. I am now happily remarried and still working.

Steve Gunders
Parents from Germany

My grandparents were both from Germany, my mother's parents from Essen and my father's from Munich. My paternal grandfather owned a wholesale tea, spice and chocolate business that sold these items to shops across Europe. My father joined his father in the family business until the war forced them into financial difficulties in1938. My parents left Munich and came to the Philippines in 1938 as a result of World War II. They left Munich on "Kristallnacht" [The Night of the Broken Glass, where Nazis destroyed synagogues and Jewish businesses throughout Germany and Austria] in 1938 and spent a number of months in Italy waiting for the appropriate papers to come to the Philippines. They left from Italy for the Philippines by boat in the fall of 1938, arriving in January, 1939. My father, speaking very little English at the time, was given his first job with a Chinese Coffee Company, acting in a sales capacity for the company. His main role was to say "good coffee" on cue from the owners of the coffee company when they were in a sales situation. Prior to the war in the Philippines, he joined Heacocks, the fashionable jewelry and appliance store in Manila. When the war started in the Philippines, Heacocks closed, so he was forced to work in a number of capacities to survive. Being from Germany, he was not interned. I was born on October 1, 1943 in the middle of the Japanese occupation of the Philippines. I don't recall very much about the war effort, but I have vague memories of American soldiers around my house and getting some candy from them. After the war my father re-joined Heacocks, which had started operations again, and rose to become the General Manager of the store several years before we left for the U.S. I also remember my Aya (nursemaid), Nena, who took care of me until I left the Philippines in 1951.

My parents made friends with several other European, American and Philippine families and I made friends with their kids. It was a great international experience for me without my even realizing it at the time. One of my closest friends was Mary Brings, the daughter of friends of my parents. We played together in those early years on swings and with other toys in our respective backyards. Our families were close friends, and she and I went to pre-school together as well. Both Mary and I started regular school at the American School in Kindergarten, and we stayed close with each other until I left for the US towards the end of the second grade. I remember getting up in Mrs. Fletcher's second grade class for "show and tell" and explaining to everyone that "We got our visa to the U.S." and we would be leaving in several months. At that point I was not sure what that meant for my future, but I knew it would be different from living in the Philippines.

In April 1951 we boarded the President Cleveland and sailed to the U.S. The ship landed in San Francisco four weeks later, and we spent several months there, while my parents deliberated their next steps in the U.S. I remember eating my first fresh cherries and other different foods I had not been exposed to in the Philippines. My parents decided to leave San Francisco and head to the east coast where my father's family had established themselves years earlier. We drove across the U.S. in my father's green Packard which he brought from the Philippines. As we drove over the Rockies, I saw my first snow!

We stopped in many cities and towns along the way to our initial destination, Boston, to visit with the family my parents had not seen since they left Germany. After several months and much discussion, my family settled in New York, where I started to go to school in Kew Gardens, Queens. I guess I must have had quite a good education in those early years at the American School because after taking some exams, I was asked to skip the 3rd grade and join the 4th grade class. I spent the next years in Queens, moving to Forest Hills in the 6th grade and stayed in that area throughout high school, graduating from Forest Hills High School one year early, in 1960.

I went to City College in New York (CCNY) and graduated in 1964. Shortly after graduating from College, I joined the American Peace Corps and spent the next two years living in a village in India. Quite a change from the U.S. and even from the Philippines! When I was on my way back home from India, I stopped in the Philippines to see how things had changed and to visit my old Aya who was then living in Catanduanes with three children of her own. That was an experience I will never forget. I also looked up an old Chinese friend who lived next door to us when we lived in a Manila suburb know as San Juan. We became good friends again from that visit, and we still stay in touch with his family that still lives in Manila today. I also took the opportunity to visit other islands and made a trip to Baguio. That visit reconnected me to the Philippines in a very real and tangible way.

I started my MBA studies in Finance at the University of Chicago in 1967. During graduate school, I worked at Time Magazine as a Marketing Research Specialist. Also while in graduate school, I married my wife Madelaine whom I had known for a number of years before leaving for the Peace Corps. Upon my graduation in 1969, we moved back to New York where I started a job as a Management Consultant with Touche Ross & Company. I worked there for thirty-eight years, becoming a partner in 1977. In 1986, I was asked to run our New York Office, and in 1988 I was asked to run the Eastern Region's Consulting Practice. In 1989, Touche Ross & Company merged with one of our competitors, Deloitte, Haskins and Sells, and we formed a new company, Deloitte. From 1989-1996 I ran the new Deloitte Northeast Consulting Region. During this period I made a number of business trips to the Philippines, which helped me to keep my connection to my past.

In 1997, I was transferred to Europe to run our Pan-European Consulting practice based in London with operations in all the major cities in Western Europe. As a result, I frequently traveled around Europe and returned to the U.S. quite often for our global management meetings. Madelaine and I lived in London for seven years.

After returning from Europe, I moved to San Francisco and continued to work for Deloitte until I retired in 2006. Since retirement, I have been on several global corporate boards, have continued to do some private consulting, and have worked to develop and lead a new global NGO known as the Sustainability Accounting Standards Board (SASB).

Sylvia Ayers Stetzelberg
Born in Ecuador

I was born In Guayaquil, Ecuador. My father was an American geologist, and my mother was a New Zealand artist. For about the first four years of my life we lived in South America, where I learned to speak fluent Spanish, but later lost it. Every so often we went back to the States for home leave or back to New Zealand to visit my mother's parents. We had a two-year stay in Nairobi, Kenya, where I entered a British school, my first formal schooling, at the late age of eight, due to long ship journeys around the world. We returned to the U.S. for about a one half year stay in New York, while my father was searching the Sahara for oil. I entered the second grade, but I was considered too old, so I was moved into the fourth grade. There I went through hell as I could barely read or multiply yet. Somehow I caught up before the next move to the Philippines. We moved to Baguio in 1954. We stayed there for four years, and I attended Brent School. I loved that school. Baguio was a paradise and the school was so small that we practically had private tutoring for classes. I loved Brent so much that when my parents moved to Manila, I stayed on another year in the boarding school. Eventually, I was homesick for my parents and moved to Manila, where I entered the American School for my 10th and 11th grades.

Ellen Bancroft Page
Missionary family

My parents had gone over independently to the Philippines in 1935 and 1936, to serve as missionaries under the same Baptist mission and met in the mountain town of Baguio where they went to "cool off" and take a respite from their work. My parents had planned to marry in the Philippines, but had too much pressure from family and friends, so they returned to the U.S. in 1939/40. They were married in the States in 1940.

As the first civilians allowed to return after the war, we moved to the Philippines at the end of 1945 on an empty American troopship going to pick up the U.S. Military to return them to the U.S. We were allowed to come back (my parents, that is—first time for us kids) because the mission my parents belonged to owned a house that was still intact after the war. The house, on an island named Cuyo, in Palawan, was obviously built by someone who envisioned it as an island paradise, but without amenities available. For three years we lived in a house built with faucets and light switches, but without running water or electricity. So we had light switches and faucets, but none worked. However, that was okay. My dad sometimes used a generator to light up the house, but mostly we used kerosene lamps or early Coleman gas lamps. There was no traffic and the island had two trucks only, which were available to hire, but I remember mostly walking everywhere. We had the beach in front of the house, and since it had a huge shallow sand bar, we played out there hours on end when the tide was out. I played with the ten children of the Filipino pastor who lived next door in a little nipa hut.

When I was six our family was transferred to Manila, and the experience was so strange that I remember it vividly. We couldn't get used to the traffic, and my parents went crazy trying to teach us to turn off water faucets. We were fascinated by the running water coming out and light switches that really worked.

For one year, we lived in Manila, where I met civilization in a compound with families, Filipino and Chinese, as I recall playing with children there. In 1951 we lived in the house of Gertrude Stewart, the lady who saved Mary's life by sneaking milk out of Santo Tomás. After a couple other locations, we moved into a house we lived in for four years. It was on Taft Avenue in a compound that was near (walking distance) to American School and to Rizal Stadium, so I could walk back and forth to swim practice. Ray Domingo and his family moved into that compound about the last year we were there.

In the Philippines we always rode on the jeepneys and buses—no chauffeur system for us. I rode a local "Direct Express" bus up to Baguio once when a swim meet kept me from going up with my parents. That was a "fun" experience up the Zig-Zag Road. As a teenager with angst, I really felt humiliated when my dad felt we couldn't afford the customs on the car we'd brought back from the States, so he sold it and bought a Thames (from England) jeepney. However, now I laugh when I see a picture of that vehicle; it brings back crazy memories. If I had had an experience like Mary's in the 7th grade, where we were supposed to share something about our state, I would have been up the creek also, for we'd lived more in the P.I. and only visited the States, and I didn't know "nothin" about it.

I went to the A.S. from 8th grade through 11th grade and cried my eyes out when I couldn't persuade my parents to leave me behind to finish my senior year. I graduated from a high school in upstate New York and went to LeTourneau Christian College in Longview, Texas, majoring in English and History. I met my husband, Martin Page, there and we have lived in Walnut Cove, NC (near Winston-Salem) since 2001.

Priscilla Litwin Dolan
Girl from Yonkers

Grandpa Gabriel and Grandma Mary emigrated to Hastings, New York from Austria and Poland. Gabriel served in the Cavalry of Franz Josef and always referred to him as "the little father". Grandpa and Grandma met while working at the Smith Carpet factory in Yonkers, New York. Grandpa contracted anthrax from contaminated wool but survived. Grandpa and Grandma went on to build their own house and have three children. My father, Peter Litwin, worked for Phelps Dodge Copper and Wire. He had been engaged to a local girl until he met my mother, who had just arrived from Cuba. The maracas won out! Years later the company sent my father to set up a factory in Venezuela. My sister, Edwina, and I attended Campo Allegra in Caracas for 7th and the beginning of 8th grades. In1958, at the end of my 8th grade, my father's company sent us to Manila. We arrived via a prop plane, NorthWest Orient Airlines, with stops in Alaska, Tokyo and Guam.

Getting off the plane, we were overwhelmed by the heat! Incredible. It was impossible to think of sitting in a classroom, but I remember running into soon-to-be-good-friend, Vicky Schulz, in the girls' room and her easy advice, "You'll get used to it." Since we didn't have a house yet, we spent our first month in a hotel on Manila Bay. We were wowed each night by the spectacular sunsets, like nowhere else in the world. More than once we were shaken awake by earth tremors. Another "You'll get used to it." And of course we did. It was the beginning of a grand adventure!

Edurne "Noonie" Neely Kowalski
Spanish / Filipino Heritage

My grandfather, Antonio Menchaca, was a very young man when he emigrated with his father to the Philippines from Bilbao, Spain. They settled in the sugar island of Negros where they worked for a Swiss hacendero (plantation owner). When they saved enough money, my great grandfather traveled back to Spain to bring back the rest of the family. Great grandfather never made it back to Spain; he died when the ship was lost at sea. Grandfather Menchaca eventually acquired three plantations of his own in Negros Occidental and married a local woman whose surname was Salcedo. They had seven children which spanned two generations. My father was the youngest, and his name was also Antonio Menchaca.

My mother's family was from Iloilo, Panay, in the Visayas, where she was born in a small town called Molo outside of Iloilo. Her father, Francisco "Paco" Zulueta, was a lawyer, judge and politician. He was Secretary of Interior for President Manuel Quezon before World War II. Unfortunately, he died in a plane crash in 1946 on government business, along with many other government officials. One of my earliest childhood memories was his funeral. The airplane was called the "Lili Marlene". I was told that my mother's side, the Zuluetas, was a melting pot of Filipino, Chinese and Portuguese heritage. Grandmother Zulueta's family (surname Salas) was of Spanish and Filipino descent. They were educators and pharmacists. The pharmacy part makes me think that they practiced holistic medicine in those days. I remember having to drink too much cod liver oil when I was growing up.

Though both families, the Zuluetas and the Menchacas, were from the provinces, Manila was always the hub with homes in both places. My mother grew up mostly in Manila, and she was in boarding school (St. Scholastica) for many years. Commuting was a way of life; it was boat travel in those days.

My father was an architect, educated at the University of Santo Tomás, though he never really had the chance to practice much because he died so young. He contracted tuberculosis during the war—no penicillin in those days—and died in 1947. I always felt that he too was a war casualty, but in a different way. My mother, Lydia Zulueta, went to the University of the Philippines, studied journalism and worked as the society editor for the *Manila Bulletin* before the war.

My parents married in November of 1940 and shortly thereafter "all hell broke loose". Their words, not mine. It was the beginning of the Japanese infiltration into Manila. My brother was born the day before Pearl Harbor, Dec. 6, 1941, and one of the family anecdotes was that the Japanese started bombing Manila that day. Mom ran to the nursery, snatched up my brother and left minutes before Philippine General Hospital was bombed. I was born during the Japanese occupation on Dec. 3, 1943 and we lived in a family compound on Singalong Street. Many family members were separated then. Those caught in the provinces were not permitted to leave, and travel was dangerous. The rest of us in Manila lived and stayed together for safety.

Before the American liberation, Grandfather Zulueta decided that we could escape the Japanese by going to Baguio where we had a house. The journey was mostly on foot but, lucky for me, since I was a baby, I was carried. It didn't work because the bombings and Japanese followed. They eventually confiscated our house in Manila for a radio command post. We decided to walk down towards the beach because we heard that the Americans were going to land there. I was told by aunts and older cousins that when the Americans landed, there was much cheering, and the soldiers really did hand out gum and candy, just as the war movies depicted. I thought the war lasted forever when I listened to all those war stories, but, in reality, it was only because a lifetime of events occurred during those short years.

After the war, we lived with my mother's side Zulueta grandparents in a house that my father designed and built for them (before the war) in a neighborhood called San Andres. My only recollection of my father was sadly visiting him at Manila Sanitarium because he was already ill. I was 3 years old. Children were not allowed inside, but he could wave to us from his room window.

After 1947 my mother went to work at the War Damage Commission, and we (mother, brother and I) moved to a small townhouse on Taft Avenue. I do know that I was in kindergarten for two years. Mom begged the nuns at St. Scholastica, her alma mater, to take me early because my brother was already at De La Salle College which was nearby. I think it was an early form of daycare even though there were maids at home. Sister Gracia told me much later during a reunion that I cried so much then.

In 1951 my mother married an American (hence the name Neely), a civil engineer with the U.S. government. With him, we moved to the small island of Okinawa, where we lived on a military base. I guess my brother and I were "military brats" during our formative school years. We became naturalized American citizens and visited the U.S. several times. It was a good place to grow up in. Small community and very structured.

In 1959 my mother and stepfather divorced. My brother had just graduated and left for the University of New Mexico where he had friends. Mom and I moved back to Manila. My mother decided that I would fit in better at the American School rather than in the local Catholic all-girls schools. Of course I was not happy at all! I had to leave all my friends, and I was the new girl at a new school. Soon everything changed. I was told to make the most of the situation and make new friends! Pretty good advice for a petulant fifteen year old.

As it turned out, I did decide to make the most of it. During my junior year at A.S. I learned to embrace change. The faculty encouraged us to participate in all the extracurricular activities. I was not athletic (still not), but I tried out for some sports teams and I joined many clubs.

One of our teachers was too easy. I found out what "open book tests" were. Another teacher was a tyrant. Several of us cried in that class on a regular basis, so I learned to always be prepared. The faculty in general gave us the best possible education to prepare us for an American college.

As a college Freshman, I went to the University of New Mexico to be with my brother. A large state university was overwhelming and impersonal, so for Sophomore year I went to Madrid, Spain, where my mother had taken up residency. At the University of Madrid I enrolled in their program for foreigners. Most of the European universities had classes for foreigners. The following summer I traveled around Europe with a friend, and I ended up at the University of Vienna summer school in Strobl, Austria. I met three American ladies who invited me to join them in Vienna that fall. We were an eclectic bunch, two high school teachers (one a Fulbright scholar) and a talented piano major. German was challenging for me, so I only stayed for one semester. Vienna was memorable because I was there during the Kennedy assassination.

That I was open to taking university classes for foreigners in other countries, where I knew only a little or none of the language, was at least in part due to my positive international experience at the American School.

Kaye Fisher Hautem
California Girl

My family and I moved from California to the Philippines in the early 50s via the President Wilson, just one of many sailings we would make on The President Lines. Dad worked for Firestone, and initially we were sent to Cebu, in the Visayas, where we spent the next three years and where my brother John was born. We lived in a compound with other expats, and my sister Jeri and I literally went to a one room school house, where we sang the Philippine national anthem every morning. I was not only the oldest in our school, but also the sole 8th grade graduate. When we inevitably moved to Manila, the transition for me was terrifying, having not really experienced kids my own age. What I learned was this: You make mistakes, you adapt, you grow. I look back on the years at the American School with a mix of emotions and memories—a special time in a special place.

Leata Thomas Selby
Georgia Girl

Adventure best describes my two years in the Philippines. After I had already moved hither, thither, and yon as an "Army Brat" my entire life, and after I had already attended two different high schools in two different states, my father informed our family that we were moving to the Philippines. He had a new assignment: Advisor to the Philippine Army as part of the Joint United States Military Advisory Group (JUSMAG).

The idea of leaving Atlanta, Georgia between my junior and senior year and my happy life with friends and classmates shifted from unbearable to exciting when we boarded the train that took us from Atlanta to San Francisco and the Presidio. Four days later found me in the air aboard an Air Force troop carrier with metal bucket seats, peanut butter sandwiches, and warm reconstituted milk (yuck!!). I was grateful that this misery was broken up with sleep-filled nights in Hawaii, Kwajalein Island, Guam, and finally Clark Air Base. A long ride in an air-conditioned car brought us to our new home, the JUSMAG Compound just outside Manila.

Military life had, unwittingly, prepared me for the novelty of a foreign country and the international mix of people and cultures. Because my stateside transcript indicated that I was not prepared for 11th grade, I had to repeat my Junior year, but I didn't mind, because the American School was a complete adventure all by itself!

Tonya Winters
Class of '61 Social Director

My father's father, an immigrant from Russia, spoke English and was an educated man. He wanted my father to be a rabbi, but my father refused. At age fifteen he left home and peeled potatoes around the world on a freighter. He was able to get false working papers for his trip around the world. This created a yearning that never left him. My dad went to Ohio State on a polo scholarship and graduated with a medical degree. My parents, who had met in New York, first arrived in Manila in 1936, just after they were married. They came to the Philippines to visit my father's brother who was at University of the Philippines Medical School and to see their first niece, Barbara.

They made the Philippines home until 1940 when things started to get "hot." My uncle had come back to the USA and my parents decided to leave, as my father was accepted at the U. of Oregon Dental School. Carol, my sister, and I were both born in Portland while my dad was in dental school.

After the war, we moved first to California, where my father practiced dentistry and then on to Hawaii, where he worked as a dentist with the Veterans Administration until 1949. In September of 1949 Lothar Lissner, a German-Jewish dentist in Manila, sent my dad a telegram that the last American dentist had died, and if he wanted the license, he should come immediately. So off we went from Hawaii to Manila on the President Cleveland, arriving in October 1949.

I have a very scary memory from 1953. We were going to the Polo Club and all of a sudden we were in the middle of gunfire. The Huks, the communist anti-Japanese Army, comprised mainly of disenfranchised peasant tenant-farmers of Central Luzon, was only one of several guerrilla groups resisting the Japanese invasion and occupation of the Philippines. After the war this communist group fought the Philippine government. They were shooting at the Philippine military when all of us were on the floorboards of our new '53 Chrysler. My father was hysterical, especially as he had just bought that new BLUE BOMB, as my sister and I called it.

I attended the American School and graduated in 1961. I stayed until 1963, attending the University of the Philippines for two years and transferring to the University of Miami, where I earned a teaching credential in 1965. I was married in 1966 and, instead of a wedding, my husband and I spent three months in the Orient: a month in Manila and then on to Hong Kong, Bangkok, Cambodia, Japan, Hawaii, San Francisco, Las Vegas and back to Miami. Obviously, a passion for travel had not left me.

After an exciting life filled with travel and adventure, Tonya passed away at home on December 26, 2013 from bile duct cancer, but not without attending and enjoying a Christmas party the day before. That was Tonya!

Mabuhay!

A greeting, a farewell, a toast !

~ POSTSCRIPT ~

Our story starts with the compelling story, Escape to Manila, a riveting account of an escape from the Nazis in Austria to the Philippines, only to endure the Japanese invasion and occupation. We go on to the stories of how classmates of diverse backgrounds shared life at the American School in Manila.

The fact that we were asked to recall and evaluate a mutual experience that took place over 65 years ago for this book is amazing in itself. I couldn't tell you five things about other decades, but remember vividly my family's time in Manila. Was it that it was so different? Made so special by the small close-knit group? We were in the heart of Manila in school in a building with history of Japanese occupation during World War II. While our stateside counterparts were taking field trips to museums, we took a field trip to Corregidor Island at the mouth of Manila Bay and saw huge gun emplacements and military defenses. For fun we went to parties, joined clubs, played sports, skipped school for a day at the beach, won folk dance contests, acted in shows and plays, ran for office, knew our teachers and were known by them, had first crushes, and even sat in a jam-packed movie theater to see the *The Ten Commandments*, which played for months. While our stateside friends were getting cars, we took jeepneys or had drivers. I don't remember anyone's religion or color being an issue. For many of us, we were world travelers who at a young age observed, participated, made do and made friends and made memories that have lasted a lifetime.
—Priscilla Litwin Dolan

WE WISH YOU ALL THAT IS BEAUTIFUL AND GOOD

IN MEMORIAM
Class of 1961

Dik Bartlett	1943 – 1994
Wilma Braat	1942 – 2013
Bobby Hamm	1943 – 1972
John Joe Hendryx	1941 – 2010
Steve Malchow	1943 – 2010
Tim McCloskey	1942 – 2009
Linda Pratico	1943 – 2000
Tonya Winters	1943 – 2013

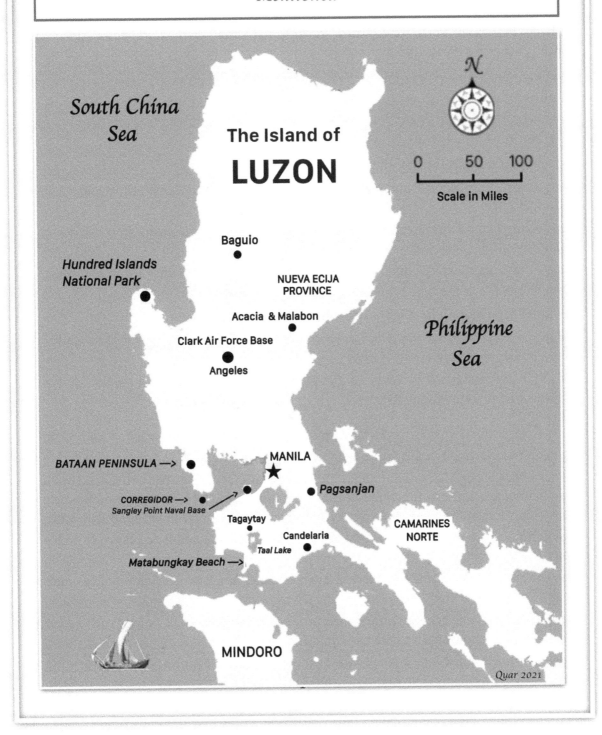

PHILIPPINE PLACE NAMES
Mentioned

The Island of
LUZON

South China Sea

Philippine Sea

N

0   50   100
Scale in Miles

Baguio

NUEVA ECIJA PROVINCE

Hundred Islands National Park

Acacia & Malabon

Clark Air Force Base

Angeles

MANILA

BATAAN PENINSULA —>

CORREGIDOR —>
Sangley Point Naval Base

Pagsanjan

Tagaytay

Candelaria

Taal Lake

CAMARINES NORTE

Matabungkay Beach —>

MINDORO

Quar 2021

Suggested Reading and Viewing

For more information on the history of the Philippines and the Battle of Manila:

Abinales, Patricio N. & Donna J. Amoroso. *State and Society in the Philippines.* Ateneo de Manila University Press, 2017.

Francia, Luis H. *A History of the Philippines.* New York, 2014.

Rood, Steven. *The Philippines.* Oxford University Press, 2019.

Scott, James M. *Rampage: MacArthur, Yamashita, and the Battle of Manila.* W.W. Norton & Co., Inc. 2018.

To learn more about the Jewish rescue in the Philippines:

Ephraim, Frank. *Escape to Manila, from Nazi Tyranny to Japanese Terror.* University of Illinois, 2003.

The documentary is *Rescue in the Philippines, Refuge from the Holocaust* by 3 Roads Communications, available on Amazon.

Another documentary by Filipino-American filmmaker Noel (Sonny) Izon, *An Open Door*, will be released soon. An extended preview is available on YouTube.

For more information on Viennese conductor Herbert Zipper:

Cummins, Paul. *Dachau Song, The Twentieth Century Odyssey of Herbert Zipper.* Peter Lang Publishing, Inc., New York 1992

Film by Terry Sanders. *Never Give Up, The Twentieth Century Odyssey of Herbert Zipper.* American Film Foundation, 2006

Acknowledgements

We would like to thank our three readers for their thorough and professional critique of the early review copy. Their comments and suggestions from their respective fields were most helpful and encouraging: Laura Rink, a published author; Lisa Mast from the field of cross-cultural relations; and Linda Victoire Byers, Advanced Placement English teacher.

Thank you to Lou Gopal, who allowed us to use historical data and old photos from his blog *Manila Nostalgia*.

Also to Aurora's historian sister, Alcestis Abrera-Mangahas, who gave us valuable counsel for the Philippine History page.

We would also like to acknowledge the hours spent by honorary classmate Peter Farquhar in bringing old photos back to life and in designing the book itself.

And a big thank-you to our artist classmate Ray Domingo for his brilliant, eye-catching cover design. It's what people first notice about the book!

List of Illustrations

Illustration Credits

AS American School
BL Bob Liese
BT A.S. *Bamboo Telegraph*
C Classmate in Photo
ISM International School Manila
K A.S. *Kawayan*

LC Litwin Collection
MB Mary Brings
MN Lou Gopal, *Manila Nostalgia*
PDI Public Domain Internet
TK Terry Kleeman
WG Warren Gerig

ABOUT THE AUTHORS

Mary Brings Farquhar

Mary Brings Farquhar is a retired San Francisco high school Foreign Language teacher. She has been a co-presenter at Apple's MacWorld Expo in San Francisco and New York, where she spoke on the topic of editing and digitizing personal history stories.

Mary has appeared in two documentaries about the Philippine rescue plan for Holocaust victims, *Rescue in the Philippines* and *An Open Door,* and has presented this little-known story to national and international audiences.

Karl Terry Kleeman was born in Dubuque, Iowa. His family's first overseas trip was to relocate to Manila in the Philippine Islands, where he attended the American School from seventh grade through his junior year in high school. He has been collecting stories from classmates for twenty years and was convinced that they were worth telling. He is the co-author of three railroad history books, most recently, *Early Railroads of Whatcom County, Washington Territory.*

Karl Terry Kleeman

Colophon

Typeface: Minion Pro & Ornaments
Cover Design by Ray Domingo
Book & Map Design by Peter Farquhar

Comments from Readers

My father, Jorma Sr., was posted to the Philippines in 1957 and of course my mother, brother and I went along for the ride. I would spend my junior year of high school at the American School. One short year for me but in a way it was a lifetime. I made friends at the American School that have been with me for decades. This collection of tales is like a gentle wind that wraps me in recollections of another time and place.

Jorma (Jerry) Kaukonen
Lead guitarist for *Jefferson Airplane* and *Hot Tuna*

*   *   *   *

The book is a remarkable story of friendship, inclusion, personal bravery and diversity. Each individual story is compelling and a testament to the many ways individuals from different circumstances can live together harmoniously, while celebrating the likenesses and differences among them. There are many lessons to be learned from these collective school experiences and I expect that the book will be well received and enjoyed by many.

Constance E. Simon, Ed.D
Chevy Chase, MD Educational Consultant

*   *   *   *

What an entrancing memoir! Congratulations on adding to the AS/ISM story. Long may it continue to unfold!

David Toze
Superintendent International School Manila

*   *   *   *

This has been such a pleasure to read and will definitely touch the hearts of many. What hit me the most was the quote from the Dutch officer. "All that is beautiful and good will come back in our lives." Although it has been over 70 years, that statement is so relatable to what we are all experiencing today where we are all suffering from a pandemic and a profound divide. I hope this will help us remember that we are all citizens of the world.

Anna Seipelt Goco
Director of Advancement, International School Manila

CPSIA information can be obtained
at www.ICGtesting.com
Printed in the USA
LVHW111048071221
705508LV00016B/221